THE AMERICAN SOCIETY
OF PLASTIC AND
RECONSTRUCTIVE SURGEONS'

GUIDE TO
COSMETIC
SURGERY

Josleen Wilson

SIMON & SCHUSTER
NEW YORK LONDON TORONTO SYDNEY TOKYO SINGAPORE

Simon & Schuster
Simon & Schuster Building
Rockefeller Center
1230 Avenue of the Americas
New York, New York 10020

Library of Congress Cataloging-in-Publication Data

Wilson, Josleen.
The American Society of Plastic and Reconstructive Surgeons' guide to
cosmetic surgery / Josleen Wilson.
p.   cm.
Includes index.
1. Surgery, Plastic—Popular works. 2. Consumer education.
I. American Society of Plastic and Reconstructive Surgeons.
II. Title. III. Title: Guide to cosmetic surgery.
[DNLM: 1. Surgery, Plastic—methods—popular works.   WO 600
W749a]
RD119.W57   1991
617.9'5—dc20
DNLM/DLC
for Library of Congress   91-2068
                                                                                           CIP

ISBN 0-671-76105-6

The ideas, procedures, and suggestions contained in this book are not
intended to replace the services of a trained health professional. All
matters regarding your health require medical supervision. You should
consult your physician before choosing to have the procedures in this
book. Any application of the treatments set forth in this book is at the
reader's discretion.
The cases and examples cited in this book are based on actual situations
and real people. Names and identifying details have been changed to
protect privacy.

As this book was going to press, the FDA called for a moratorium on the sale
and use of silicone gel–filled breast implants pending further review by the
Agency of the safety of these devices. In light of this development, any person
considering breast implants or concerned about existing implants should
discuss the relevant portions of this book with his or her physician.

ACKNOWLEDGMENTS

We wish to thank the twenty distinguished members of the American Society of Plastic and Reconstructive Surgeons who contributed their time and expertise to the development of this book. During extensive interviews they were dedicated, generous, and forthcoming with a wealth of information. No clocks ticked, no phones were permitted to ring, and no questions went unanswered. Although we would like to name each of them individually, they have pledged to remain anonymous, at the request of the ASPRS.

Special appreciation has been particularly earned by the reviewers from the ASPRS Public Education Committee, whose considerate and careful evaluation of the manuscript ensured its medical accuracy and enlightened its content. Despite such in-depth appraisal, the reviewers never tried to prevent the author from exposing controversial issues, or from presenting more than one side of a story. Their sole concern was how to best serve the reader. We are also grateful to Toni Sciarra, this book's editor, for her encouragement, steady hand, and a vision that remained clear and unwavering at all times.

We would also like to express our gratitude to Pamela Rasmussen, communications director of the ASPRS, who piloted this sometimes overwhelmingly cumbersome project through its many complex stages. Without her administrative skills, painstaking follow-up, and talented editorial support, this book would never have been accomplished.

—JOSLEEN WILSON   —ASPRS PUBLIC EDUCATION COMMITTEE
NEW YORK CITY   CHICAGO

CONTENTS

Part IV Recontouring the Body   223

FOREWORD

One might well ask why we need another book on plastic surgery when we read, see, and hear so much on this subject in magazines, on television and radio, and in other books. The fact is that much of the information that reaches the so-called public is partial, at best, or misleading and erroneous, at worst. What Josleen Wilson has written here, in contrast, is authoritative and thorough without being tedious. This book also has that rare combination of reliability and readability. In an almost conversational style, she presents facts and perspective that anyone interested in plastic surgery in general or a specific operation should have.

This is not a glib book that tries to market plastic surgery to the unwary or the uncritical. From the many plastic surgeons and patients Ms. Wilson consulted, she has been able to produce a balanced picture of the surgery of appearance. Not only will the reader learn what plastic surgery can do but what it cannot do. Limitations as well as complications and unfavorable results are freely discussed. For these reasons particularly, this book is different from most accounts of aesthetic surgery. It seeks to inform rather than to entice. There are no magic wands here—no Pygmalian miracles. Although plastic surgery can achieve some remarkable results, it is a human endeavor and it shares with all others the reality of disappointment for the patient and surgeon alike. Fortunately things go right much more often than they go wrong. For those difficult situations, this book offers helpful advice.

As the author has emphasized, this book is not a substitute for consultation with a competent and caring plastic surgeon but it is a good place to begin. For the would-be patient these pages are helpful for you to read or reread after consulting with a plastic surgeon because you might find additional or differing information that should prompt you to have another conversation with your surgeon before embarking on an operation or a treatment.

As a practicing plastic surgeon doing the kind of procedures described here, I have found, as have my colleagues, that a better informed patient lessens the surgeon's task and increases the likelihood of success.

—Robert M. Goldwyn, M.D.
Editor, *Plastic & Reconstructive Surgery,*
Clinical Professor of Surgery, Harvard Medical School

A SPECIAL NOTE

The author and editors reluctantly use the masculine singular pronoun "he" throughout this text when referring to a plastic surgeon. Although it is true that 95 percent of all plastic surgeons are men, that is no reason to contribute to the continuing masculine dominance of the language, no matter how small the effect. However, the alternatives—pluralizing, the use of s/he, or he or she—seemed too awkward when used continuously in a book of this size. We apologize to present and future female plastic surgeons—and their number is growing.

BEFORE YOU BEGIN
THIS BOOK

It's not unusual for people to be unhappy with some aspect of their appearance and want to improve it. According to a survey by *Psychology Today*, 60 million people don't like their chins, and 6 million claim to be unhappy with their eyes. Another recent survey by *USA Today* found that 40 percent of 8,000 men and women who responded gave their bodies a C, and 14 percent said they'd choose liposuction to remove fat from their stomachs and thighs. In today's climate of greater acceptance of plastic surgery, advanced techniques, and lower complication rates, chances are that many of these dissatisfied people will seek help from plastic surgery.

Plastic surgery is booming. Some sources estimate that more than one million Americans undergo cosmetic surgery every year. The four most popular procedures are liposuction, breast enlargement, collagen injections, and eyelid surgery.

The consumer is faced with myriad choices: What responsibilities should I assume? What can be left to the surgeon's discretion? What must I know to make an informed decision? The American Society of Plastic and Reconstructive Surgeons (ASPRS), the medical organization to which nearly 4,000 board-certified plastic surgeons belong, has responded to this dramatically expanding need for information. The *ASPRS Guide* tells you what to expect from cosmetic plastic surgery and gives you the information you need to make your decision, based on your unique needs.

Perhaps in no other medical specialty are there so many valid means to accomplish the same ends. The *ASPRS Guide* is the first book to present different—and sometimes opposing—points of view, and makes your choices easier to comprehend. It provides a clear perspective on what is possible and what is probably risky, what is on the cutting edge and what is tried and true.

The *ASPRS Guide* walks you through the first office visit: Do you tell the surgeon what you want, or will he tell you what procedures you should have? Should you bring a photo of your-self from ten years ago? Of the nose you want? Of the breasts you'd like to have?

The book takes you into the operating room: What surgical techniques can you choose from—and what difference do they make in the outcome? How much discomfort will you have? It follows you into recovery: When can you go back to your normal activities? How can you camouflage the incision lines and swelling? The book also grapples with the psychological issues, explaining why your emotions can sometimes surprise you during the pro-cess of recovery. Perhaps most important, the guide tells you in detail how to find a well-trained, experienced plastic surgeon.

The information is organized into types of cosmetic problems: changing inherited traits, minimizing the effects of aging, and recontouring the body.

With few exceptions, this guide is limited to cosmetic surgery procedures. The specialty of *plastic surgery* encompasses both *reconstructive* surgery (for repair of birth defects and deformities caused by accidents or disease) and *cosmetic* (aesthetic) surgery (facelifts, nose reshaping, fat suction, eyelid surgery, and others).

ASPRS believes that the number of people having cosmetic surgery is on the rise because the results help people feel better about themselves. Moreover, first impressions are more impor-tant in our society than ever before, because we are so mobile. We are concerned with making a good impression because we are meeting new people all the time. Businesspeople today are under pressure to work longer and remain competitive with younger people. Some believe that if they can look better, they will feel better and others will relate to them better. Appearance is so important that an article in the *Harvard Law Review* in 1988 documented that discriminatory practices based on appearance were more widespread and serious in employment decisions than those for sex or race. Research cited in the article showed that physically attractive people are thought to be more intelli-gent and outgoing than unattractive people (although the ex-tremely glamorous are seen as less competent). Other studies show that if two equally qualified people go in for a job inter-view, the more attractive candidate will get the job. In an ideal world, less emphasis might be placed on appearance, but our perceptions of appearances are deeply rooted in our culture and our subconscious.

Several new surveys and studies have focused our attention

on appearance and what we think about it. Much of the growth in the number of people seeking cosmetic plastic surgery is attributed to a widening public acceptance. Public-opinion surveys show that the number of people who approve of plastic surgery for both themselves and others is up 50 percent since 1982. The number of people who disapprove is down 66 percent. Acceptance has come partially because public figures—movie stars, fashion models, and other trendsetters—are much more open about their decision to have cosmetic surgery and about discussing what it's done for them.

Plastic surgery is no longer a luxury reserved only for the very rich. Some 30 percent of people who choose cosmetic surgery have family incomes of less than $25,000 a year; about 35 percent have incomes between $25,000 and $50,000; and only 23 percent earn over $50,000.

Technical advances have taken cosmetic surgery far beyond the hackneyed "nose job." The scooped nose with the pinched tip and the facelift stretched so tight that it looks painful are problems that largely belong to the past. Today, cosmetic surgery is performed with greater safety and more delicacy and skill, resulting in more individualized, natural-looking improvements.

Plastic surgery today is also not limited to women. In 1990, about 16 percent of all facial cosmetic surgery patients were male. This statistic represents a significant change. In the past, surgery for men had a clandestine aura, and was limited largely to actors, male models, or athletes with broken noses. But today's job market is tougher, and society is more youth-oriented. Men from every walk of life are paying more attention to fashion and grooming, and choosing cosmetic surgery. Some men choose surgery because their wives have had it done with good results. Others, especially those whose jobs depend on first impressions, choose surgery because they want to make it past the "first cut." For the most part, men choose surgery for the same reasons women do and have to make the same decisions.

Nose contouring ranks as the number one procedure requested by men, followed by eyelid surgery, fat suction, and facelifts. Men often choose eyelid surgery because bags under their eyes make them look fatigued, which they feel may affect their business dealings and, thus, their livelihood. Liposuction around the abdomen can take care of the pot belly many men develop as they grow older.

Cosmetic plastic surgery is both a science and an art that is always changing as new techniques and technology are perfected. Because of its changing character—and because it sometimes feeds people's fantasies and reacts to beauty trends—plastic surgery is ripe for exploitation by the media and by self-proclaimed practitioners.

Plastic surgeons are conscious of the relentless pressure put on women to focus on their appearance. As one eminent physician makes clear, there are those who "market *inferiority* to women" by subtly pressuring them to seek improvement at all costs. Ethical plastic surgeons resist this trend and try to take as their patients only those whose motivation comes from *within.*

It's true that plastic surgery is the darling of the media: Either they play up a horror story that makes it seem that anyone who chooses plastic surgery is taking her life in her hands; or they glowingly describe a new "tuck" or "lift" or "bob" that makes cosmetic surgery sound like something you can have done on your lunch hour.

The media are abetted in these extremes by a recent influx of inadequately trained doctors who will operate on virtually anyone. Any doctor can call himself a cosmetic surgeon and perform plastic surgery, even if he has no formal training in the specialty.

All of this leaves consumers in a tough spot. Cosmetic surgery is *not* simple. But, in the proper hands, it is most often safe and successful. (The incidence of serious complications is estimated by several reliable sources to be 1.5 to 2 percent, approximately the same as for other forms of major surgery.) A happy outcome depends on choosing the right physician *before* surgery. That is what this guide is designed to facilitate.

To our knowledge, the *ASPRS Guide* is unique in the attention paid to the manner in which the research was gathered and evaluated. The Public Education Committee of ASPRS invited twenty of the nation's most prominent plastic surgeons to be interviewed for each chapter based on their areas of expertise. All gave unstintingly of their time and expertise in extensive interviews. These doctors represented various surgical approaches, different areas of the country, and a range of practices. However, no individual surgeon's name is mentioned, so that no favoritism could be attached to participation and the widest possible consensus could be presented.

These specialists, each a leader in his field, voluntarily and anonymously gave their time and effort, without compensation, so that consumers—and the specialty of plastic surgery itself—would benefit. With this book in hand, you have access to the insights of the country's most experienced plastic surgeons.

The *ASPRS Guide* has another advantage that is rare indeed in popular medical literature: Each section of the manuscript was carefully reviewed in exacting detail by a select committee convened by ASPRS; it was reviewed again after final editing. Controversial issues were explored, differences in technique were examined, and helpful answers were hammered out. More important, the reviewers assiduously attempted to rid the manuscript of bias. Their task was to make certain that, as much as possible, the *ASPRS Guide* reflects the knowledge of the society's impressive membership, as well as the principles and ideals of the organization itself.

We chose to use drawings rather than photographs to illustrate each procedure because, even when fairly taken, photos can be misleading. You will never have the same postsurgical result shown in a photograph because no two people ever begin with exactly the same problem, nor do they heal the same way after surgery. More problematical is that before-and-after photos are often taken in different lighting, and at different angles, with makeup or without makeup.

The finely made drawings executed by medical illustrator Jackie Aher zero in on the information you need most: the problem, the incisions, the procedure, the potential for scars, and the outcome.

People who are ambivalent about cosmetic surgery make poor candidates for such procedures. At the other end of the spectrum, there are a few plastic surgery "junkies," people who become addicted to surgery and have repeated procedures. However, recent surveys among surgeon members of ASPRS report that fewer than 20 percent of patients come back for second procedures; most of these come back once or twice over a period of five to ten years.

Cosmetic surgery is an option that you may select, depending on your own needs and circumstances. If you have a cosmetic problem that bothers you—whether you want to minimize the effects of aging or to change something fundamental in your appearance—then it is your right to have it successfully corrected.

The single most critical factor in successful cosmetic surgery is the surgeon. Your life and your looks will be in his hands.

PART I

YOU AND YOUR PLASTIC SURGEON

Is Plastic Surgery Right for You?

COSMETIC PLASTIC SURGERY IS NOT A CHOICE TO MAKE LIGHTLY. How do you know if cosmetic surgery will give you the result you want? How do you know if the result will be worth the expense and discomfort? Is there any way that you can tell beforehand if cosmetic surgery is the right choice for you? The two most important questions you can ask yourself are: Why do I want surgery? What do I expect surgery to do for me?

THE MOST SATISFIED PATIENTS

You are most likely to be satisfied with cosmetic surgery if you have a problem that you feel self-conscious about, and if the operation can improve it. If an aging appearance has dampened your self-confidence, a facelift can help you look refreshed and you are likely to be happy with the results. If you are self-conscious about your nose and rhinoplasty can make the change you want, there is an excellent chance you'll be satisfied afterward.

The best candidates for cosmetic surgery, then, are people who are self-conscious about a specific part of their body and want it changed. They like themselves and are well-adjusted, but having this one problem corrected would round out the picture. Afterward, they get on with their lives and are a little bit happier. In a year or so, they don't even think about the old problem anymore. That is the ideal surgical candidate. There is no hidden agenda.

Other patients who can benefit from plastic surgery are those with a cosmetic defect that over the years has eroded their self-esteem. The person with a large, hooked nose, for example, or the woman with extremely large breasts may have a skewed self-image because the problem first developed during adolescence, an emotionally vulnerable age. Psychologists who have studied surgical candidates believe that a cosmetic problem at this age often affects a person's feelings about herself for the rest of her life.

For these patients, cosmetic surgery can boost self-esteem and self-confidence, which often translates into better performance at work and a more comfortable fit in the world at large. These individuals usually derive tremendous pleasure and satisfaction from plastic surgery, but adjusting to their new appearance can take longer than they expected because their lifelong image of themselves must also change.

THE LEAST SATISFIED PATIENTS

A less-satisfied patient is someone who hopes that cosmetic surgery will bring about a significant life change. These individuals secretly hope that their relationships with other people will change overnight, or that someone they love will return the feeling. Those who expect such miraculous turnabouts in their relationships after surgery almost always feel disappointed. Although cosmetic surgery can have an indirect effect by invigorating the self-image you project, its impact usually stops there. For example, one young man thought his girlfriend had lost interest in him and that people at work had turned against him. He thought if he had cosmetic surgery to reshape his nose that other people would like him more. He was reasonably satisfied with the rhinoplasty, but disappointed that nothing had changed in his life.

Sometimes, only after a cosmetic operation is over does someone realize that such a hidden agenda existed. One woman who had a facelift and rhinoplasty reluctantly admitted, "Deep down I hoped my husband would find me more attractive. We've been having problems and I hoped this would help, but it hasn't."

There is another, very small group of people who seek cosmetic surgery because they are psychologically disturbed. They may have a small cosmetic flaw, yet their full attention is riveted on it. They may lose sleep over a small bump on the nose that no one else even notices and they may blame all of their troubles on it. These patients will never be satisfied with plastic surgery because they expect it to make life perfect.

Patients who concern plastic surgeons most are those who return for repeated procedures because they have unrealistic expectations, or who use plastic surgery as an antidote for an unhealthy lifestyle. These "scalpel slaves," as people "addicted" to cosmetic surgery are often called, are usually women who have a history of seeking multiple procedures, quite often for minimal problems. Their expectations are often unrealistic; they may be seeking to look like someone else altogether, or to stop the clock from ticking. They frequently feel that plastic surgery isn't really surgery and that there are no risks involved. That attitude is a clue to the surgeon that something isn't quite right.

Experienced plastic surgeons are usually adept at spotting troubled candidates during the consultation and refuse to operate on them. In these unusual cases, the surgeon usually recommends psychological counseling. That doesn't mean, however, that everyone with a history of mental illness or emotional disturbance is automatically refused plastic surgery.

One woman who wanted a breast reduction had had a psychotic episode in the past. Her emotional problem had been related to tremendous life stresses and had nothing to do with her breasts. She said she had always been embarrassed and self-conscious about her large breasts; she had deep furrows on her shoulders from bra straps and she wanted the operation. No hidden agenda was attached to the surgery, except the desire for the physical change. She had the operation and she did fine.

TIMING IS EVERYTHING

Timing is a critical factor. How will surgery, at this time, fit into the overall panorama of your life? If there's too much going on in your life, it may be better to wait. Surgery should never be something that you squeeze into a long weekend. Cosmetic surgery procedures, even those that seem fairly simple, can drain you of strength. If you have work or family obligations nipping at your heels during the recovery period, it may actually take longer for you to get back on your feet.

If you're going through a personal crisis, it may be best to postpone surgery. Divorce, death of a partner, or even the termination of psychotherapy can bring on depression and a deep sense of loss.

Surgery imposes an additional stress on the body and mind, and before the beneficial results of cosmetic surgery are apparent you usually look worse than you did before. You need to be in good physical and emotional shape to cope with these stresses. In addition, if you are among the few people who have a complication with plastic surgery, you will need sufficient emotional reserves to recover from it. Judge the timing in your life carefully before deciding to have surgery.

YOUR PERSONAL RELATIONSHIPS

Altering your appearance will not change established relationships. If you are trying to win back a lover or an emotionally distant spouse, or to change the way your boss responds to you, disappointment is almost certain. However, if you think it will be easier meeting new people or going on job interviews, and if you just generally hope for a little boost in self-confidence to help face a new situation in life, then cosmetic surgery may help you.

Elizabeth, a fifty-year-old secretary, had had the same boss for many years; when he retired, a younger man took his place. Elizabeth was certain the new man would want a younger woman to work for him. She felt depressed and self-conscious about her aging, tired appearance. Without telling anyone, she took a three-week vacation at a spa, where she had a facelift and rhinoplasty. When she came back, she said she felt "reborn." Actually, Elizabeth looked very much the same, but younger and more alert, which gave her self-image a boost. Her new young boss told her how much he valued her experience.

This is a perfect example of using a cosmetic surgery procedure as one of several ways to cope with a changed life circumstance. New people in your life may respond more positively toward you because you feel better about yourself and are more outgoing. In other words, what *you* do with your changed appearance affects your life the most.

It's also important for you to think about the effect your decision will have on the people you are close to. Is your partner comfortable with the idea? Discuss plans for cosmetic surgery with family members and close friends. Their approval or disapproval can influence how satisfied you are with the result, and this is something you should be aware of *before* the procedure is performed.

PREPARING FOR CHANGE

Procedures that involve a significant change in your body shape, such as breast reduction or nose reshaping, require a different emotional adjustment than procedures such as a facelift or chemical peel. Psychologists point out that self-image is set in our late teens and early twenties. Even as we grow older we continue to see ourselves as we looked then—that is, until we are forced to acknowledge the subtle changes of aging. After a facelift or chemical peel you look in the mirror and quickly adapt to the alteration because it has restored your image of yourself.

By contrast, a rhinoplasty or breast reduction alters that basic body image. No matter how much you wanted the surgery, it will take more time for you to get used to the change. You have to be more prepared for it. This is particularly true for older patients. Older people have lived with a particular body part longer and must redefine a body image that has been set for years.

ARE YOU A PERFECTIONIST?

If the result of the surgery is somewhat less than you had hoped for, will you be devastated? If your answer is "yes, it must be exactly right," tell your surgeon how you feel. Perfection is in the eyes of the beholder, and what *you* want may not be possible. Listen carefully to what the physician tells you about what the surgery can be expected to achieve and the problems that sometimes occur. Living tissue is subject to many variables and even the most gifted plastic surgeon cannot guarantee a perfect result. Think carefully before you proceed with surgery.

EXTRA CARE FOR MEN

When it comes to choosing cosmetic surgery, men have the same issues to consider as women, but they may need to prepare themselves more to cope with the recovery period. Men are programmed by society to be stoic and doctors feel that many men make light of surgery. Men often don't provide themselves with an adequate support system to care for them after surgery. A man may say, "I'm fine," when he really means "I feel lousy, please help me." A man should prepare his support system in advance, just as a woman should (see chapter 5).

SELF-ANALYSIS: IS PLASTIC SURGERY RIGHT FOR YOU?

This evaluation is designed to help you decide if your expectations about cosmetic surgery are realistic and if surgery is the right choice for you. The overriding question you must answer is: Is this operation, at this time in your life, to your advantage emotionally and physically? To answer this fundamental question, you should know where you stand on these specific issues:

- Why do you want this operation, at this time in your life?
- What do you expect it will do for you physically? Emotionally? Socially?
- What are your expectations that you tell others about?
- What are your "hidden expectations"—the reasons you don't want people to know about?
- Is your concern about your cosmetic problem out of proportion to what others think about it?
- Do you expect the operation to improve your relationships at work?
- Do you think it will alter a personal relationship you have with someone now?
- Do you think it will make it easier to form new relationships?
- If you are in psychotherapy, have you discussed having plastic surgery with your therapist?

Finding a Plastic
Surgeon

What you are about to read is the most valuable information you can have when it comes to achieving a satisfactory result from plastic surgery. Given the competition among doctors and lack of regulations governing medical specialties, selecting a surgeon for your operation is your most important task. In the next few pages is a step-by-step plan to help you find a well-trained, experienced surgeon—someone you can rely on and someone who will do the best possible job for your specific needs. In broad strokes, you can divide your search into three steps:

- Gathering a select list of names.
- Checking the credentials of each name on the list.
- Interviewing the two or three doctors who pass your credentials check.

Most people believe that they are protected by state or federal laws that mandate the training and qualifications of doctors who call themselves medical specialists. In fact, no such laws exist. Anyone who has a basic medical degree can obtain a license that allows him to practice whatever type of medicine he wishes, including plastic surgery. Nor is there any law to prevent physicians—regardless of training—from *advertising* themselves as plastic surgeons. Indeed, they may accurately state that they are "board-certified," but fail to mention that their certification is not in plastic surgery, or that the "board" that certified them is not recognized by the American Board of Medical Specialties (ABMS).

If you choose a physician who is allowed to perform your particular procedure at a hospital, you have some protection: You know that your surgeon has been assessed by a peer review committee and is generally considered to have the training needed to perform that particular procedure. Even this safety net has holes, however, since any doctor can legally set up his own surgical facility and bypass hospital privileges altogether, free from the watchful eyes of other physicians.

The situation is worsening as more and more new doctors enter the lucrative field of plastic surgery and many older, established physicians switch specialties. Doctors can pay to take short, expensive cram courses in fat suction, chemical peels, or other money-making procedures, and can hang a certificate from an official-sounding organization on their walls.

Although these practitioners may have learned the basics of a given procedure, they may not have the training needed to ascertain whether a person is a good candidate. They also may not be able to quickly diagnose and properly treat any complications that occur. Plastic surgery is *surgery*. It has all the potential risks that any operation has and some additional ones.

Plastic surgeons agree that their procedures can be learned and done well by other doctors, but the current environment—the intense competition for patients and the loosening of government restraints on advertising—has made it tough for consumers to separate the legitimate from the questionable.

Does this mean your task is hopeless? Not at all. In fact, now—more than at any time in the past—you are likely to find a well-trained, experienced plastic surgeon who practices somewhere near you.

WHERE TO LOOK

There are nearly 4,000 board-certified plastic surgeons in the United States, far more than ten or twenty years ago. Good cosmetic surgery can be obtained in many communities coast to coast. Given some information, you should be able to make a choice with confidence, regardless of where you live in the United States.

JET-SET PLASTIC SURGERY

California, Florida, New York, and Texas are considered by many to be the U.S. ultracenters for plastic surgery. The level of competition, the abundance of surgeons, and the large number of patients seeking surgery all enhance the quality of care in those areas. The reputation of those centers attracts even more surgeons to move into the regions, so the ultracenters tend to maintain their status quo.

California is one place where innovations, both good and bad, thrive. New surgical techniques often start in California. Many refinements in facelifts and nasal surgery originated in California.

However, not all California trends have been so productive. Acupuncture facelifts, electrical facial "rejuvenators," unproven peel formulas, and fat injections to the breast also started there. Good and bad, these innovations filter quickly across the country.

It's also interesting to note that many people who live in the ultracenters of plastic surgery travel to *other* parts of the country for surgery, because prices are lower or because they want to get away from home for a while.

There are many reasons why someone might want to go out of town for surgery. Price is one factor. There is usually a direct correlation between the price of surgery and a surgeon's overhead. The higher the overhead, the higher the fee.

Another reason to travel, of course, is to obtain the services of a famed plastic surgeon. Going to someone whose reputation is so solid that he is known around the world relieves you of the pressure of making a choice. But Europe and South America do not offer any sensational plastic surgery secrets that American doctors don't know and practice. Unless you are accustomed to living or traveling abroad, having surgery performed in a foreign country—where you may not know the language, and where you may have problems with the food, accommodations, or travel arrangements—may create more stress than the surgery itself.

One very common reason for going out of town for surgery is to get away from home. Some people love the idea of getting on a plane, checking into a hotel, having the surgery, and recuperating in privacy with room and maid service. When they go home, it's all behind them, and no one even has to know they've had surgery. This is a very appealing choice for the right person. However, a problem may arise if you overestimate your desire to be alone. You may start out thinking you want to go through surgery by yourself and may wish afterward that you had your mother or a friend with you to hold your hand, keep you company, cheer you up, and take care of you. Recovering from plastic surgery is like recovering from any other kind of surgery—it's nice to have someone around until you're feeling better. Remember, depending on the procedure, you may not be able to travel for a week or more after surgery.

Some of these drawbacks are now overcome by the latest trend—cosmetic surgery resorts. These recuperative hideaways range from moderately priced, comfortable rural retreats to chic, expensive spas patronized by film stars and foreign royalty. They offer all-inclusive postoperative care, including around-the-clock nurses, massages, facials, and spa cuisine. Sometimes the resort also includes the operating facility; other times surgery takes place at a local hospital or at your surgeon's office, and you are transferred to the spa afterward.

At least one prominent plastic surgeon goes to a different part of the country each time he has *his* surgery, because it gives him a chance to visit another city. His opinion: "Some of the best surgeons I know practice outside of the California-Florida-New York-Texas sphere. They choose to live outside of the competitive stream in a quieter, less pressured environment. Today, you can find superb cosmetic plastic surgeons everywhere in the country."

GETTING STARTED: GATHERING A CHOICE LIST

How do you begin to look for a plastic surgeon? Should you ask a friend, consult your family doctor, ask your local hospital, or look in the yellow pages? These are some of the possibilities, but each has its drawbacks.

A friend who has had good results from plastic surgery can be a good source of information, but you may not get the same outcome. Do not make a decision based on one patient alone. When you do get a name from a friend, such a referral is most helpful if she had the same procedure you're thinking of having. If you're having a facelift and your friend had an abdomino-plasty ("tummy tuck"), her referral may not be as helpful as you'd like.

Your friend may insist that her doctor is "the best." However, when it comes to medicine, and plastic surgery in particular, there is no such thing as the best, just as there is no one best painter or one best chef. The truth is, even when they hold diametrically opposed opinions, competent, skillful plastic surgeons usually end up with good results.

Your family doctor should also be able to give you the name of a plastic surgeon, although other doctors are not always knowledgeable about different fields of medicine and the credentials of their practitioners. Ask your doctor how many patients he or she has actually referred to the recommended plastic surgeon and what feedback they offered later. More specifically, would your doctor send a member of his or her own family to that plastic surgeon?

You can also call a major hospital in your community and ask for names of board-certified plastic surgeons on staff. Make sure you ask for the names of doctors who have privileges to do the particular operation you are seeking.

Do you know an operating room nurse, or someone who knows an operating room nurse? Nurses who work in operating rooms often have the informed, inside story on surgeons.

Looking up a name in the yellow pages can correctly tell you a surgeon's address and telephone number, and often *nothing else*—even if that doctor lists himself under a plastic surgery specialty heading. Doctors are allowed to list themselves under any heading they desire; there are no credential checks performed. Selecting a name from an ad tells you only that the doctor can afford to spend money on advertising. Of all your sources, yellow pages and other ads are the least informative. Exceptions are group listings sponsored by the American Board of Medical Specialties or other organizations representing physicians certified by member boards.

ADVERTISING AND PLASTIC SURGERY

Patients often are lured into consultations by deceptive advertising. Doctors can claim just about anything they want in ads as long as they stay within the letter, if not the spirit, of the law. There have been some instances when a physician used photos of a model or other person in an ad, implying that he was responsible for his or her good looks. However, the model had never had plastic surgery, or had had her surgery done by another doctor. Or, the use of photos may imply that the pictured results can be duplicated for everybody.

When you read ads, be aware that you are being solicited, that someone is trying to sell you something, and that ads cost money that in turn will raise a doctor's overhead. That doesn't mean every doctor who advertises is looking to take advantage of you. Nor is it always the young doctor starting out who resorts to advertising to attract patients. Medical corporations and hospitals advertise. So do some experienced, well-trained physicians trying to get the word out about their services to a broader number of consumers.

In the past, a plastic surgeon's reputation and practice were built over a five- to ten-year period as he or she worked to get referrals from colleagues and patients. Young surgeons built their reputations by accumulating extensive experience, getting consistently good results, and receiving peer recognition for their contributions to medical journals. Now, many are forced by competition and lack of awareness of their services to resort to advertising and self-promotion.

Until 1975, the American Medical Association and other specialty societies did not permit their members to advertise. That tradition changed when the Federal Trade Commission ruled that such restrictions interfered with free competition.

The ASPRS has recommended to the Federal Trade Commission that physicians who advertise be required to state the full name of their certifying board and whether it is "self-designated." The society also suggests that the FTC encourage states to enact laws defining and banning deceptive medical advertising. This would include ads that lead consumers to believe that a particular plastic surgery procedure is painless, free from any chance of complications, or beneficial to everyone. In addition, ads that imply a physician has superior qualifications should be allowed only if the claims can be substantiated.

Doctors who get their names in the paper sometimes have hired publicists who send promotional articles to magazine and newspaper editors. These releases usually wind up in the magazine's files under specific topics, such as plastic surgery; if a story is written on that particular topic in the future the doctor may be called for an interview.

Most journalists try to check on their sources and call the people with the best credentials for interviews and quotes. But they don't always discover the best sources or, even if they do, they can't always reach them for an interview. Sometimes a journalist's deadline pressures, inadequate research, or inexperience means that a less than credible source gets his name mentioned in a national story. For this reason, mention of a doctor's name in a magazine or newspaper story does not guarantee first-rate performance.

One valuable source for names is the ASPRS. You can call the society, giving your address and the procedure you're interested in (call toll-free 1–800–635–0635). Within a week, the ASPRS will send you the names of ten board-certified plastic surgeons who perform that procedure in your area. You can show this list to your family doctor and ask if he or she is familiar with any of the names. You can also check a hospital that you hold in high regard to find out if any of the surgeons on the ASPRS list are on its medical staff.

At your local library you will find the names of board-certified plastic surgeons listed by state and city in two comprehensive reference books: *The Directory of Medical Specialists* and *The Compendium of Certified Medical Specialists*.

Your objective is to come up with a list of three or more names. Getting the list together is only the first step. If some of the names turn up several times—for instance, if your friend recommends a surgeon whose name is also given to you by your hospital or by the ASPRS—that is a name you definitely want to consider. (The fact that a name is not duplicated on more than one list, however, doesn't necessarily mean that a doctor is unqualified. The ASPRS sends only a partial list of names, and some good people may be left off.)

HOW TO CHECK CREDENTIALS

Although good credentials do not guarantee a good surgical result, they are an important screening tool. You have a greater probability of success if you are in the hands of a fully trained, experienced surgeon. What constitutes good training?

What Is a Plastic Surgeon?

Plastic surgery encompasses both reconstructive and cosmetic (or aesthetic) surgery. Cosmetic procedures evolved out of reconstructive surgery, in which body parts and facial features are rebuilt after trauma, disease, or birth defect. The level of skill required for reconstructive surgery can enhance a physician's ability to perform cosmetic procedures.

Physicians who call themselves cosmetic surgeons often do not have this background in all aspects of plastic surgery. It is common today for physicians to receive their original training in an unrelated specialty, then switch to cosmetic surgery in later years. They may justify the switch by taking a weekend workshop, studying videotapes of cosmetic surgery procedures, or completing an official-sounding "fellowship" in cosmetic surgery. While these are all good methods of obtaining continuing medical education, they cannot *replace* an appropriate, accredited residency program. Most fellowships and workshops are brief when compared to a residency program in plastic surgery. In addition, these workshops and fellowships can be sponsored by anyone, and usually operate away from the intense review that accompanies an accredited residency in plastic surgery.

Board Certification

The American Board of Medical Specialties (ABMS) exists to promote high standards in patient care through the establishment of criteria for physician training. Its associate members include six of the major organizations within the medical community, including the American Medical Association. The ABMS recognizes one certifying board per specialty, each of which tests and certifies physicians in their fields of expertise.

In 1941, the ABMS designated the American Board of Plastic Surgery (ABPS) as the only one of its bodies authorized to certify plastic surgeons. The nineteen directors of the American Board of Plastic Surgery evaluate the education, training, and knowledge of physicians who desire to practice the specialty. To be eligible to take the rigorous exams, applicants must first graduate from an accredited medical school in the United States or Canada. (Graduates of medical schools in other countries must meet additional requirements.) They must then complete three or more years of approved residency training in general surgery. (Many applicants opt to extend this training to five years.) Alternatively, applicants may complete a residency in orthopedic surgery or may be previously certified by the American Board of Otolaryngology (ear, nose, and throat medicine). Finally, applicants must complete at least two years of approved residency training specifically in plastic surgery.

Fulfilling these requirements qualifies physicians as eligible to begin the certification process. Certification comes only after they practice plastic surgery for two years or longer, are judged to meet the high ethical standards of the ABPS, and pass exhaustive written and oral examinations. These tests cover all aspects of plastic surgery, ranging from standard cosmetic surgery procedures to reconstructive surgery. Only after passing these exams may physicians call themselves board-certified plastic surgeons.

Some other boards recognized by the American Board of Medical Specialties require their members to also be trained in specific plastic surgery procedures. For example, ear, nose, and throat specialists, who are certified by the American Board of Otolaryngology, are trained to perform procedures on the head and neck. In addition, ophthalmologists do eyelid surgery, and dermatologists may perform skin treatments, such as dermabrasion and chemical peels.

Physicians certified in plastic surgery are trained to perform such procedures on every part of the body and to cope with complication's that may occur. Although certification in the specialty does not guarantee a good result, it is the most reliable bottom line for patients.

Be wary of self-designated organizations that sound impressive, but are recognized only by their own members. A self-designated medical "board" is free from external checks and balances.

Go to the library. Look in the Marquis Who's Who book called the *Directory of Medical Specialists*. This book lists most doctors in the United States who are certified by an ABMS-member board. Listings will document where the physician went to school, which specialty he was trained in, what board certified him, whether he is on the faculty of a medical school, and what professional societies he belongs to. If you are gathering names of plastic surgeons in a specific area, look at volume 2, which lists all certified plastic surgeons, ophthalmologists, and otolaryngologists by state and city.

In addition, the ABMS publishes its own directory. It is called the *ABMS Compendium of Certified Medical Specialists* and is available in most large libraries. You may also call the ASPRS (1–800–635–0635) or the ABMS (1–800–776–2378) to check on a doctor's credentials. The ASPRS can tell you if a particular doctor is certified in plastic surgery, or has completed the required training and is working toward certification. The ABMS can tell you which of its twenty-three recognized boards, if any, have approved the physician you're considering.

CREDENTIALS CHECKLIST

Good:
- Recommended by a friend who had similar procedure
- Recommended by family doctor
- Listed by ASPRS
- Board-certified in specialty related to your procedure
- Completed residency in specialty related to your procedure, e.g.:
    Plastic surgery—all areas of the body
    Otolaryngology (ENT)—head and neck
    Ophthalmology—eyes
    Dermatology—skin

Uninformative:
- Yellow pages listing
- Other advertising
- Recommendation by your hairdresser
- Media mention

Warning:
- No hospital privileges for procedure desired
- Certified in unrelated specialty
- Completed residency in unrelated specialty

Professional Medical Societies

Physicians belong to a bewildering variety of professional societies and many doctors advertise their membership. Some professional societies have stringent membership requirements, whereas others are relatively lax.

Physicians may also point to the *number* of procedures they perform as a substitute for formal training. However, *quantity* alone cannot be used to judge depth of skill. We all know duffers who have played golf for decades and still shoot well above par.

If a doctor tells you he belongs to a particular society, get the *exact* name and then ask what the requirements for membership are. Of course, even the most demanding set of requirements cannot screen out every questionable physician, but it offers additional reassurances. The largest, and among the most stringent, of the societies that represent certified plastic surgeons is the American Society of Plastic and Reconstructive Surgeons (ASPRS). It boasts a membership of more than 4,000—including 97 percent of the physicians in the United States who are certified by the American Board of Plastic Surgery. In addition to requiring its active members to be certified by the ABPS, the society subjects its applicants to review by their peers. Once they are accepted into active membership, physicians must continue to earn this status by adhering to a strict code of ethics and completing a minimum number of continuing education hours every three years.

Another prominent organization of certified plastic surgeons is the American Society for Aesthetic Plastic Surgery. Composed of about 900 surgeons, most of its members also belong to the ASPRS and have a particular interest in the cosmetic area of plastic surgery.

Making Phone Calls

If a doctor who has been highly recommended does not appear in the *Directory of Medical Specialists,* and his status cannot be confirmed by the ASPRS or ABMS referral services, call his office and ask for a copy of his curriculum vitae (CV). You're looking to discover the nature of the doctor's training, not how many medical meetings he has attended or what his hobbies are. Look for completion of an accredited residency program in a specialty relevant to the cosmetic procedure you wish to have. For example, if his residency is in otolaryngology and your procedure involves the head and neck, *that* would be a relevant specialty. Remember, "fellowships" alone are not enough.

If the CV says he is "board certified," it should also name the specific board that tested him. If it does not, *cross his name off the list.* If the board is named, but your research indicates it is not recognized by the American Board of Medical Specialties, consider whether you still want to pursue this particular surgeon. If so, call back and ask for an explanation of his formal training in the procedure you are considering. Unfortunately, the office staff is frequently uninformed on this subject and may suggest that you come in for a consultation with the physician. Do so if you continue to be interested in the physician in question, but remember that you will probably be charged for the meeting.

Ask for a range of fees for the procedure you're considering. No one can quote you an exact price over the telephone, because the actual costs depend on variables such as how much "work" you need to have done. However, most reputable doctors can tell you what ballpark you're playing in.

On the telephone, you can also ask how often the doctor performs the particular procedure you want. As a rule, a plastic surgeon renowned for his breast reconstructions also does good facelifts, and vice versa. However, a few plastic surgeons become heavily involved in one subspecialty and, as time goes on, tend to concentrate exclusively on one area of the body. An ethical surgeon will tell you straight out how experienced he is in a given procedure. There isn't a magic number that defines competence, but the answer should make you feel comfortable. The surgeon should tell you if he's had a lot of experience, if he's done the procedure a few times, or if he hasn't done it for several years. If the last is the case, he will usually refer you to another colleague.

Hospital Privileges

Even if your surgery will be performed in your doctor's own surgical facility, he should have privileges to perform the procedure at an accredited hospital in the community. Your physician should meet the same standards of training and qualifications that you expect of a hospital-based surgeon who is subject to approval by a body of his peers.

If you are told the doctor operates "in his own facility," but also has hospital privileges at a particular hospital, call that hospital to double-check. Ask specifically if the doctor is allowed to perform your procedure, using the hospital operating facilities. If the doctor tells you that he doesn't need to have hospital privileges, *cross him off your list.*

The Consultation

WHEN YOU HAVE COMPLETED YOUR CREDENTIALS CHECK AND YOUR phone calls, you should have two or three thoroughly screened names. Should you make appointments to see all of these doctors? There is no rule that says you must. If you've been selective in your screening up to this point, you may not have to look very far. Start with one interview at a time. If you're comfortable with the first surgeon you meet, you may decide to look no further. If you want to have a second or even a third consultation, do it.

However, if you have had three consultations with physicians from a carefully compiled list and still can't decide who to choose, ask yourself why you are shopping around. Are you looking for a cheaper price? (There are no bargains in plastic surgery.) Or a doctor who guarantees the result? (No good doctor will offer you such a guarantee.)

Perhaps you're looking for something very specific that you haven't yet found. It may be that the type of procedure you're looking for isn't possible in your particular case. Perhaps deep down you are ambivalent about having plastic surgery. You might wish to more closely examine your motivations and needs before consulting another doctor. Perhaps you're just not ready yet. People often become interested in plastic surgery and then let it ride for several months before making a decision.

If the plastic surgeon you consult advises against surgery, by all means get a second opinion. If the second surgeon concurs, it's likely that you should start looking for ways to accept that reality. Continuing to seek plastic surgery may mean that you end up with an unethical doctor who will operate on you simply because you insist on it.

PAYING FOR CONSULTATIONS

A consultation may cost $50 to $100 or more. Some plastic surgeons offer free consultations, but most top professionals charge and this fee is not covered by insurance. Depending on the procedure, a consultation may take from fifteen minutes to an hour, which means time and record-keeping expense for the doctor. The investment is worth it to you. After you have chosen a doctor, you may wish for a second consultation before you actually schedule surgery. Most of the time, plastic surgeons will not charge extra for an additional consultation.

BRINGING QUESTIONS

Take a list of key questions with you to the consultation. That way, you can review your list to make sure everything has been covered.

You can also jot down the information the doctor gives you. You don't have to write down everything he says, just the pertinent details that you might otherwise forget. The doctor will probably also give you some written material to take home with you to read later.

QUESTIONS TO ASK

Here are the questions that should be fully explored during the course of the consultation:

- From a physiological perspective, is this the proper time in your life to have cosmetic surgery? Would you be better off waiting a few years?
- What procedures are available to improve the problem you have? Which would be best for you and why?
- Are there other ways to perform your procedure besides the technique preferred by your surgeon? The surgeon should tell you what other surgical options, if any, are available to you. (For instance, if you are having breast reconstruction, the surgeon should tell you about free-flap techniques, even if he prefers to use implants.)
- What results can you probably expect, given your skin, bone, and body type?
- How long can you expect the results to last?
- Where will the scars be located, and how noticeable will they be? Will they improve with time, and how long will that take?
- Is any part of the procedure painful?
- What type of anesthesia does the doctor recommend? Who will administer it? (See chapter 4.)
- Will surgery be done in a hospital, an office-based facility, or a freestanding clinic? Do you have a choice?
- What is the difference in cost between the hospital and the outpatient facility?
- Is there much pain or discomfort after the operation?
- What kind of care will you need following surgery? Will you need someone to take you home? Will you need someone to take care of you for a while? For how long?
- What are the full instructions for postoperative care? When can you resume physical activity?
- When can you go back to work?
- Will there be much bruising and swelling? How long will it last? When can you wear makeup?
- How many days must pass before you can expect to feel comfortable in a social setting?
- How many weeks or months does the entire healing process take?

■ What is the total cost of the procedure, including fees for the surgeon, anesthesiologist (if any), operating facility, and supplies?

■ Will follow-up visits for postoperative care be charged separately?

■ Is any part of the cost usually covered by insurance? (For a definite answer to this question, you will have to check with your own insurance carrier.)

■ What complications can occur? Are these complications common or rare? Are they likely to occur during surgery or after surgery?

■ If a complication arises that needs further treatment, do you have to pay additional medical bills?

■ If the results are not what you hoped for, can the operation be repeated? What are the chances for success the second time? Will you have to pay for this second operation?

BRINGING A FRIEND

For most people, a one-on-one meeting with the doctor offers the best opportunity to establish rapport and understanding. However, your circumstances may be unique and you may feel differently. A teenager or young person should bring at least one parent. A married woman considering breast surgery is encouraged to bring her husband. If you are particularly nervous or uneasy, bring a friend or family member who can act as a backup in terms of remembering what went on during the consultation.

If you do choose to bring a friend or relative, it should be the person who will go through the operation with you or help you afterward. It should be someone you trust and who is supportive. The doctor can't be expected to relate to both of you at the same time. His main interest is you. The friend's role is to listen quietly. You can compare notes afterward.

THE DOCTOR'S OFFICE

The purpose of an in-person consultation is to discover if the surgeon clearly understands your needs and whether he will be committed to your welfare. The doctor's staff should be professional and pleasant. The office should have a relaxed yet efficient atmosphere.

It's a good sign if a doctor's staff thinks well of him, but there's a line and you must judge it for yourself. Does the staff seem to be selling you on the doctor? A good surgeon doesn't need, or want, this kind of obvious promotion from his staff.

A surgeon's office should look well kept and professional, although the "look" of a plastic surgeon's office is decidedly different in various parts of the country. Certain cities are known to have high standards of medicine (such as Boston and New York), but the offices tend to have an academic, even worn, look. Some of the best university offices are mere cubbyholes.

Southern California and Texas favor more chic and glamorous motifs, sometimes with theme decor or impressive art collections. Many Boston plastic surgeons would be appalled at a Los Angeles–type office. And a Boston office would probably look seedy to a California physician.

The one thing that never changes, no matter what the office looks like, is the character of the doctor. The office may be modern and glitzy, or frumpy and traditional, but you're still looking for the quality of the human being who practices medicine there.

GIVING YOUR MEDICAL HISTORY

Before meeting the doctor, you will be asked to fill out a questionnaire about your medical history. The purpose of history-taking is to avoid complications later on. Giving a complete medical history means that should a complication arise, your plastic surgeon will better know how to cope with it. Further, reviewing your medical history during the consultation is an opportunity for both of you to establish rapport.

MEETING THE DOCTOR

You will probably like the physician you meet, because plastic surgery tends to attract individuals who are personable, sensitive, and appreciative of the aesthetics of life. Many are interested in art and have extensive collections on display, or they may be painters or sculptors themselves. The specialty also demands that its practitioners be detail-oriented.

For you to feel satisfied and happy with the results of plastic surgery, you must feel that you have achieved more than a good technical result. You also should have a positive experience. In the event that you develop a problem or a complication after surgery, you should still feel satisfied that the doctor and staff have taken good care of you.

Good plastic surgeons understand the need for personal, hands-on care throughout the process. Even though they may have done the procedure 500 times, it's a once-in-a-lifetime experience for you. Your surgeon should be concerned about everything that concerns you. That kind of attention can turn an average experience into a positive one for you.

The most ethical plastic surgeons thrive on happy patients and successful outcomes. As one well-known surgeon says, "We don't like failure. I take it as a personal affront if something goes wrong, so I do everything I can to assure a good result. If something should go wrong, I want to be there myself to take care of it." It is interesting that of all the medical specialists, plastic surgeons have the highest job satisfaction rate, probably, they say, because the majority of their patients are happy with their results.

Just because a doctor has an engaging personality and is easy to talk to, doesn't guarantee that he is a good surgeon. Likewise, a doctor may be abrupt and still be an excellent surgeon. Occasionally, a doctor will give a little speech to inform you fully of what you need to know, but he becomes nervous if you interrupt and ask questions. Perhaps he's afraid he'll leave out something important if you interrupt his discourse. A good compromise is to allow this type of doctor to deliver his talk, then ask questions after he's finished.

How would you feel about having a surgeon who doesn't like dealing with questions and answers? Again, it's your choice. You have a lot of power in this decision-making process.

PATIENT'S WATCH LIST

Beware if the doctor:

- Seems too eager to do surgery, or says he can schedule your surgery the next day because "we had a cancellation." (Never choose a doctor who will do the operation overnight or that afternoon. You should always have plenty of time to think about it.)
- Toots his own horn and praises himself (or claims to be the first or only doctor to do a particular procedure).
- Urges you to consider additional unrelated cosmetic procedures (for example, you come in for a facelift and he talks to you about breast surgery, or vice versa).
- Guarantees a good result and doesn't mention potential risks.
- Relies on sensational advertising.
- Says he charges more because "I'm the best."
- Offers cut-rate prices.

CONSENT FORMS

During the consultation, the doctor should explain the procedure, the risks involved, and the probability of success for you. He should voluntarily discuss the possible complications and willingly provide the answers to all the questions on your key list. He or one of his staff will also explain the costs involved (see chapter 4) and may give you written material concerning your particular procedure.

All of the information the doctor gives you, both spoken and written, is ultimately preparing you to sign an informed-consent form should you decide to go forward with the surgery. If you are underage, a parent will also have to sign this form. A consent form may sometimes be rather intimidating because it usually spells out every imaginable complication.

There is an interesting side note regarding informed consent. Studies have shown that patients forget about 60 percent of what they hear in the consultation, especially when it comes to complications. No one wants to go into surgery dwelling on the possible consequences if something goes wrong. Even so, it's important that you fully understand potential complications so you can weigh the risk/benefit ratio for yourself.

At the end of the consultation, the doctor will ask you to read the consent form. If there is anything in the form that surprises you, or something the doctor has not explained, ask him about it. When you are comfortable with the contents of the form, sign it.

BEFORE SIGNING THE CONSENT FORM

Before you sign the consent form and set a date for surgery, can you answer yes to the following questions?

- Do you have a clear idea of the result you can expect?
- Are you clear about the result the doctor expects?
- Are these two pictures the same? (Do you and your doctor agree on the surgical objectives?)
- Do you know the incidence of complications for your procedure?
- Do you know what kind of scars you can expect?
- Have you chosen a good time to schedule surgery, with adequate time for recovery?

DEFINING THE PROBLEM

Describing the cosmetic problem you want fixed may not be easy. You might know exactly the procedure you want. It's more likely, however, that you have an idea of what bothers you, but don't know the best procedure to correct it. Maybe you're not even sure what troubles you; you just have a vague idea that something isn't right. It's part of the surgeon's job to help you identify the cause of your discontent.

Ethical plastic surgeons try *not* to tell you what they think personally about your appearance. They know that their observations, like everyone else's, are subjective—and that their comments can persuade you to have surgery you may not want or need. If you are unsure of what procedure you want done, the surgeon should ask you questions to help *you* zero in on the problem. For instance, a reputable surgeon will ask you to describe the cosmetic problem that bothers you and why you want it changed. You may say that your face shows signs of aging, but you don't know if you need a facelift, a chemical peel, a browlift, or eyelid surgery. The plastic surgeon can then tell you which procedure or procedures will give you the best result at this time in your life.

A plastic surgeon should not try to sell you on every possible procedure he can perform. If you come to the doctor because your face is aging and he tells you he can do a great tummy tuck on you, or give you breast implants, look out. A doctor who creates dissatisfaction where none existed is a doctor you don't need.

The doctor will also ask you about your motivations. Good plastic surgeons are sensitive to the psychological component of cosmetic surgery and are alert for underlying emotional problems. That's why well-trained plastic surgeons ask open-ended questions: "How are you feeling?" "What makes you think of having the surgery now?" These questions help you focus on your real wishes.

It's in your best interests to be honest about your motivations, what you hope to achieve, and why you want to have the surgery. You may think that if you hold back information the doctor may more readily accept you. However, a doctor who doesn't have all the facts may end up recommending the wrong procedure and you will be the one to suffer. So don't cheat yourself by not being totally honest with your physician.

Many people today are so well informed about plastic surgery that they know how to keep a "hidden agenda" hidden. Let's say you tell your doctor that you want breast augmentation because your small breasts have always bothered you. As far as it goes, your statement is true. But there's more to it. Suppose your marriage is falling apart and deep in your heart you hope that the breast implants will bring back your husband.

Just how serious is that secret you're keeping from your surgeon? Chances are you will still be satisfied with your surgery. It probably will *not* save your marriage, although you may be happy with the surgical results anyway. But if this "hidden agenda" is a top priority and you deliberately mislead your surgeon, you are the one who will be disappointed.

Since you are spending your money and taking the risks, it's in your own best interests to be as honest as you can with your doctor. If you can talk about your secret wishes, your surgeon may be able to help you get a better grasp on the situation and view it more realistically. Patients who are open with their doctors and are clear about why they want surgery are the patients that a good surgeon will accept, and these are the patients who are most likely to be satisfied with their results.

During the consultation, the doctor will delve into your medical background and possibly your psychological history. He will ask if you take any prescription medications. Because they may interact with anesthetic agents or cause bleeding problems, dosages may have to be adjusted or temporarily discontinued just before and after surgery. Over-the-counter medications can also cause problems. It's important that you describe any chronic disease you suffer from such as heart disease, hypertension, or diabetes. Even if the condition is well controlled, you will require additional monitoring during surgery; it's also possible that your plastic surgeon will want to consult with the physician who treats your illness.

It's to your advantage to be completely honest with the doctor during this phase of the consultation. Some patients are afraid to tell the doctor about their drug or alcohol habits. But withholding this information may cause potential complications from anesthesia, thus endangering your life. If you take drugs, tell your doctor.

It's also important for you to tell the plastic surgeon if you are currently being treated by a psychotherapist or if you have had emotional problems in the past. Your plastic surgeon will want to talk to your therapist and may call him or her during the consultation with your permission. This conversation is a precaution on your behalf, to make sure that you all agree that plastic surgery at this time in your life is in your best interests.

For instance, people prone to depression or extreme mood swings are especially vulnerable after any kind of surgery because of metabolic changes brought on by surgery and anesthesia. Your therapist and plastic surgeon can make sure that the timing is right for you and that you are adequately prepared for surgery.

Occasionally, plastic surgeons encounter patients with severe emotional problems who believe that cosmetic surgery will resolve their problems. Experienced plastic surgeons usually can spot someone whose desire for surgery is deeply rooted in a longstanding psychiatric condition and such a person usually will not be accepted for surgery.

PHOTOGRAPHS—YES OR NO?

Some doctors show before-and-after photographs because they feel that a picture helps the patient visualize the benefits of the operation as well as its limitations. Other doctors hesitate to show postop photos because a prospective patient may not have the features that lend themselves to the same result.

Some surgeons have a book of photos on display in the reception area for patients to browse through; others frown on this practice because they feel photos should always be accompanied by a personal explanation from the doctor or his staff. Postop photos also can be misleading. They may be taken in better lighting and at better angles than the preop photos. The pictured person may be wearing a new style of makeup, may have just come from the hairdresser, or may have lost weight following surgery.

Keep in mind that physicians usually show photos only of their good results, not of outcomes that were only fair or poor. A before-and-after photo is never a promise. No two people start with the same coloring, the same bones, or the same skin.

If the doctor doesn't volunteer to show pictures and you would like to see them, by all means ask. If the surgeon shows you pictures of good results, you can also ask to see photos of a result that didn't turn out so well.

COMPUTER-IMAGING MACHINES

An imaging machine looks like a computer terminal with a monitor and a keyboard. The surgeon takes a picture of you with a video camera and your image is transferred to the screen. Using a pencil-like "mouse" the doctor can draw right on the screen, changing your image in front of your eyes.

An imaging machine can be helpful, but it is only a two-dimensional sketch. A computer-clever surgeon can turn your head upside down on the machine, but he could never do that in real life, no matter how good a surgeon he is.

A computer-imaging machine can help you look into the unknown to get some ideas. It is sometimes useful for people who are uncertain whether they want surgery. When they see the change they could get, they realize it's not going to give them what they want. In other words, the machine can help people choose *not* to have surgery because they wouldn't be happy with the result.

Some surgeons use drawings, some use clay models, and others draw on photographs. Like these other methods, the computer is only a tool. The nose you can create on the computer may not be possible with skin and bone. The imaging machine cannot take into account your skin elasticity, your cartilage and bone structure, or the way you heal. It cannot judge the blood supply to the surgical area. It cannot judge the skill of the surgeon who is actually going to operate on you. A doctor can be a whiz with a computer, but much less skillful with a scalpel. Some plastic surgeons also feel that using a computer-imaging machine takes up valuable time that would be better spent talking to the patient.

That being said, computer-imaging machines are sometimes used by good doctors. They are also sometimes used by not-so-good doctors. If a doctor uses a computer to deceive you into thinking you will have a perfect, guaranteed result, he's just as likely to deceive you by some other means. Your final focus should not be on the computer image but on the individual who uses it.

PREDICTING RESULTS

Your age, skin type, general health, genetic background, and the nature of the problem you wish to correct will influence the surgery's ultimate result. Another variable is the blood supply to the area to be operated on. The face heals faster than the legs because of its more ample blood supply. Another important factor is the presence of a hidden infection in your body that may migrate to the incision site during cosmetic surgery. That's why your surgeon will order a urinalysis, blood count, and other tests before surgery. Your ability to heal is also influenced by the degree of sun damage to your skin and whether you smoke, and if you are willing to stop smoking for at least a week or two before and after surgery. (Smoking constricts the blood vessels and decreases nourishing blood flow.)

The surgeon can consider such known factors before surgery and say with some degree of certainty whether there's a strong chance that this particular patient, with this complexion, this build, and this previous scar elsewhere on the body, will end up with a good scar, meaning one that is nearly invisible. Everybody heals differently, however, and there's no way to exactly predict the outcome. Five incisions done by the same surgeon, the same way, on five different people will all heal differently.

There is another aspect of predictability. Some procedures can be done quickly, with less probability of complications. For instance, the success of upper eyelid surgery is fairly predictable. However, as surgical procedures become more complicated, such as the facelift, the risks go up, and the probability of good results decreases.

On the plus side, most of the procedures done today have been perfected over several decades. The technical aspects of the surgery have been refined, the scientific knowledge of tissue is broader, surgeons are more skillful and better trained, and anesthetics are vastly improved. Surgeons say that plastic surgery procedures can be done better and more safely today than ever before. By choosing the best-qualified surgeon, you give yourself the best possible chance for a successful outcome.

PREDICTING SCARS

So many variables contribute to scarring—the blood supply to the area, your skin type, your physician's technique, and your general health—that even the most experienced plastic surgeon cannot predict exactly what kind of a scar an incision will leave. No two scars are alike, even in the same person.

Look at other scars on your body if you have any. If they are minor, you are likely to heal well again this time, although you can't be certain. If they are severe, you have a higher than normal chance of healing poorly again and you may not want to have a cosmetic surgery procedure on your face, such as a facelift, chemical peel, or dermabrasion. However, there is no certainty that you will scar the same way again; many people have a bad scar from previous surgery on their abdomen, for instance, but heal well after a facelift. Talk it over with your plastic surgeon.

Here are some general ground rules that can help predict what kind of scar you will form:

- Older skin scars less than youthful skin.
- Thinner skin scars less than thicker skin.
- Lighter skin scars less than darker skin.
- Scarring is less noticeable on the face, where skin is usually thin. Scars are worse on the back, shoulders, and other parts of the body where skin is thickest.
- Skin heals best in areas with a healthy blood supply, such as the face. Scars are more pronounced on the legs and other areas where circulation is poor.
- Scars are less conspicuous when the incision is made in an area where the skin is relaxed, and worse when they run across lines of tension. Thus, scars may pull and widen on the chest because the weight of the breasts creates constant tension. Elbows and knees, which are frequently bent and flexed, can also be problem areas.
- Scarring may also have a genetic component. Members of some families all share a tendency to develop significant scars.

Plastic surgeons always try to place incisions strategically, so even if the worst happens and an "angry" or "ropey" scar results, it will be out of view. Fortunately, most scars fade and flatten with time. If a raised scar develops, your plastic surgeon may inject it with steroids to flatten it; however, this treatment, which softens skin, may also cause the scar to widen.

SCAR REVISIONS

Keloids are thickly puckered, dark-colored, itchy clusters of irregular scar tissue that continue to grow beyond the site of the incision. They can occur anywhere on the body, but are most common over the breastbone and shoulders. They also occur more often in dark-skinned people than in those who are fair. However, the tendency to develop keloids lessens with age.

Steroids injected directly into the scar may reduce itchiness and cause some shrinkage. The scar tissue can also be cut out, although the same kind of scar may form again. In a typical operation to remove a keloid, the scar is removed and the wound is closed with two layers of sutures. A skin graft sometimes is used to avoid stretching the skin too tightly over the wound. To discourage recurrence of the keloid, steroids may be applied directly to the wound during surgery, or a small amount of radiation therapy may be administered soon after the operation. Other preventive techniques include wearing a pressure garment over the area for six months to a year or applying a sheet of silicone gel to the wound for a month or more.

Plastic surgeons can often improve other old scars on the body that have resulted from previous surgery or accidents. No scar can be removed completely, but many scars can be made less noticeable. Scar revision may be performed in your surgeon's office, in a freestanding surgical facility, or in a hospital. Costs vary widely, depending on the complexity of the operation, where the surgery takes place, and the kind of anesthesia used. Thousands of successful scar revisions are performed each year. In addition to keloids, the most common scars that require revision are:

Facial scars. A facial scar that crosses the crease between the nose and mouth can be made less conspicuous by using a technique called Z-plasty. This technique, which can be used on many other areas of the body as well, involves removing the old scar, then making two additional incisions on either side to create small flaps that can be rotated to cover the wound. It allows the surgeon to change the direction of the scar so that instead of going across the crease the scar more closely conforms to the natural skin fold. The repositioning makes the new scar less visible. This kind of procedure is normally performed under local anesthesia.

Some facial scars can be softened with dermabrasion (see chapter 11).

Hypertrophic scars. Thick, red, angry-looking scars are called hypertrophic. This kind of ropey scar often will grow lighter and flatter with time, and for this reason scar revision is not undertaken for several months, or for even a year or longer after the wound has healed. An application or injection of steroids may help improve the scar in the meantime.

If surgery is recommended, the excess scar tissue is removed and the incision occasionally is repositioned so that it will heal in a more normal pattern. This surgery may be done under a local or general anesthetic depending on the scar's location. Steroid injections may be given again during surgery (and regularly for up to two years afterward) to prevent the thick scar from reforming.

Burn scars. Burns or other massive injuries resulting in the loss of a large area of skin may form hypertrophic scars that can cause muscles, tendons, and joints to contract. Revising these scars often involves creating a zigzag incision using the Z-plasty technique, which releases tension on the scar. When large areas of skin are involved, skin grafts may be needed to restore full function, and you will probably be instructed to wear a special support garment or bandage over the area for up to a year. This kind of extensive surgery often requires more than one operation. However, the result is a much thinner scar that more closely follows natural skin folds.

If you have any kind of scar revision, it's important to closely follow your surgeon's recommendations during recuperation. Your degree of improvement depends on the size and direction of your scar, the nature and quality of your skin, and how well you care for the wound after the operation.

Cross off your list any surgeon who promises a good result, who says the procedure is "real easy, I do this all the time, no problem, you'll look great." The probability of success may be 95 or even 98 percent, but even in the most capable hands, the best surgical candidate may still have a significant complication.

The word that all plastic surgeons use is *trade-off.* There is a trade-off in every procedure. It may be a scar; it may be a risk of complication. It's up to the plastic surgeon to tell you what the possible trade-offs are. If the swap seems like a poor one for you, you don't have to make the trade. If it seems reasonable, you can choose to go forward.

CONSULTATION CHECKLIST

In a consultation, you should use your judgment and intuition to evaluate the plastic surgeon just as you would when meeting anyone new. After the consultation, ask yourself if the surgeon met these basic criteria:

- He was willing to discuss his credentials in detail.
- He has privileges to perform your procedure at a reputable hospital in your community.

- If he has an office-based surgery facility, it is approved by one of the three watchdog agencies. (This is not a must, since many office-based facilities are not accredited, but it is an extra assurance of quality. See chapter 4.)
- He displayed a caring attitude.
- He answered all of your questions.
- He openly volunteered information.
- He readily told you how often he does the procedure.
- He asked what you would like plastic surgery to do for you.
- He didn't try to "sell" you on procedures to fix problems that hadn't bothered you before you walked into his office.
- If you were uncertain of what procedures you wanted, he tried to help you focus on what was bothering you.
- He spent adequate time with you.
- He took a thorough medical history and reviewed it with you.
- The physical examination was carried out carefully and professionally.
- He was the type of person you would feel comfortable with if something were to go wrong.
- At the end of the consultation, he asked you to call back if you had any further questions.
- If you have already booked surgery, you are still treated with consideration and attention when you call the doctor's office.
- If you were undecided at the end of the consultation, the doctor suggested that you discuss the procedure with your spouse or family, take printed material home with you, and think about it.

ABOUT POSTOP CARE

Ask the doctor if he will personally see you for follow-up visits after surgery, or if you will be checked by a staff person. Cosmetic surgery patients may feel let down after the procedure because the immediate postop results—bruising and swelling—often don't look the way they imagined. In the first few days postop it's common for people to question why they ever had surgery at all. You want to be sure that the person who consults with you after surgery will be able to tell if your feelings are typical or if you're a little the worse for wear and need a bit of encouragement. An important part of the job of the plastic surgeon and his staff is to be responsive to you.

In addition, although major complications seldom occur, if they do happen it can mean everything to you to have your surgeon on the spot. Even minor complications should receive the personal attention of your doctor.

It's not easy to judge beforehand how your doctor will react to a postoperative problem. It helps to notice what he does before surgery. If you call him with a question, does he take your call or get back to you the same day? If he orders a mammogram for you and says he'll get back to you in a couple of days, does he do it?

HOW YOUR DOCTOR EVALUATES YOU

In a consultation, you evaluate the doctor, and the doctor also evaluates you. There's a lot of selectivity on the part of surgeons. As one prominent plastic surgeon has said, "We earn our living by the patients we operate on, and we earn our reputations by the patients we refuse to operate on."

There are several reasons why a surgeon may reject a particular patient. The individual's general medical health may be poor. Someone who had a recent heart attack, for instance, would be advised by most plastic surgeons to wait until his or her cardiologist approves the operation. Someone else may have other medical problems, such as blood clotting problems, uncontrolled high blood pressure, or a heart irregularity that could be life threatening; these patients should not be accepted.

Or, the doctor may feel that no matter how good the result, he is facing a patient who will never be satisfied. For instance, one thirty-year-old woman consulted with a plastic surgeon about having her prominent nose reshaped and insisted that the physician examine her mother as well. The patient's mother had a small, turned-up nose and the daughter hoped to re-create that feature for herself. Although much could be done to make her nose smaller and to give the tip more delicacy and projection, it could never look like the mother's. The daughter's bones were simply too big and her skin was too thick. Even if the surgeon achieved a wonderful technical result, the patient might feel disappointed because the nose wouldn't match her ideal.

It is your responsibility to make your surgeon aware of your expectations, but a good plastic surgeon will help you zero in on your feelings. If it becomes apparent that you are not likely to be satisfied with the probable result, your doctor will probably refuse to perform the operation. A good surgeon usually prefers to disappoint a patient temporarily by refusing to operate rather than having a disappointed patient after the surgery.

YOUR SATISFACTION

If you understand the limits of what can be achieved, and still believe the benefits are worth it, you are likely to be satisfied with surgery. For instance, a person whose facial skin has lost its tone with age, but who also has extensive wrinkles from sun exposure, may look fresher and better after a facelift. However, she won't get a miraculous result. If she understands these limitations and accepts them, she will be viewed as a good candidate for surgery.

If an individual's goal is viewed as unrealistic by one plastic surgeon, it may help to get another opinion. If the second doctor echoes the first, it may be best to wait a while and reconsider surgery in the future.

MAKING YOUR CHOICE

You may decide at the end of the consultation to go forward with that particular doctor or to think it over for a few days. You may also decide to see someone else for another consultation.

It's not unusual for a prospective patient to leave the consultation disheartened to learn that the surgery is more complicated and more serious than she or he had hoped. Some people go through a period of ambivalence and then decide later to have the operation.

If you choose to go forward with the surgery, the doctor will sometimes recommend a second meeting, or you may ask for one. A second consultation with your chosen doctor is usually recommended if you feel uncertain or if you have so many questions that they can't be answered at one time. In addition, if an important person in your life is against your having plastic surgery, let your doctor know. Unless you're underage and your parents refuse to sign the informed-consent form, surgery is *your* choice. However, your plastic surgeon may be able to help you resolve any conflicts that exist by inviting the dissenter—whether it's your partner, parent, or closest friend—to come with you for the second consultation.

SCHEDULING SURGERY

Once you have made a decision, it's time to schedule the operation. Some surgeons will work out the date with you while you are still in the office. Others will call you later, letting you know the possible dates from their end.

Most patients want their surgery as soon as possible after they have decided upon it. Some people like to schedule surgery on their vacations or over an extended holiday. Others like to take only a few days off work and get back as soon as possible.

It's important for you to accurately assess how much time you need for recovery. With some minor procedures you may feel well almost immediately, although bruising and swelling will last longer. More extensive procedures can have a serious impact on your body, requiring two weeks or more before you feel back to normal.

Think twice about having surgery over a Christmas and New Year's holiday. Although many students and working people choose this time slot, it can be depressing to face New Year's Eve with a bruised and swollen face.

If there is a long interval between consultation and operation, it's helpful to return for another visit with the doctor a month or so before the operation. This gives you a chance to rethink your plans, ask any further questions, and let the doctor reassure you if you become nervous.

Ready for Surgery

AFTER YOU HAVE CHOSEN A PLASTIC SURGEON, YOU HAVE TWO other important decisions to make: where to have the surgery and what kind of anesthesia you want. The decisions depend on your own preference and the recommendation of your doctor.

CHOOSING BETWEEN A HOSPITAL AND OTHER OUTPATIENT FACILITIES

If you have followed the guidelines laid out in chapter 2, the doctor you have chosen has operating privileges in an accredited hospital. He may also have his own in-office surgical facility, or he may operate in a freestanding surgery center. Where he chooses to operate most of the time usually depends on what he deems most efficient and productive for his patients and practice. A doctor whose office is located across the street from a major hospital and who has his own team on staff there may forego setting up his own facility.

The advantages of hospital care are extensive backup equipment and personnel who are available to handle any emergency. There are also adequately staffed and serviced rooms on site in case you need to spend one or more nights under medical care. The drawbacks are the additional cost, the frequently impersonal nature of large institutions, and the fact that nurses and other staff members may be uninterested in cosmetic surgery patients or may even resent having such patients to care for.

Freestanding surgical facilities and office-based operating rooms are becoming increasingly common around the country. Such facilities usually consist of one or more fully equipped operating rooms and an adjacent recovery area. The advantages of these types of outpatient facilities are privacy, a relaxed atmosphere for you, usually less expense and, in the case of an office facility, a staff devoted exclusively to plastic surgery patients.

A drawback may be that your doctor, if he operates exclusively in his own office, has less opportunity to share information and be reviewed by his colleagues. There is also the danger that an unaccredited office-based facility may not have the necessary equipment or personnel to cope with an emergency.

Remember, too, that if the unexpected happens and you need medical care overnight or longer, you will usually have to be transferred to a hospital. Don't accept a motel or other substitute unless you know that it has the necessary medical personnel and equipment.

No federal laws govern the facility in which a doctor operates. Legally, he can perform surgery anywhere he chooses without anyone monitoring it. This situation may change if a new bill before Congress requiring regular accreditation of facilities is passed. At present, however, if your doctor operates in any facility outside of a hospital, it will be up to you to discover whether it is properly equipped and staffed. Take a tour of the facility and don't hesitate to ask questions. Does it have access to a nearby hospital? Does the doctor have privileges to do this same operation in a hospital? Who's going to administer the anesthesia? If the doctor hesitates to answer questions or becomes very abrupt or arrogant about answering, you may be in the wrong place.

Ask whether the facility is accredited. Although many good facilities are not yet accredited, it is one extra reassurance to look for. Three national organizations license or accredit office facilities. The American Association for Accreditation of Ambulatory Plastic Surgery Facilities (AAAAPSF), an organization founded by ASPRS, has approved more than 400 plastic surgery office-based facilities. In addition to inspecting the facility itself, the AAAAPSF makes sure the physician is certified in plastic surgery and has appropriate operating privileges at a local accredited hospital. A great facility and an inadequate surgeon may not give you a good result. Similarly, an excellent surgeon operating in an inadequate facility may be unprepared to handle problems if they arise. Thus, it's important that both the surgeon and the facility be top-grade. The AAAAPSF requires that its facilities be reinspected every three years.

The Accreditation Association for Ambulatory Health Care (AAAHC) and the Joint Commission for the Accreditation of Healthcare Organizations (JCAHO) also accredit outpatient surgery facilities, using slightly different criteria. In contrast to the AAAAPSF, neither organization limits its scope to plastic surgery offices or requires that surgeons be certified by the American Board of Plastic Surgery. Nonetheless, accreditation by any of these three organizations means that at least the facility has been evaluated by an outside group and has met certain standards. You can call the ASPRS (1–800–635–0635) or AAAAPSF (1–708–949–6058) to check if a certified plastic surgeon's facility is accredited. The AAAAPSF will send you a list of all accredited facilities in your area.

SELECTING TYPES OF ANESTHESIAS

There are hundreds of different anesthetic agents, and combinations of them, that are used to induce varying degrees of anesthesia. Three basic types of anesthesia are used for plastic surgery procedures.

With *local injection* only the immediate area to be operated on is numbed. Local injection is used mainly for minor procedures such as removal of moles and correction of small scars. Sometimes a local injection is used for minor surgery on the upper eyelids and for insertion of chin implants.

With *local injection plus sedation* you are given sedatives either orally or intravenously before receiving the local injection. This is the most common type of anesthesia used for cosmetic surgery procedures. It is usually used in facelifts and browlifts, upper and lower eyelid surgery, dermabrasion, nose reshaping, chin and cheek implants, ear pinning, and breast augmentation. At the minimum, this type of anesthesia should be administered by your plastic surgeon or a certified registered nurse anesthetist (CRNA). Beware of facilities that trust this job to less-than-qualified staff.

With *general anesthesia* you sleep through the entire procedure. This is the second most commonly used type of anesthesia. You may elect to have general anesthesia for any of the procedures mentioned above; in addition, general anesthesia is usually used for breast reduction and lifts; suction lipectomy (liposuction), when large areas of the body are involved; abdominoplasty ("tummy tuck"); and cosmetic surgery on small children.

General anesthesia is usually administered by an anesthesiologist, a physician whose medical specialty is putting people to sleep during an operation. However, it may also be given by a CRNA under a physician's supervision. (Again, do not trust this vital task to anyone else.) The anesthesiologist assesses the condition of your heart, lungs, and circulation before the operation, decides what specific agent is needed and how much, monitors your condition during the operation and immediately afterward, and determines what to do should an emergency develop.

The choice of anesthesia used depends on the procedure you're having, your personal preference, and your doctor's recommendation. For many procedures, local anesthesia with sedation *or* general anesthesia can be used; the decision is up to you, although your doctor will probably have a preference.

There are many advantages to having a local with sedation instead of general anesthesia. The surgeon can communicate with you during the operation. You can go home sooner and will feel better faster. Another significant advantage is that local with sedation can be administered by the plastic surgeon or a specially trained nurse. Therefore, this type of anesthesia can reduce your overall bill by $1,000 to $3,000.

However, given the option, some patients and surgeons prefer general anesthesia. From your point of view, you sleep through the whole operation and seemingly only a few minutes pass. With the use of new anesthetic agents, postop nausea and vomiting following general anesthesia have been greatly reduced. It's possible to have general anesthesia in the morning and go home that same day. Some plastic surgeons prefer to use general anesthesia because it means another specialist will be present to monitor your vital signs and administer the anesthetic agent, leaving them free to concentrate on the surgery.

Common myths are that you should not have general anesthesia when you are having a facelift because your skin relaxes too much; or, that you have to be awake so that the surgeon can monitor your facial movements. Despite what anyone might tell you, neither of these myths is true. It is certainly possible to have general anesthesia with a facelift and some plastic surgeons even prefer it. However, as mentioned, general anesthesia is expensive. It also may make you feel a little more under the weather for the first day or two.

In addition, there is an element of risk with any kind of anesthesia, but more so with a general. Rarely, an individual will have an unexpected reaction that can be life-threatening. It's important for you to know, however, that all types of anesthesia commonly used today have been used safely and effectively for many years. If you do not have a personal preference, ask your surgeon which method he prefers to use and why.

HOW ANESTHETICS ARE ADMINISTERED

Local Injection with Sedation

You are first given a sedative orally or intravenously. When you are sedated to the point that your speech slurs, the area to be operated on is completely numbed by injections of a local anesthetic such as lidocaine. This may hurt a little, but you will not remember it later.

During surgery, you may feel a little pressure, pulling, or a slight vibration, but you will feel no pain. Most people fall asleep and feel nothing at all. The sedative is short-acting; when you awake from time to time, the doctor or anesthetist will give you a little more medication. At no time, even if you wake up, do you experience pain at the surgical site.

After surgery, you may fall asleep again, but you should be able to go home within a few hours depending on the length of the procedure and how much sedation you received. (Make sure you have someone to drive you home.) Some people will need more time to recover before going home, and if the surgery was done in a hospital you may be kept overnight. It takes time to recover from any kind of anesthesia, even after you are at home. You can expect to feel a little groggy for one to three days after sedation. A few people experience a little nausea and vomiting postop.

General Anesthesia

Before the operation, the anesthesiologist talks to you and assesses your fitness for anesthesia. You will probably be given some medication to reduce anxiety and then an intravenous line is inserted into a vein in your arm. A sugar or saline solution is given through the IV to help avoid dehydration during surgery. Other drugs can also be given rapidly through the IV if needed.

The anesthetic agent is injected into the intravenous line and you are asleep within a few moments. After you are asleep, a tube is inserted into your mouth to deliver additional anesthetic gases. If you are having surgery on your face, the tube is attached to your teeth to avoid distorting your mouth and to allow the surgeon to see your features clearly. Some plastic surgeons do not like to use general anesthesia for surgery on the nose and face for this reason, but others say they have no problem.

You will sleep through the entire operation. When you wake up, you may feel cold. General anesthesia dilates blood vessels in your skin, so you lose body heat during surgery.

It may take several hours before you feel awake and strong enough to go home. If you are in a hospital and the anesthetic makes you feel very dizzy or nauseated, you may stay overnight. After you are at home, it may take a week or longer before all traces of the anesthetic are cleared from your system and you feel normal.

DRUG ALLERGIES AND ILLNESSES

If you are prone to severe allergies, ask your plastic surgeon specifically which drugs you will be given for anesthesia, as well as any postoperative medications that will be prescribed for you. Then check with your allergist (if you have one) to make sure you aren't sensitive to any of these drugs.

If you develop a severe cold or other upper respiratory illness, your surgery may be postponed until you recover, particularly if you have a fever. If you have an illness going into surgery, any diagnosis of postoperative problems, such as infection or pneumonia, may be harder to make. Further, a preexisting illness increases the chance of complications after surgery such as infection or bleeding.

MEDICATIONS

Certain common drugs can cause problems during surgery. During the presurgery consultation with your plastic surgeon you were asked to list the names of any medications that you take. This is vital information for your surgeon and gives him a lot of insight into preventing problems during and after surgery. For example, hormone drugs may cause bleeding, and you may be asked to discontinue birth-control pills or hormone replacement therapy until after surgery. If you take vitamins, your surgeon will need to know which ones and in what amounts. Vitamin E, for example, is believed by some to cause bleeding.

Many people take aspirin regularly. However, aspirin interferes with the ability of the blood to clot, which can lead to excessive bleeding during surgery and may hinder the healing process. Your doctor will tell you how long before surgery he wants you to stop taking aspirin (usually at least two weeks before) and at what point you can resume (usually two to three weeks after the operation.) Both over-the-counter and prescription drugs may contain aspirin. Check the labels or ask your pharmacist whether the drugs you are taking contain aspirin or aspirin derivatives.

You *can* use products that contain an aspirin substitute such as Tylenol or Anacin-3. However, if you take any medications containing ibuprofen, such as Advil, your doctor will probably advise you to discontinue them also for forty-eight hours or more before surgery. Other drugs in popular use today, particularly among athletes and people who suffer from arthritis, are called nonsteroidal antiinflammatory drugs (NSAID). Among these are Feldene, Naprosyn, and Indocin. Because these agents inhibit blood coagulation, most plastic surgeons advise patients to discontinue them for two weeks prior to surgery. If you take one of these drugs, discuss this issue with your plastic surgeon.

SMOKING ALERT

Smoking can interfere with healing after surgery, particularly in the cases of breast reduction, facelift, "tummy tuck," and other procedures that involve the creation of skin "flaps."

Smoking constricts blood vessels and decreases blood flow all over the body. Even more important, the carbon monoxide in cigarette smoke greatly reduces the blood's ability to carry oxygen, which is essential for wound healing. Smoking slows healing, and if a skin "flap" was used, the wound may not heal at all.

In a landmark study conducted by New York University's Institute of Reconstructive Plastic Surgery, cigarette smoking figured as the major cause of serious wound-healing complications in a significant percentage of the 1,186 facelift patients who participated. If you smoke cigarettes and inhale, you are at least twelve times more likely than nonsmokers to heal poorly after a facelift. Translated, this means a prolonged healing period and a consequent delay in returning to your job and social activities. Worse, the final results of the operation can be marred by unsightly scars.

If you have general anesthesia and also smoke, you may develop a hard cough that can cause internal bleeding. For all of these reasons, smoking is against the rules for cosmetic surgery patients.

If you cannot give up smoking for one to two weeks before and after the operation, your surgeon may want you to rethink your decision to have plastic surgery. People choose to have plastic surgery to improve their looks and sense of well-being, so it makes little sense to jeopardize the results by failing to forego smoking for several weeks. If you are a smoker trying to quit, this may be an excellent opportunity to give up the habit altogether.

PAYING FOR SURGERY

Physicians are paid according to the services performed without regard to the outcome. Most plastic surgeons expect full payment in advance for cosmetic surgery. Since insurance does not usually cover cosmetic procedures, you must pay the bill beforehand. Collecting before surgery, rather than after, helps the doctor keep his administrative costs down because it eliminates the paperwork of billing and collecting debts, and it prevents financial problems as much as possible from disturbing the physician-patient relationship.

Since some procedures may be considered both cosmetic *and* reconstructive (i.e., medically advisable or necessary), check with your insurance carrier *before* surgery to see if you are covered. For example, rhinoplasty may be covered if it will correct a defect that interferes with breathing, and fees for breast reduction may be reimbursed if you have physical problems such as back pain and difficulty in breathing. Even eyelid surgery may be reimbursed if your vision is obscured by heavy upper lids.

Many physicians prefer that an assigned staff member talk to patients about fees and payment, so don't be surprised if you have to fill out forms and discuss payment with a person other than your doctor. Fees for the same procedure vary from doctor to doctor, depending on the experience of the surgeon, how busy his practice is, and where he practices. Generally, the more experienced surgeons with busier practices will charge more. However, a higher price tag doesn't necessarily mean you're going to get a better result. Assess your own financial limitations; at the same time, don't skimp on your surgery or shop for bargains. It's the only body you have.

Costs also vary depending on whether one or several procedures are performed at one time. The price tag for the surgeon's services may be $3,000 for a rhinoplasty and $5,000 for a facelift. If they are done at the same time, however—requiring one anesthesia bill and one use of the hospital or other outpatient facility—the total cost may be reduced. Make sure you find out what *all* the fees are, including costs for an anesthesiologist, the surgical facility, laboratory tests, and devices such as breast implants.

If you have surgery in a doctor's office, the fee will often include the use of his operating facility. If an anesthesiologist is to be used, your surgeon probably will collect a separate check from you in advance for this service.

If you go to a hospital, be prepared to provide a certified check upon admission. This is an *estimated* fee. You may receive a bill later for additional costs. The anesthesiologist's bill will be given to you before you leave the hospital or mailed to you shortly thereafter.

In a freestanding surgery center, the method of payment varies depending on the arrangement made with the doctor.

If complications require additional care or more surgery, payment depends on your doctor's policy, which you should ask about beforehand. Some surgeons feel that you shouldn't have to pay additional fees to correct complications. You will, however, have to pay hospital costs or other costs, if they are necessary.

Training Institutions

What if you want a certain procedure that is beyond your means? Some people in this situation lower costs by going to a teaching hospital, where their surgery is performed by residents in plastic surgery. These are doctors who have completed three to five years of training in general surgery and are finishing the two-year plastic surgery program required for board certification. They may not have the experience of surgeons who have been in practice for years, but they are not beginners.

In addition, every operation they do is supervised by a board-certified plastic surgeon affiliated with that teaching hospital. This senior attendant, who is usually in private practice and may in fact be a well-known plastic surgeon, usually operates with each resident and always monitors the surgery, stepping in if anything goes amiss.

If you decide to go to a teaching hospital, you will probably not have your choice of doctors, but you can ask who will be operating on you and who the supervising physician will be. Meet both doctors and evaluate them just as you would a doctor in private practice. If you feel unsure or uncomfortable, go elsewhere.

The ASPRS Financial Plan

The ASPRS has established a financing plan to help make plastic surgery more accessible to those who have a desire for it. The plan is available through participating doctors who are members of the ASPRS. Basically, the financial plan is a loan that does not encroach on your savings accounts or use up credit-card limits. This plan will finance your surgeon's fee and the facility fee if the operation is performed in your doctor's office. It cannot be used to cover operating-room fees elsewhere or the anesthesiologist's fee.

Monthly payments are manageable and there is no minimum financing amount. The independent agency that supervises the plan runs a credit check and evaluates your ability to pay. The ASPRS's goal is to help you choose the best surgeon for your needs, *not* to encourage you to spend beyond your means. If you are interested in this plan, ask the surgeons you are considering if they are members of ASPRS and if they participate in the program. If they have not yet signed up, perhaps they will do so for you, or they may accept credit cards or participate in some other financing plan. In addition, you can call the ASPRS hotline (1-800-635-0635) and ask for a list of certified surgeons in your area who offer some type of financing plan.

PHOTOS BEFORE SURGERY

You can expect to have preop photos taken by a trained photographer, the doctor himself, or a member of his staff. These are often taken from several different angles and sometimes help your surgeon plan customized variations in your procedure. During surgery, the photos may be pinned on the wall or, if in slide form, displayed in a viewer. Since you don't look the same lying down as you do standing up, these photos can be a helpful guide to your doctor.

Several weeks or months after your surgery, postoperative photographs also will be taken for your medical record. Neither pre- or postop photos can be shown to anyone else without your permission. Your surgeon may ask you to sign a consent form giving your permission for these photos to be used in lectures that your doctor gives or in articles that he writes for medical journals. Some doctors also ask in their forms for permission to use your photos for *public* education, such as for magazine and newspaper articles. In these cases, your doctor usually promises to keep your identity anonymous. You do not have to give your permission if you don't want to, although most people are willing to have their pictures used for purposes of education.

Postop Planning

COSMETIC SURGERY ISN'T OVER UNTIL YOU ARE BACK TO YOUR NORmal activities and beginning to see the first beneficial effects of the surgery. (Most people *feel* good before they completely *look* good.) Your recovery depends heavily on the preparation you do in advance.

Many people don't take sufficient time off to rest after an elective procedure because they feel self-conscious about reaching out for help. They have work sent home from the office, or they expect to cook meals and clean house while they are recuperating. Often, cosmetic surgery patients wind up feeling resentful and miserable, and may take even longer to recover than usual. In fact, the most important thing you can do to help yourself postop is to make sure that you have a support system in place and ready to go.

YOUR SUPPORT SYSTEM

When you have a problem to solve or you are sick, do you like to go off by yourself and take care of yourself? Or are you someone who likes to be taken care of by others and benefit from their emotional support? Even if you consider yourself a loner, you may need to change your ways during your recovery from cosmetic surgery. Surgery is too big an event to carry off without cooperation from your spouse, children, a close friend, or parent. You can keep it from everybody else if you want, but you need at least one support person.

Schedule surgery during a week when you can have someone stay with you. Like any operation, cosmetic surgery is a shock to the body and it tends to make you tired and weak. Discuss with your doctor the extent of the care you will need afterward.

When operations are done on an outpatient basis, as many cosmetic procedures are, people tend to think that because they are allowed to go home on the same day, they will feel physically fit. However, many plastic surgery procedures are still considered major surgery; the effect of the anesthesia alone may take several days to dissipate.

Do you and your support person accept willingly that you will need time to recover? Sometimes the person you live with is a big help for a day or two, waiting on you hand and foot, and then expects you to be back to normal. He or she may withdraw support just at the critical time that you begin to feel a natural letdown.

PREPARING YOUR SUPPORT SYSTEM

To set up your postop support system, you need to know the answers to these questions:

- Do you fully understand how extensive the operation is?
- Do you know how long it will probably take to recover?
- Do you know what type of pain to expect?
- Do you know to what degree your activities will be limited after surgery and for how long?
- Are your live-ins or support people also aware of the extent of the surgery?
- If you will need a lot of help, are you expecting too much from one person?
- Have you allowed yourself enough time away from your responsibilities to recover?
- Are you prepared for postoperative letdown?

Also, others tend to be less sympathetic after cosmetic surgery than they would if you had had your appendix out. It's good to clarify beforehand what your support person's role will be, and how long his or her help will be needed, so you do not feel neglected or guilty during recovery.

RECOVERY SCHEDULE AND DOCTOR'S ORDERS

How quickly you recover from plastic surgery depends on the extent of the operation and the kind of anesthesia you had. For most procedures, recovery proceeds predictably through three stages: During the first twenty-four to forty-eight hours you feel the most discomfort; by the end of the first week you feel much better; and by the end of the second or third week you are usually back to your normal work and social activities.

Every surgeon has his own postop instructions for patients. A booklet or set of photocopied pages may review the procedure, list possible problems, and outline how to take care of yourself following surgery.

In follow-up visits your plastic surgeon will remove stitches and check your progress. Although most people recover without complications, if you notice anything that you don't think is right, call your doctor. Special signs to be alert for are any unusual pain at the surgery site, fever, or pain elsewhere in the body.

Most people who have been well informed by their surgeons are alert for potential complications. However, one side effect of plastic surgery catches many people off guard: It's not uncommon for depression to occur at some time during the recovery process.

POSTOP EMOTIONAL ADJUSTMENT

Cosmetic surgery patients may feel blue afterward as they go from being healthy and vigorous to looking and feeling terrible. Occasionally on the very first day postop patients will lament, "Why did I ever do this?" Postop depression may start during the first three or four days after surgery and may last anywhere from a week to several weeks.

Surgery causes certain metabolic changes that may trigger depression. Also, some people tend to respond to stress by becoming depressed. At the request of many plastic surgeons, research has been conducted about the source of postop depression. A recent study on the psychological effects following facelift showed that although about a third of the fifty women studied experienced postoperative depression, it was no more severe than the moodiness that can occur following any surgical procedure. None had serious clinical symptoms of depression (such as loss of sleep or appetite). Those who were most vulnerable were people who were already somewhat depressed before surgery or who had a history of depression. In addition, women who were normally assertive and busy seemed to feel more depressed after surgery because they couldn't immediately resume their activities. All of the women recovered their emotional balance. Some eventually felt less depressed than they had been before they had the operation.

Feeling postop letdown is not unusual and you can expect depression to lift naturally within a week or so. Some people opt to stay home until they look great, but it's usually better, emotionally speaking, to get up and get out. As soon as your doctor gives the go-ahead, take a brisk walk, go to the movies, and start using makeup (see below). If you can't shake the blues, make sure you tell your doctor so he can help you get through it or can refer you to another professional.

WHEN OTHERS UNDERMINE YOUR SURGERY

In the first two weeks after surgery, you will be especially vulnerable to comments from other people because your results are not yet what you want them to be. For a little while you may look worse than before. You can never totally predict the response you will get from friends and family. A spouse, friend, or relative may think that cosmetic surgery is frivolous and may disapprove of you for having it done. A loved one may feel threatened by the change in you and may expect that the surgery will somehow alter your feelings for him or her. Your partner may feel that you had surgery because you're interested in finding a new mate. These feelings may be unconscious, but because of them the people closest to you may not always be supportive.

This may be particularly true if your surgical change involves changing a cultural trait such as a Semitic nose or Asian eyes. Criticism may be harsh if friends or family think you are trying to deny your cultural heritage. Consider this and make sure you are prepared for it before you go ahead.

It's difficult to fully protect yourself against undermining comments. Terry, a middle-aged homemaker and mother of four, had a glamorous neighbor with whom she had coffee every morning. After Terry had a rhinoplasty and facelift, her friend stopped coming by for coffee. Terry was distressed. She happened to mention it to her doctor, who suggested that the neighbor now felt competitive with her. It would take some time for the neighbor to get used to the change and it was possible that she would never adjust.

TELLING OTHER PEOPLE

Most people who have cosmetic surgery want the change to be subtle. Paradoxically, they also want people to notice it. Fortunately, both things usually are possible. In general, after you have had cosmetic surgery other people will say you look terrific, but they will rarely realize why unless you tell them. People may think you've been on vacation, have a new hairstyle, or have new makeup. Something is different, but they probably won't know what.

If you would like others' recognition, then let people know about your surgery so that they can provide support for you. Otherwise, you will feel disappointed if they don't notice. If you do *not* want people to notice, try changing something else right after surgery. Change your hairstyle or color, switch from glasses to contact lenses or vice versa, or lose a few pounds. People will attribute the change they observe to the new style rather than to cosmetic surgery.

CAMOUFLAGE COSMETICS

Your surgeon can advise you on when it is physically safe for you to resume your usual activities. Only you can judge how comfortable you feel about how you actually look. New makeup products especially designed for cosmetic surgery patients are now available that will help you to look as good as you feel.

It may take days, weeks, or even months before you can fully appreciate the results of cosmetic surgery, but there's no need for you to hide in your room or for your surgery to be obvious to everyone. While almost everyone has some sort of temporary side effects, such as swelling and bruising, there are makeup techniques that both men and women can use almost immediately to disguise them. Deftly applied, these products need not be apparent. You may use special camouflage products recommended by your plastic surgeon, commercial camouflage products available in many large department stores, or perhaps a standard makeup that you already use.

You can purchase the makeup you'll need prior to surgery. It is important that the products are hypoallergenic and fragrance-free. If you are happy with the products you currently use, purchase new ones with new applicators so you know they are as hygienic as possible.

Camouflage cosmetics are usually more adherent than everyday makeup, so be sure to use a cleansing cream that thoroughly removes all your makeup. Then use a gentle, alcohol-free toner applied with a cotton ball to remove any cleanser residue. Follow this with a moisturizer formulated for your skin type (oily, dry, or combination).

Generally speaking, makeup can be used soon after surgery to cover discolorations. It can also be used to hide incision lines after the stitches have been removed and the *incision is completely closed.* Since everyone heals differently, always check with your surgeon before using camouflage cosmetics.

It takes a little patience and practice to master camouflage techniques, but most postop patients feel it is well worth the effort. Camouflage cosmetics let you enjoy the results of your cosmetic surgery almost immediately. For more detailed and visual information on camouflage cosmetics, ask your surgeon for the ASPRS brochure and video on the subject.

Camouflage cosmetics include three basic types of products: *concealers* to hide incision lines and discoloration; *contour shadows* to disguise swelling; and *color correctors* to neutralize color in reddened skin.

Concealers

Thicker and more opaque than regular foundation, concealers can cover healed incision lines and discolorations following a facelift. Concealers also can cover scars on any part of the body.

Choose a concealer that is opaque and waterproof but creamy enough so that it doesn't pull or drag on the skin. If possible, choose a product that matches your skin color. If the concealer blends with your natural skin color, you may not have to use a foundation on top of it.

Because concealers are so thick, it takes patience to apply them smoothly. Use a makeup sponge, a small brush, or your fingertips. Be sure your hands and any applicators are clean. Then put a dab of concealer in the palm of your hand, and using your fingertips, work the concealer into a smooth consistency. Dot it lightly over the discolored area, then gently spread it evenly over surrounding skin. To disguise incisions, concealer can be applied with a small brush directly into the incision line. You may need a second application for complete coverage, but apply it sparingly. Two thin layers often look more natural than one thick one.

If the concealer does not match your skin tone, you will need to cover it, as well as the rest of your face, with your usual foundation to achieve an even skin tone. Pat the foundation on gently to avoid removing the concealer.

To set the makeup, use a clean, soft brush or cotton ball to lightly dust your skin surface with a loose, translucent face powder. The powder increases the durability of the concealer, so you won't find the discoloration creeping through as the day goes on. If you use blush, apply it as a final touch.

Concealer should not be used on the thin, delicate skin around the eyes. Concealer is thick and will build up in the crease above your eyelids. Instead, normal fluid foundation can be applied directly over incision lines. If a lid is discolored, apply the foundation over the entire lid and browbone. Use clean cotton swabs to apply makeup gently to this fragile skin. You can also gently apply foundation to the incision line just under your lower lashes and blend it into the surrounding skin. Using another cotton ball or soft brush, lightly dust the eyelid with a loose, translucent face powder to set the makeup.

If you don't normally use foundation, you can disguise discoloration with eye makeup alone. Apply eye shadow directly over the incision line to define the crease of the eyelid and camouflage the effects of surgery. Muted shades like browns and grays attract less attention than bright colors. Stay away from iridescent shadows, which can cause allergic reactions and may pick up light and show wrinkles. For liner under the eye, use dry, wet, or cream shadow. You can also use a soft pencil liner as long as it doesn't drag or pull on your skin. Use a water-soluble, fiber-free mascara that will be easiest to remove.

Contouring

Contouring can be used anywhere on the face, but it is most often used to disguise the swelling that accompanies nose re-shaping or chin augmentation. Contouring creates dimension using light and dark shadows. It is based on the painter's palette: Things that are light appear to come forward and things that are dark appear to recede. Contouring uses two separate prod-ucts: one about two shades lighter than your normal foundation, called highlighter; and one about two shades darker than your normal foundation, called contour shadow. If you are happy with your normal foundation, you can purchase the same prod-uct two shades lighter and two shades darker. If you prefer, you can use pressed powders to achieve the same effect.

Blending is the most critical element in highlighting and con-touring. The idea is to create an illusion of angles without seeing stripes of makeup. Learning to skillfully highlight and contour can be a tremendous asset if you are recovering from nose re-shaping. After rhinoplasty, the nose may remain noticeably swol-len and the area around it may be slightly puffy for several weeks, and the swelling does not disappear completely for sev-eral months.

Begin contouring by adding dimension to your cheekbones. Apply highlighter along the ridge above each cheekbone to bring it forward. Then apply contour in the hollow below the cheek-bones to make this area recede. Blend by gently patting with your fingertips or a makeup sponge. Blusher can be applied between the highlighter and contour.

To narrow your nose, apply highlighter down the center, from brows to tip. Apply contour along the sides of the nose, starting from where the brows begin and continuing toward the nostrils. Blend with your finger or a sponge. The idea is to make the cheekbones more prominent and the nose thinner without see-ing stripes of makeup.

To make a swollen chin appear shorter after augmentation, apply contour shadow to the bottom. If swelling makes your chin protrude, contour shadow can also be applied to the chin's center. Until you have practiced the subtle techniques of con-touring, it's best to use them only in the evening.

Color Correctors

Color correctors disguise yellowish discolorations or the pink-ness that follows chemical peel and dermabrasion. Lavender neutralizes or removes yellow. Green has a similar effect on red. A sheer application of color corrector will even out your skin tone.

You can use a concealer to cover *small* areas of redness, but if your problem is overall redness, a better solution is to use a green color corrector. Color corrector has the same sheer con-sistency as foundation and can be applied lightly with a makeup sponge. For natural skin color, apply foundation over it, using a fresh makeup sponge. Pinkness after chemical peel or der-mabrasion may last three months to a year, so learning this tech-nique can be a great advantage.

Lavender color corrector is used on yellowish areas and is especially good on the tender skin around your eyes where you don't want to use a heavy concealer. Apply it with a cotton swab and blend gently with your fingertip. When a bruise changes color from yellow to blue, you will have to switch to eye makeup or foundation.

PART II

**CHANGING
INHERITED
TRAITS**

6

Changing Your Family Profile

Inherited traits can bother people of every age. Little children may wish to correct protruding ears that lead playmates to tease them. Older people may wish to improve a problem that for one reason or another they were unable to have corrected earlier. Teenagers also may desire certain cosmetic surgery procedures, particularly nose reshaping.

Changing a physical trait you are born with can be an emotionally loaded experience. You may hate your nose, but it's still *your* nose. It may be the trait your mother loves most about you. You may have inherited your father's chin or your grandmother's jaw. These traits are points of "clan" identification, binding you to your family in subtle ways.

This is particularly true of families with strong ethnic identification. Although the second, third, or fourth generations may be interested in plastic surgery, the first generation may be likely to find it frivolous or, worse, offensive. Changing your family profile is sometimes seen as rejection of the family itself.

An increasing number of African-Americans and Asians are seeking plastic surgery, particularly to alter the look of their noses. They often want the bridge of their noses taller, the base narrower, and the tip more projecting. In addition, Asians often look for doctors specifically skilled in building up small or flat noses and creating eyelid folds to make eyes appear larger. However, most people wish to retain their ethnic identity while making these changes.

Someone with strong ethnic identification should talk to his or her family before deciding on plastic surgery. One young African-American woman was certain that she wanted her nose reshaped, yet following rhinoplasty she fell into a profound depression because her family couldn't accept the change. She felt that she had betrayed her parents. On the other hand, if you truly are unhappy with one of your features, the alteration possible through cosmetic surgery may be worth whatever lack of understanding you must overcome on the part of your family and friends.

Even if your family supports your choice, an operation to change an inherited trait alters the body shape you grew up with. After surgery, you will be different. No matter how much you wanted that change, it may be a shock at first, and it may take you some time to get used to your new look.

Anytime anyone considers cosmetic surgery to correct an inherited trait, they need to consider carefully the possible ramifications. Parents should not routinely seek surgery for their child's protruding ears if they don't bother *him*. Teenagers needn't rush for surgery if they are unhappy with their noses. Feelings and self-image change with maturity. Evaluation is personal and often emotionally subtle. Hold these thoughts in mind while reading this next section.

Each of us is unique. Although most people just want a nose or chin that they like better, if you have decided to go forward with surgery, you may want to have more than one consultation with your surgeon. Taking a little extra time lets you better understand how cosmetic surgery will affect your overall appearance and also gives you time to discuss it with your family. At the very least, it will give you time to prepare for change.

The Nose

THE SEARCH FOR A BETTER-LOOKING NOSE IS ONE OF THE MOST popular reasons for seeking plastic surgery in the United States. Rhinoplasty is the most common cosmetic procedure for men and the fifth most popular overall. Modern rhinoplasty *(rhino* meaning "nose") goes back about a hundred years and first became popular in the United States in the 1930s. Early rhinoplasties often removed too much cartilage, resulting in the characteristic scooped-out or "ski-jump" nose. Some noses were made too short and some had a pinched look.

A standard method of performing "nose jobs" soon developed. Until the sixties and early seventies, rhinoplasty continued to be done "by the book." Every plastic surgeon followed the same steps, regardless of what the nose originally looked like. If a patient had a nose that was too long with a hump, but had a beautiful tip, the surgeon still followed the recipe and operated on the whole nose.

However, that approach has now been abandoned in favor of new techniques that allow custom design, more precise control, and better ways to avoid problems. The resulting nose fits the face so well that it is no longer obvious surgery has been performed. The current trend is to correct less, rather than more, and to operate only on the part of the nose that needs improvement. Given the scenario of a long nose with a bump on the bridge, but a good-looking tip, today's surgeon would shorten the nose, rasp down the bump, and leave the tip untouched. The reconstructed nose would look more natural rather than like a transplant.

However, what one person considers unattractive, another may think perfectly fine. Like anything else, noses are a matter of personal perception. If your nose bothers *you*, you can usually get the change you desire through modern techniques of rhinoplasty.

THE POSSIBILITIES

The wide range of possible improvements is amazing. Rhinoplasty can:

- Reduce the overall size of the nose
- Remove a hump on the bridge
- Reshape a tip that appears too bulbous, too short, or too long
- Narrow the span of the nostrils or the base of the nose
- Increase the angle between the nose and upper lip
- "Tuck in" a low, hanging columella (the short column of skin and cartilage that runs from the tip of the nose to the upper lip), or make it longer or narrower

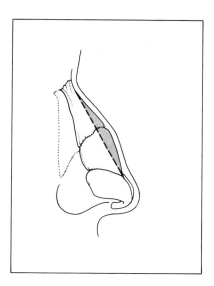

Incisions are made on both sides of the nose inside the nostrils to provide access to cartilage and bone. The hump is removed using a sawing instrument, a chisel or rasp, leaving the bridge flat and bones and cartilage spread further apart. The bones are then freed from their base along the dotted line and brought closer together to form a narrower bridge.

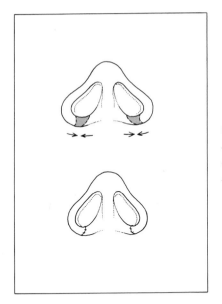

To narrow the base of the nose, wedges of skin are removed on both sides and the nostrils are brought closer to the center, leaving minute scars where the edges were stitched together.

DIFFICULT SURGERY

Difficult, sometimes even impossible to correct, is a very short nose and columella. In some people, the columella is so short that the tip does not project at all and appears to be "tethered" to the lip. The surgeon's challenge is to create a natural-looking projection in the tip. This is a technically formidable operation and results are often less than ideal.

The patient who has a combination of thick skin and a short columella also presents a challenge that is difficult to fully overcome. In some cases, an experienced surgeon will advise against surgery.

Tip Revision

Most experts in rhinoplasty agree that the bridge of the nose is merely a line to the tip. The shape and angle of the tip define the whole look of the nose. Reshaping the tip is one of the most difficult and least predictable aspects of rhinoplasty. Plastic surgeons are always looking for new techniques that will give them more control over the outcome. Listening to a surgeon talk about reshaping the tip is like listening to an architect describe the physics of why a building stays erect.

The tip of the nose is the meeting place for two pieces of cartilage that slant upward from both sides of the lip to the bridge and down again, like a pair of arches. When the point where these two arches meet is too thick and bulbous, the goal is to remove some of the excess cartilage and alter its shape without weakening the arches. If too much cartilage is removed, the arches will collapse.

Different surgeons use different techniques to reshape the cartilage in the tip. Overall, *less* surgery seems to give better results. By removing just a small amount of cartilage, the arches can be bent and their angle can be significantly reduced. As long as the surgeon preserves the integrity of the arches, the tip will hold up.

Years ago, a short tip was impossible to improve; now surgeons can remove cartilage from under the arches and layer it on the top to give projection to a stubby nose.

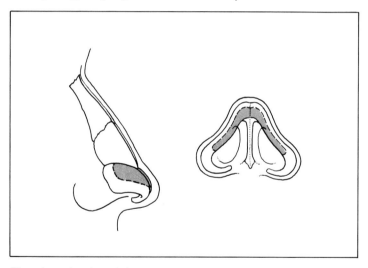

To reduce the size of the nasal tip, cartilage in the shaded area is removed.

Noses That Are Too Small

A genetically small nose may be too short or too flat. In other cases, the bridge may be depressed in the middle, forming what is known as a "saddle nose." Asian patients often request rhinoplasty to build up a flat nose, typically asking for a "taller" nose. A plastic surgeon now can use cartilage or bone taken from elsewhere in the body to build up noses that are too small. For those who had a rhinoplasty in the past and ended up with a nose that's too small, today's plastic surgeon can perform a "touch-up," using grafts to lengthen the framework and build up the bridge.

Grafts may come from cartilage removed from the ear or elsewhere in the nose. A sliver of bone also can be taken from the outermost layer of the skull, a rib, or hip bone and carved to the right shape. The body accepts these grafts made from your own tissue without difficulty. Other surgeons use plastic implants, such as silicone, to reshape the nose. Both techniques have their advocates; however, the majority of plastic surgeons prefer using cartilage or bone—living tissue—for such implants.

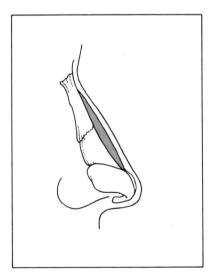

Using internal incisions, a bridge that is too low or flat can be built up with pieces of bone or cartilage taken from areas such as the skull, rib, or ear.

BEST CANDIDATES

The best candidates for rhinoplasty are people who are physically well, are psychologically stable, are realistically expectant about the results and, of course, have anatomical problems that can be helped by rhinoplasty. While rhinoplasty can reshape your nose, it cannot reshape your life nor can it satisfy an unrealistic search for perfection. Someone who perceives a tiny little bump as a gigantic hook may never be satisfied even if the surgeon is technically successful.

Rhinoplasty for Teenagers

An estimated 11 percent of all rhinoplasties are performed on individuals who are eighteen years old or younger. Until recently, it was generally held that nose surgery should be delayed until the age of sixteen or seventeen for girls and a year or so later for boys. However, new studies suggest that correcting nasal deformities need not be delayed until a teenager is fully grown.

The value of such early surgery is psychological. Many leading plastic surgeons believe that performing surgery on the nose early in adolescence, before the body image solidifies and self-consciousness peaks, can avert years of distress and perhaps permanent emotional scars.

The decision of whether or not to perform rhinoplasty must be based on the teenager's social and emotional adjustment, as well as on his or her physical development. The nose grows at a different rate than the rest of the body. By the time a person is thirteen or fourteen years old, the nose is 90 percent grown. Nose surgery that is performed before this growth spurt is complete may stunt or change the development of the nose. To decide if a teenager is old enough for rhinoplasty, the surgeon has to evaluate the whole nose, not just the flaw, in relationship to the body.

If the nose is large enough, particularly on a young girl who is at least thirteen years old, there is no reason to wait until she's sixteen or seventeen to alter it. At age thirteen, a girl is just beginning to be concerned with her appearance. The nose hasn't yet become an integral part of her persona. There is no known medical complication caused by doing surgery at this early age.

Boys generally mature later than girls, so a boy may need to wait until age fourteen or fifteen before his nose is large enough for surgery. Sometimes, however, a thirteen-year-old boy has quite a large nose even though he is still growing. The surgeon will probably evaluate the boy's nose in relationship to his overall body growth. If his nose has a large hump and the tip is bulbous, the surgeon can remove the hump and narrow the tip without reducing the overall size of the nose. The deformity will not reappear even as the boy continues to grow.

This is not to say that every teenager who dislikes his or her nose is a candidate for plastic surgery. Hypercritical attitudes about various parts of the body are extremely common in adolescence, and often these perceptions are not shared by parents and more objective observers, including the plastic surgeon. As teenagers mature, their desire for conventional appearance often fades and they begin to appreciate their own individuality.

In addition, if a teenager says, "I don't really want this operation, but my mother wants it," this attitude signals a poor candidate to a plastic surgeon. An example of a *good* attitude is when a teenager says, "I'm dying to have my nose done. I've wanted it done ever since I was ten years old, but my mom likes it the way it is. Now I'm old enough to make my own decision."

Older Adults

As a result of the aging process, your nose may become longer as the skin loses some of its elasticity or gravity may cause the tip to droop. Rhinoplasty in older adults can have excellent results as long as physical and psychological factors favor it.

If you are over forty, the most important thing when contemplating rhinoplasty is to ask yourself why you want surgery now and why you didn't want it many years before. There's an old belief that when a man waits until he's middle-aged before coming for a rhinoplasty, it's a sign that he has a sexual problem. Both the nose and the penis are protruding, midline organs, and the notion that a man subconsciously transfers sexual problems to his nose is still common, even among doctors, although there's no evidence that this is true.

There are many reasons why a man or a woman may seek rhinoplasty at a later age. The nose may actually have changed with age and often elevating the tip of the nose will give a younger look. The individual may have developed a breathing problem caused by some deviation in the septum that didn't bother him when he was younger but has become a nuisance as he grows older. Perhaps he couldn't afford surgery when he was younger or perhaps his nose just bothered him more and more as the years passed.

For both men and women, plastic surgeons prefer to make rhinoplasty in older patients more subtle and less dramatic, so they can more easily adjust to their new look. Certain surgical problems also have to be taken into consideration when rhinoplasty is performed on older adults. Surgical risks do increase as we age. After age forty, nose tissues are thicker and harder to sculpt. Bones grow more brittle. During surgery, there is a possibility that the bones in the nose may break in several places rather than along the exact line planned by the surgeon. Should this happen, it's not a disaster; however, it does make the procedure more complicated.

The skin of the nose also has less elasticity as you grow older. If a major reconstruction is undertaken in an elderly individual, the skin may not immediately shrink to the form of the new skeleton, leaving excess, loose skin. In this case, the surgeon may make a small external incision and cut away the excess skin. This procedure is simple, but will leave a slight scar over the bridge of the nose.

The main factor in deciding whether to have rhinoplasty in later years is your ability to adjust to your changed appearance. Abandoning your old self-image takes some time since you've lived with it so long (no matter how much you may have disliked it).

SOME SPECIAL CONSIDERATIONS

Changing Racial and Ethnic Characteristics

Special techniques are sometimes needed to correct a problem while retaining ethnic individuality. Most rhinoplasty is done from inside the nose. Bone and cartilage are reshaped through the nostrils, and the skin redrapes itself over the new framework. If the skin is thick, as black and Asian skin tends to be, it may not redrape well. In addition, such skin makes it more difficult to adequately examine abnormalities and assess the results of surgery. To overcome this problem some surgeons are now using an "open" approach to rhinoplasty, in which a tiny incision is made at the base of the columella. This allows a better view of the cartilage structures in the nose. In some surgeons' hands, the open technique seems to give better and more predictable results, although it leaves a small scar.

Rhinoplasty to correct a broad, wide nose with a very short tip will produce a dramatic change. The bridge will be higher, the nostrils narrowed, and the tip more projecting. In contrast, simply narrowing the nostrils is a more subtle refinement.

Singers

Some people believe that rhinoplasty increases the nasality in a singer's voice. Changes *do* sometimes occur in the resonance, timbre, and nasality of the voice, especially when singing. For the most part, however, these are positive changes, with the voice becoming less nasal and more resonant.

Models and Actors

What about the model or actor who seeks plastic surgery because an almost imperceptible "flaw" shows up on camera? Such problems can affect the professional's livelihood. One young model had a beautiful rhinoplasty, but a tiny remaining irregularity—unnoticeable to the human eye—cast a shadow that the camera always detected and magnified. This was a very subtle and difficult correction to make because it required only a millimeter of difference, but it was successfully performed in a second operation.

Likewise, an actress said that although her nose was a hundred percent improved after rhinoplasty, she still wasn't fully satisfied. A year later, her plastic surgeon performed a second operation to refine her nose to the point where she considered it professionally acceptable. Most plastic surgeons would accept patients like these because, given the special needs and visibility created by their professions, their requests are usually appropriate.

If You Are in Psychotherapy

If you are in psychotherapy, even if it's simply for routine support rather than a diagnosed mental illness, you should always consult with your therapist before deciding to have plastic surgery. Your plastic surgeon should also talk to your therapist. Psychotherapy will not keep you from being accepted for surgery, but your emotional stability is a consideration for both you and your doctor.

If your dissatisfaction with your nose is viewed as a separate issue, unrelated to any emotional problems, you are likely to be accepted for surgery. One schizophrenic woman had been in and out of hospitals for several years. Her nose had been broken in an accident and the resulting deformity caused her great distress and made her illness worse. In this case, although surgery didn't cure her schizophrenia, it allowed her to put aside the problem of her appearance.

However, some psychiatric patients make their perceived nose deformity—if it is real at all—the focal point for all their troubles. In this case, plastic surgery cannot help and may even make the situation worse.

THE CONSULTATION

In the consultation, the surgeon must visualize both the immediate and long-range look of your nose in relationship to your face. A well-trained surgeon creates a nose that best matches the rest of your facial features. His task in the consultation is to evaluate the anatomy of your nose and envision its potential relationship to your whole face and body.

This is why surgeons warn against bringing in a photograph of someone else and requesting a similar nose. What can be achieved depends on *your* anatomy. Plastic surgeons like to compare the structure of the nose to that of a tent, whose unique size and shape is determined by the framework (bone and cartilage) that supports it and the thickness of the canvas (your skin) that covers it. During the surgery, the skin is separated from the framework, and bone and cartilage are literally sculpted to assume the desired shape. The skin is then redraped over the new framework.

The surgeon will assess the shape of your nasal bones and cartilage, the shape of your face, your age, and the quality of your skin. In the fifteen to thirty minutes of the consultation, he will discuss the many variables that might influence the procedure and whether the imperfection can be improved. (Surgery tends to be more difficult, with less predictable results, for instance, if you have broken your nose in the past.)

Your skin type is the most important factor in the success of your surgery. Sometimes the results of rhinoplasty will barely show because thick skin maintains its old shape over its new

framework. Some surgeons will not do surgery in this case because they know the result will be less than desired.

Can *you* tell if your skin is too thick for surgery? Not really. A
nose may look bulbous just because of extra cartilage under the
skin. The lower half of the nose is comprised of a different type
of skin than the upper half. Skin on the tip is usually thicker
than skin on the upper part of the nose. The tip of the nose is
filled with tiny glands, with small holes visible in the skin's surface. If these little glands become thick and heavy, as they do in
the so-called alcoholic nose, the skin gets rigid and the nose
appears bulbous. It doesn't mean that the nose can't be improved, but special techniques and an innovative surgeon may
be necessary.

A plastic surgeon can examine the skin and usually tell
whether your skin will redrape well. Sometimes it's a matter of
waiting. A teenager whose skin is oily and coarse, who suffers
from acne, or whose face and nose are pudgy with baby fat is a
poor candidate for rhinoplasty. But it is possible that after the
adolescent matures a bit, both skin and face will change. As
teenagers shed their baby fat, and as acne improves or disappears, it is sometimes possible to make improvements with rhinoplasty.

Your plastic surgeon will also ask you candidly about your
expectations. Keep in mind that the desired result is improvement, not perfection. An obviously disfigured nose, with a large
hook or hump, will show dramatic results. On the other hand,
slightly flaring nostrils or a tip that is a bit too large may be
improved, yet the results may be subtle. The intention is not to
create a "new" nose that draws attention to itself but rather one
that blends into the overall features of the face in the proper
proportions.

If the surgeon thinks there are drawbacks to surgery for any
reason it is his responsibility to let you know what can be done
and what problems may occur. It is your responsibility to listen
carefully.

In nine out of ten cases, the procedure is complete in one
operation. But there is always the possibility that during surgery
a newly fractured bone can move a little bit, producing a little
bump after healing. Sometimes even the healing process will
create a little bump. These are the kinds of unpredictable things
that can lead to a second operation.

Experienced plastic surgeons estimate that they can predict

the results fairly well for about half of their rhinoplasty patients. For the other half, predictions are less reliable because of the individual's skin type or other anatomical characteristics.

That doesn't mean the results won't be satisfactory. Patients are usually very happy with the improvement that can be achieved. Part of the surgeon's job is to describe the possibilities so that you have a realistic surgical goal.

Even if you think you are a poor surgical candidate, don't disqualify yourself without consulting a plastic surgeon. Only a professional evaluation can determine your potential for rhinoplasty. In this day and age, there are very few people who cannot be helped.

RHINOPLASTY WITH FACELIFT

It is increasingly common for plastic surgeons to suggest rhinoplasty in older patients seeking a facelift. As the face ages, the nose droops. In some cases, if the face is rejuvenated but the nose is not, the face still looks old. One woman in her sixties asked for a rhinoplasty because a hump had appeared on her nose. After examining her, the plastic surgeon told her that the tip of her nose had dropped, and the bump, which had always been there, was now emphasized. Today, some surgeons say, 80 percent of facelift patients have something done to their nose as well, even though originally they may not have asked for it.

If you feel you are being talked into a procedure you don't need, or pushed into changing a nose you've lived with all your life simply because you are vulnerable to the promise of looking younger, just say no. You know best what you're satisfied with and what makes you feel unhappy. It's up to you to evaluate whether the surgeon's suggestion makes sense for you.

Lucy visited a plastic surgeon for a facelift evaluation and was told that he could also refine the tip of her nose, which was decidedly turned up. As a young girl Lucy had always received compliments about her "cute" nose, and although she sometimes wished that she looked more sophisticated, she never thought she needed surgery. Now, in her fifties, Lucy was surprised by the surgeon's suggestion. The surgeon explained that as she grew older, her nose would grow longer and more bulbous in the tip. Lucy recalled that she had seen this happen in her elderly aunt, who had the same turned-up "family nose," but wasn't convinced she wanted surgery. Although she saw the surgeon's point, she chose not to have rhinoplasty. Lucy reasoned that, "If it gets bad later on, I can always go back and have it done."

More plastic surgeons today evaluate the whole face—the brow, eyes, neck, chin, and nose—when they do a facelift. In terms of your recovery, there's no reason not to have rhinoplasty done in conjunction with other facial procedures. Some surgeons, however, hesitate to do multiple procedures in one longer operation because it takes more time and therefore requires more extensive anesthesia. If your surgeon feels he can do multiple procedures in a reasonable number of hours and *you* want them all done, there is no reason not to proceed.

RHINOPLASTY WITH CHIN AUGMENTATION

For some individuals, the impression that their nose is too big is actually caused by a chin that's too small. In such cases, rhinoplasty is often combined with chin augmentation. Many leading plastic surgeons say they advise chin implants for more than half of their rhinoplasty patients. Sometimes a chin implant is used *instead* of rhinoplasty. By making the chin larger, the nose appears smaller. Because some surgeons carve their own implants, the size can be quite small if necessary, and the overall look of the chin implant may be very subtle.

It is not necessarily axiomatic that a large nose is accompanied by a receding chin. Your surgeon will judge your chin by looking at your profile. Even subtle augmentation can enhance the profile.

Costs

Costs for rhinoplasty vary widely. A recent study of physicians determined that surgical fees for rhinoplasty range between $1,500 and $6,000, depending on the length and complexity of the operation and who performs the surgery. Although seldom required, hospitalization and the use of an anesthesiologist can considerably increase the overall cost.

Since cosmetic rhinoplasty is performed on a voluntary basis, insurance plans normally do not cover it. However, if surgery is deemed necessary to improve breathing or otherwise correct the *function* of the nose, the surgeon's fee and other costs may be partially or even fully paid by your insurance carrier.

An injury or fracture in childhood can sometimes cause a nasal hump to appear in adolescence and therefore some people assume insurance will cover rhinoplasty to straighten the bridge. However, most insurance companies will say no to this. The results of most traumatic injuries suffered in childhood—car accidents or a fall out of a high chair or down a flight of stairs— usually show up at once and are not delayed until adolescence. If the abnormality can be shown to be a direct result of injury or trauma, insurance is likely to cover surgery.

DEVIATED SEPTUM

There are numerous deformities of the septum, the "wall" inside the nose that divides it into two chambers. Insurance companies will provide some coverage for correcting a deviated septum, provided it truly obstructs breathing. The truth is that about 75 percent of us have deviated septums; it is the norm, not the exception.

The septum is made of bone and cartilage and covered with mucous membranes. A deviation means that the septum is bent or deflected to one side. If a deviation is severe, it can cause blockage of one or both nasal airways and, as the natural air flow is hampered, a true health problem can result.

The deviation present in most noses rarely reaches a point at which breathing is affected. A physician can usually determine whether there is a significant nasal obstruction, or whether breathing difficulties stem from allergies or other ailments. If you have a deviated septum that interferes with your breathing, your insurance may cover that portion of the operation.

BEFORE SURGERY

Smoking

Smoking interferes with healing by constricting blood vessels and reducing the blood's ability to carry oxygen to the body's tissues. Smoking is especially bad for rhinoplasty patients because smoke irritates the nasal passages. Your doctor may insist that you stop smoking for at least one to two weeks before and after surgery. If you don't, you risk a less favorable result.

Allergies

If you suffer from allergies or hay fever, schedule rhinoplasty at a time of year that you can expect your symptoms to be quiescent. If such timing is not possible, modern drugs prescribed for allergies should enable you to control your symptoms fairly well, and you should be able to go through the procedure and recovery period quite comfortably.

THE PROCEDURE

When done alone rhinoplasty usually takes from an hour to two hours or longer, depending on the extent of your surgery. The time varies from surgeon to surgeon, and from operation to operation. Rhinoplasty is usually performed on an outpatient basis in your surgeon's office-based facility, in a freestanding surgery center, or in a hospital. Patients who have their operation in a one-day surgery facility will enter in the morning and remain for several hours following the procedure.

If you have surgery as a hospital inpatient, you'll stay one to three days. Patients who have complicated nasal problems or other general health conditions may prefer to be in a hospital.

The most common choice of anesthesia for rhinoplasty is a local with sedation. This will allow you to be awake during the operation, but relaxed and insensitive to pain. General anesthesia is sometimes given if you prefer it or if your surgery is especially complex. For example, since it is important to prevent coughing or other movement during surgery on the septum (which bleeds easily), general anesthesia is more likely to be used if your operation involves surgery on this delicate structure.

Rhinoplasty is one of the most difficult of all cosmetic surgery procedures because it is usually performed from inside the nose. It is a "feel" operation. The surgeon must readjust the bone and cartilage framework underneath the skin, sculpting it to the envisioned size and shape without clearly seeing what he is working on.

Surgeons use a wide variety of techniques, depending on their own preferred methods, your anatomy, and the desired result. There are, however, some basics that apply to most rhinoplasty operations.

The incision is usually made inside the nostrils. The skin is separated from the underlying bone or cartilage and mucous membrane, and then a series of surgical steps are taken to cut, trim, or augment the bone and cartilage. The exact order of the steps varies according to the problem and the surgeon's technique.

A hump is removed by using a chisel or a rasp. If your nose is too broad, the nasal bones are surgically freed from their base near the cheek and brought closer together. The tip of the nose is reshaped either before or after the remodeling of the skeletal structure. The problem with tip revision is that the skin closer to the end of the nose is usually thick and sometimes drapes poorly even after the cartilage underneath has been remodeled. The tip may end up looking pudgy and round. Surgeons constantly look for new ways to improve their tip revision techniques.

If the nostrils appear too flared or wide after the nose has been surgically narrowed, small skin wedges are removed from their base. This external procedure leaves a small scar at the base of each nostril, but the marks are virtually invisible after healing.

The incisions are sewn together with very fine stitches using an absorbable suture material. This internal suturing dissolves and eventually falls out by itself. Small external stitches, if needed, are made of nonabsorbable nylon and have to be removed in three or four days.

Following surgery, a splint composed of tape and a plastic or plaster overlay is applied to your nose to stabilize the new shape. Some surgeons also cover your eyes with a pressure bandage to help reduce swelling during the first day. Nasal packs may be inserted into your nostrils to immobilize the septum, particularly if surgery on that delicate structure has been performed as well.

RECOVERY

If you have had local anesthesia plus sedation, you will probably fall asleep for a while following the surgery. When you wake up, your face will feel puffy and your nose may ache. The most uncomfortable period is the first twenty-four hours. For the most part, there is minimal pain and sometimes a dull headache that can be controlled by medication. If you have had your nose packed, that may add to your discomfort because you must breathe through your mouth. If extensive work on your septum was done, more packing is used and your discomfort level may be somewhat increased.

After twenty-four hours most people begin to feel more normal as the effects of the initial trauma and the anesthesia wear off. Except for going to the bathroom, however, you should plan to stay in bed for the first day after surgery, with your head elevated on two pillows to help reduce swelling.

Also plan on a liquid or soft-food diet for the first two days (which is probably all you will feel like eating anyway) to keep facial motion to a minimum. Your teeth are more sensitive following rhinoplasty and they may hurt if you try to chew.

Cold compresses on your eyes—either homemade packs from ice shavings or commercially available eye masks that you freeze—may reduce postoperative bruising and swelling. They may or may not actually help, but they can't hurt and some people feel better when they use them for a couple of days. Some people experience extensive swelling and bruising in the first forty-eight hours, whereas others don't. By and large, you can expect to look much worse than you feel. Although you may be up and about after forty-eight hours, your plastic surgeon will advise you on the proper schedule for resuming your normal routine.

Bleeding. A small amount of bleeding from the nostrils is usual during the first twenty-four to forty-eight hours after surgery. The amount of bleeding varies from person to person and, to a degree, depends on how much surgery was performed. If there was a good deal of work done on the septum, there may be more bleeding.

Occasionally, vigorous bleeding occurs from one or both nostrils. There are particular times when this might happen, such as when scabs inside the nose break away, most likely during the first forty-eight hours after surgery, after the first week, or at about the tenth day. Such bleeding usually stops by itself, provided you remain quiet and keep your head elevated. If the bleeding persists, you should contact your surgeon. He may repack your nose to help stem the flow. If that is not effective, more complex corrective procedures may be necessary.

Nasal Congestion. A stuffy nose, similar to the symptoms of a mild cold, is common after a rhinoplasty because of swelling and coagulated blood along the incision lines. As the swelling both inside and outside the nose diminishes, so does the congestion. Congestion may come and go for several weeks.

Blowing Your Nose. After rhinoplasty, your nose is going to be sore and your surgeon will probably ask you to refrain from blowing it for at least a week. Once the tissues are healed, it should be all right to blow your nose.

Wearing Glasses and Contacts. If you wear contact lenses you can put them in as soon as you feel like it. If you wear glasses, you can usually put them on while the splint is on, letting their weight rest on the splint. After the splint comes off, however, glasses may have to be taped to your forehead for several weeks until your nose completely heals. Your doctor will advise you specifically about when and for how long you can wear glasses.

Removing Packing. If used, nasal packing usually is removed either forty-eight or seventy-two hours after surgery. If extensive work has been done on your septum, the packing may remain in place for as long as five days. As soon as the packing comes out, you will feel much better.

Feeling Better

You will have to take it easy for at least the first week to ten days. If external stitches were used on your nostrils or columella, they will be removed before the first week is over. The protective splint is often removed within a week of surgery, although it may remain in place for up to ten days. In addition, your surgeon may advise you to continue to wear the splint at night. By the end of ten days, all dressings, splints, and stitches will be removed.

Bruising around the eyes will begin to fade within a few days following the operation. When the dressings and splints are removed, you may look terrific, or you may look terrible. If your skin is thin and your bones are delicate, you might look good even this soon after surgery. However, your nose may swell again within a few days. If your skin is thicker, the swelling and puffiness will probably still be obvious when the splint comes off.

Washing Your Face. Once the splint comes off, you can wash your nose with soap and water, but be gentle during the first six weeks or so. If you have very oily skin, an astringent or other skin-care product is usually all right to use. Follow your surgeon's advice about skin care after surgery.

Washing Your Hair. You can wash your hair on the day the splint is removed or even sooner if your surgeon agrees. Your head should be washed tilted back, not forward, and the best place for shampooing is probably in the shower, where your head does not have to be tilted at all. If you wish, you can dry your hair with a hair-dryer on moderate or low heat.

Cosmetics. Using cosmetics to cover bruises is permitted after the splint has been removed. However, surgeons often advise patients to refrain for several weeks from using any cosmetic that requires hard rubbing for application or removal (see "Camouflage Cosmetics" in chapter 5).

Sunbathing. After the packing and splint are removed, your surgeon will probably tell you that a limited amount of sunbathing is all right, as long as you strictly avoid getting sunburned on your nose for about three months after surgery.

Picking Up Your Life Again

Some surgeons severely limit the physical activity of rhinoplasty patients for many weeks, but most let patients return to their normal routine about three weeks after the splint is removed. After the second week, you can resume moderate activity; and after three weeks, full activity (with the exception of contact sports). Your bones and cartilage should be completely healed by six weeks after splint removal.

To permit proper healing, activities that raise blood pressure, such as jogging, swimming, or even bending, should be avoided during the first few weeks. This is true as well for sexual relations or any other activity that might result in an inadvertent bump to your nose. After two weeks sexual relations can be resumed with a certain degree of caution. Three weeks is usually a better waiting period; follow your surgeon's advice. The decision to return to work depends on how you feel and look, including the degree of swelling and discomfort you have.

Looking Better

It's unrealistic to expect an immediate transformation after surgery. Healing is a gradual process. However, your nose will probably look fairly normal as soon as the obvious swelling goes down, usually by the time the splint comes off. After the first week or two, you can go out in public feeling normal. You will not look as if you've just had surgery, because the residual swelling is generally not obvious to others.

Although your nose will look better day by day, some subtle swelling will actually be present for months and the tip retains its swelling the longest. Your nose may also feel softer, since swelling is not as hard as cartilage. Although your nose won't look bad, it just won't look much different. It may also look more swollen on some days than on others. Gradually, over the next several months the new tip will appear. Final results of rhinoplasty may not be fully appreciated for a year or more.

Protecting Your Nose

Some rhinoplasty patients worry about injuring their "new" nose. While the nose is soundly knit at six weeks, the bones heal differently than those in the leg or arm. They are thinner, more delicate structures that heal by forming a layer of scar tissue, which joins the fractured edges. However, the healed nose is no more vulnerable to injury than a nose that has not been operated on. If you are in an accident or suffer a sports injury, for instance, the likelihood of damage to your nose is no greater than if you hadn't had surgery.

TROUBLESHOOTING: WHAT CAN GO WRONG

Postoperative infections are rare. Sinus infections can flare up, although they rarely are the direct result of the operation. Most often they are due to preexisting abnormalities in the internal structure of the nose. Infections are treated with appropriate antibiotics and sinus drainage, if called for. Risk of infections and other complications can be minimized by closely following your surgeon's advice on follow-up care.

Most problems that can occur after rhinoplasty are minor and require no surgical treatment. However, about 10 percent of the time, a minimal, follow-up operation may be desired.

Occasionally, a small blood clot develops under the skin, causing swelling and increased bruising. However, this is not a serious complication. Left alone, the clot is usually absorbed by the body without treatment, or your surgeon will drain it during a follow-up visit. Small burst blood vessels and other tiny blemishes sometimes appear on the skin's surface as well. These are usually quite minor, but are permanent.

Very rarely, a significant nosebleed develops that requires medical care, and possibly even another trip to the operating room. The risk of severe blood loss from nosebleed is extremely small and a transfusion is almost never needed.

Nasal surgery should not create breathing problems if none existed before. In fact, if a deviated septum or an unusual bone formation has caused a breathing problem *before* surgery, it can usually be corrected during the operation. However, if you have difficulty breathing due to allergies or hay fever, rhinoplasty may make the symptoms worse for a few weeks to a few months. In addition, if you have a septal deformity that is not corrected at the time of the rhinoplasty, it can obstruct your breathing even more *after* surgery.

SCARS

Since most cosmetic rhinoplasties are performed from inside the nose, there is no visible scarring. Only when the procedure calls for the narrowing of flared nostrils, or when the surgeon elects to enter the nose from the outside for some other reason, will an outside incision be made, leaving behind a scar that is usually barely visible in the crease of each nostril, at the base of the columella, or over the bridge of the nose.

FOLLOW-UP VISITS TO THE DOCTOR

You will probably see your surgeon once a week for several weeks. The intervals between checkups will then grow longer and about a year after surgery you'll have your final visit. Follow-up visits usually are part of the initial fee paid for the surgery.

If you require a minor adjustment or revision related to your original surgery, your surgeon will not usually charge for this secondary procedure. However, a fee may be charged for the use of the operating facility.

AGING

One of the most persistent myths about rhinoplasty is that as time passes a nose that has been operated on looks worse. However, although our bodies do react to the forces of gravity, rhinoplasty does not accelerate the process. In fact, the small amount of scar tissue that builds up inside the nose after surgery may keep the nose from drooping. Although the results of rhinoplasty are permanent, tissue naturally will continue to age. A rhinoplasty can be repeated later to make your nose smaller or larger, if you so choose.

SUCCESS

In 90 percent of patients, rhinoplasty is successful in a single procedure. Still, a second operation is always a possibility, although in most cases it is a relatively minor procedure. There may be a small residual bump on the nose, or sometimes a slight unevenness in the tip. In rare instances, the fractured bones "wander" slightly and an adjustment is necessary. Even the most skilled surgeons perform minor secondary corrections in about 5 to 10 percent of their patients.

Revisions are usually delayed until the swelling has subsided and the scars inside the nose are well healed. Six months is considered a minimum wait by most doctors, but the interval varies, depending on how rapidly you recover from the original operation. During this waiting period, it's not unusual to decide that you like your new nose just the way it is and to cancel the revision.

SATISFACTION

Every surgeon talks about the positive personality changes that often occur after this procedure. Many people seem to blossom after a nose operation. For some, a new self-image leads to more confidence, a more outgoing personality, and a brighter outlook on life. A new sense of confidence is the most frequently observed change. Plastic surgeons' observations have been supported by a recent survey by Marcia Kraft Goin, M.D., a psychiatrist on the faculty of the University of Southern California at Los Angeles. Dr. Goin followed the postoperative progress of 120 rhinoplasty patients and found that 90 percent were glad they had the surgery. Although 20 percent said they felt depressed during the first thirty days after the operation, their depressed feelings disappeared within six months.

Temporary blues after rhinoplasty are generally attributed to two causes. First, it takes time before you see the true results of the surgery. Second, rhinoplasty changes the body shape you grew up with. Unlike a facelift, which returns your features to the way they were, rhinoplasty creates a whole new shape you've never had before. No matter how much you wanted that change, it may be a shock at first and it takes time to get used to it.

In Dr. Goin's study, patients who felt depressed following surgery were usually those who were most anxious before surgery. According to her findings, men were no more or less susceptible to postoperative depression than women, although it's hard to draw conclusions because only 17 of the 120 rhinoplasty patients were men.

Plastic surgeons have varying opinions about rhinoplasty in men. Some say men are excellent surgical candidates because they are less demanding and less likely to seek the "perfect nose." Others feel that men have a higher dissatisfaction rate than women and are more likely to require additional operations before they are happy with the rhinoplasty. Doctors believe that it's hard for men to decide what they want and then clearly express their choice to their surgeon. A man may say he wants a very subtle rhinoplasty, for example, when he really wants something more dramatic. In addition, some psychologists and plastic surgeons believe that the nose plays a greater role in a man's self-image than in a woman's, particularly in relation to his sexual identity. For instance, a man with a large hooked nose may say he wants it made smaller, but he worries that reducing the size of the nose may make him look feminine.

Doctors also say that men have trouble expressing themselves when they feel dissatisfied. They tend to feel vaguely discontented. "They just seem unhappy," says one surgeon. "You have to drag it out of them, that they want something more done to the nose."

Most people in Dr. Goin's survey chose rhinoplasty because they hoped that it would affect their life in some positive way. Primarily they hoped it would boost their self-esteem and change the way others perceived them. According to the survey, all of these goals were accomplished to some degree. Seventy-seven percent of the patients surveyed had hoped for a general, unspecified positive change following rhinoplasty and 51 percent said that they achieved it. Forty percent said they hoped the operation would boost their self-esteem and 36 percent said later that it did. Another 30 percent said they wanted the surgery to change the way they were perceived at work and 22 percent reported that it did.

The Ears

YOUR EARS ARE AS DISTINCTIVE AS FINGERPRINTS AND AS COMPLEX as labyrinths. Your ears may be unusually large or unusually small. They may have well-defined, circular lobes or almost no lobes at all. They may be slightly pointed on top or completely round. They may stick out prominently or lie close to your head. Your ears may even be radically different from each other.

Ears differ from race to race. Polynesians generally have large ears, whereas Africans often have ears that are quite small. The size and shape of the earlobes also varies from race to race. Despite their dazzling variety, most of us don't notice our ears much. Occasionally, however, the size or shape of the ears is so extreme that it causes embarrassment. In these cases, plastic surgery can help.

PROTRUDING EARS

The most common cosmetic procedure performed on the ears is otoplasty, which "pins" prominent ears closer to the head. About 5 percent of the human race has protruding ears, although not every culture considers this a flaw.

One of the persistent myths surrounding protruding ears is that you can cause them yourself by sleeping on folded ears or that you can prevent them by sleeping with a scarf or nightcap tied around your head. This is not true. The shape and size of the ear is determined long before birth; after birth, almost nothing can be done to alter its shape except plastic surgery.

There are many reasons why ears appear to protrude. It may be that the shell-like curve of the ear is too large; or the fold inside the outer rim of the ear, called the antihelix, is too shallow or missing altogether. Sometimes the lobes protrude at an odd angle.

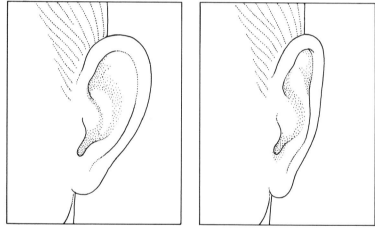

Before and after otoplasty. Viewed from the front, it can be seen how the creation of a fold in the cartilage makes the ear lie flatter against the head.

Otoplasty can be quite simple or quite complex, depending on the reason for the ears' protrusion. The optimum result is a natural shape with natural curves, without being set too far back. It is impossible to achieve an exact match between both ears, but as long as surgery is not overdone and as long as natural curves are achieved, no one will notice that the ears are slightly different from one another.

Best Candidates

Otoplasty usually can be performed on a patient any time after the age of four, when ear growth is almost complete. (Surgery does not stop further growth of the ears.) When disfigurement is severe, it is recommended that a child be operated on early to avoid possible emotional stress from teasing when he or she enters school.

Most surgeons will not operate until the child becomes aware of the abnormality and asks to have his ears "fixed." If the child personally desires the change, he is usually cooperative during the process and happy with the outcome. For some children, this awareness comes as early as three and a half or four years old. For others, it may not occur until eight to twelve years of age. If a child does not want his ears changed, most plastic surgeons will follow the wishes of the child, regardless of what the parents think.

Should you encourage your child to have his ears fixed? If your child is feeling stressed because he is being teased about his ears, you probably should consider it. However, if your child doesn't seem to notice his protruding ears, or doesn't complain about teasing, plastic surgeons suggest that parents merely stay alert for problems. For example, although there is no scientific rationale, physicians have observed that children with protruding ears tend to become combative, possibly because they are teased and ridiculed at school, which makes them defensive and angry.

After age four, otoplasty can be done on patients of any age. It's not unusual for an adult who didn't or couldn't have the operation as a child to come in years later for otoplasty.

The Consultation

Almost every well-trained plastic surgeon does otoplasty, but it's not as common a procedure as nose reshaping. Even a very busy and successful plastic surgeon may only do a few otoplasties a year. Simply look for a physician who performs enough otoplasties on a regular basis to make you feel comfortable.

Every otoplasty is individually designed. After examining the patient, the surgeon will choose the most effective technique to correct the specific problem. Even when only one ear seems prominent, otoplasty is usually performed on both ears to achieve a better balance. Occasionally, otoplasty is done on only one ear, such as when the opposite ear appears completely normal and projects just five eighths to three quarters of an inch from the side of the head.

Costs

Costs vary widely. A recent survey of ASPRS members estimated that surgical fees range from $1,000 to $4,000 or more, depending on whether one or both ears are corrected and on the complexity of the operation. Additional expenses depend on where the surgery takes place and the kind of anesthesia used.

Otoplasty in a young child is sometimes covered by insurance if the disfigurement is considered a birth defect. Teenagers and adults, however, usually have a more difficult time proving that surgery was required because of an actual defect and insurance is less likely to provide coverage.

The Procedure

Depending on the extent of the surgery, the procedure usually takes about two hours. Otoplasty is usually performed on an outpatient basis in a hospital, doctor's office-based facility, or freestanding surgical center. It may also be performed in a hospital on an inpatient basis.

Either local anesthesia with sedation or general anesthesia can be used for otoplasty. Adults over the age of eighteen usually choose the local option, which allows them to remain aware but insensitive to pain. General anesthesia is often preferred for young children because it's more difficult for a child to lie still for the length of the operation. Children also may feel anxious about the surgery and some react by becoming more, rather than less, stimulated by the sedation that is usually given with local anesthesia. In addition, children tend to recover more quickly from general anesthesia than do adults. A child aged four to six will probably only feel tired for a few days following general anesthesia, whereas an adult may feel slightly groggy for a week to ten days.

However, some children tolerate local anesthesia surprisingly well, with little or no sedation, because they are so eager to have the operation done. Parents should discuss the options with the surgeon and make the best choice for their child.

It's important for parents and physician to thoroughly discuss the process of anesthesia with the child beforehand to dispel any fears the child may have. When they're properly prepared, most children cope well with their apprehensions about surgery and they soon forget all about the operation, no matter where or how it was performed.

Otoplasties have been done since the late 1800s. It was originally thought that merely removing some of the skin on the back of the ear would flatten it. Eventually, however, surgeons began to remove strips of cartilage as well so that they could better reshape the ear. As scar tissue forms, it "glues" the altered cartilage into its new shape, producing a permanent change in the angle of the ear.

Although surgery is performed from the back of the ear, if it is not skillfully done it can produce sharp ridges, rather than smooth curves, in front. The specific technique used depends on what is causing the ears to stick out. One of three basic techniques is usually employed, and sometimes a combination of two or more. If the fold inside the outer ear isn't properly formed, one approach is to make an incision in the back of the ear and remove enough skin to expose the underlying cartilage. The surgeon then removes some of the cartilage or simply uses sutures to fold in the cartilage to reshape the ear. The outer incision is then closed with stitches.

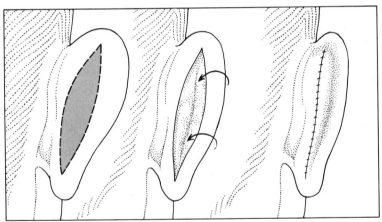

From the back of the ear, incisions are made to remove skin, and sometimes cartilage, in the shaded area. Sutures pull the remaining cartilage together and recontour the ear. The thin scar fades with time.

Sometimes the surgeon achieves the same effect by scraping the cartilage in the front of the ear to weaken it, then stitching the back to hold the ear closer to the head. Or, the surgeon may

remove a segment of cartilage from the "shell" area in the middle of the ear, then roll back part of the ear to create a fold.

Recovery

After surgery, the patient can expect to be in the recovery room
for an hour or two. When feeling ready to move around, he or
she can be driven home to rest in bed. A patient who has had
general anesthesia in a hospital setting may choose to stay overnight.

The head will be wrapped in a bulky bandage, leaving the face
open. The ears may throb or ache a little for the first one or
two days. The throbbing is usually relieved by a nonaspirin pain
reliever or, if necessary, a prescription medication. If the head
is kept elevated with two or more soft pillows, there is less swelling and greater comfort.

Most patients who receive local anesthesia plus sedation are
up and around in a day or two following surgery; those who
have general anesthesia may require an additional day or so in
bed. Within a few days, the bulky bandages are removed and
patients are asked to wear a headband for several weeks to protect the new ears from damage during sleep or play. The headband is usually worn day and night for two weeks, and then only
at night for the third week.

The stitches in the skin behind the ears are usually removed
at the end of the first week following surgery. Although the
throbbing soon stops, many people find that for several weeks
after surgery their ears hurt when they lie on them. Sleeping on
two soft pillows will help.

The ears are likely to be swollen and red after surgery, and
may look a little puffy and pink for several months. Numbness
in the ears may persist for several weeks after surgery and may
return in cold weather. One of the most common side effects of
otoplasty is an acute sensitivity to cold weather, especially in the
first year. Wearing a hat, scarf, or earmuffs will help.

Most adults can go back to work about five days after surgery.
Children can expect to return to school after seven days or so,
but must be careful about playground activities for several more
weeks. Parents should consider letting their child's teacher know
about the surgery so he or she can keep an eye on the child
during school hours and recess.

Sports and exercise should be resumed with care. A blow to

the ear could cause it to lose its new shape or might cause bleeding around the cartilage. Long walks and stretching exercises can be resumed after one week. Swimming is usually not recommended until after two or three weeks to avoid any chance of swimmer's ear, an infection that could spread to the incision site. Vigorous exercise, such as jogging, hiking, or use of muscle machines, usually can be resumed after three weeks. Contact and ball sports should be avoided for at least six weeks or longer. For adults, normal sexual activity is safe after one week.

Troubleshooting: What Can Go Wrong

Thousands of otoplasties are performed successfully each year. Nevertheless, there are some potential risks involved. Blood clots and infections occasionally occur. If a blood clot does form, it may be allowed to dissolve naturally or the surgeon may choose to draw it out with a needle. Infection—signaled by a painful, swollen ear—may occur in the cartilage and poses more of a difficulty. Infections may persist for a long time and can cause scar tissue to form in and around the ear. They are usually treated with antibiotics, but in a few extreme cases may require surgery to drain the infection, plus a later operation to repair the ear.

Scars

Since the incisions are made in the back of the ears, faint scars, about two to three inches long, are concealed in the creases. Very rarely, heavy scarring (keloids) develops in the incisions. There is no way to predict who will develop keloids and who won't; these scars may simply disappear on their own after a period of time or they can be treated with steroids injected directly into the scar.

Success

Occasionally, the new ears look mismatched or artificial. Additional corrective surgery can be performed later. Rarely, a setback ear may protrude again. When relapse does occur, it is almost always in the first few weeks following surgery, before the scar tissue has firmly welded the ear in place. A relapsed ear can be corrected through further surgery a few weeks after the original operation. Successful otoplasty is a permanent procedure.

Satisfaction

Most people are happy with both the procedure itself and the result. Other than the need to wear a headband for a short while, it is an easy operation to recover from. Children who have been teased at school are usually thrilled that they're now "like everybody else." Young children quickly forget about the operation and often even forget that they ever had prominent ears.

Occasionally, however, patients are disappointed with the results because they wanted ears that match perfectly or ears that lie very flat against the head. Good otoplasty aims for normal-looking ears, and normal ears are neither perfectly matched nor do they lie squashed against the side of the head. If patients and their parents (if appropriate) have thoroughly discussed their expectations with their surgeon before the operation, they should be prepared and know what to expect.

OTHER EAR PROBLEMS

There are a variety of other, less common ear imperfections, including a "lop ear," when the top seems to fold down and forward; a "cupped ear," which is usually a very small ear; and a "shell ear," when the curve in the outer rim, as well as the natural folds and creases, are absent. Some people have overly large earlobes or lobes that are stretched out of shape by heavy earrings. As we grow older the earlobes also may develop creases and wrinkles, which sometimes can be quite obvious in someone who has had a facelift or chemical peel (young face, old ears).

Some of these flaws can be helped by cosmetic plastic surgery, but for others the correction leaves scars that are worse than the original condition. Although it is seldom done, large earlobes can be reduced. Holes for pierced earrings that have become stretched out over time, or completely torn, can be repaired. Wrinkled lobes can be smoothed with chemical peel, dermabrasion, or injections of fat or collagen. Excessively large ears can sometimes be reduced as well, but this is complicated surgery that is done only in extreme instances. If someone is born with-

out the external part of the ear, or if the ear is severed or damaged in an accident (such as from an automobile accident or a
dog bite), the whole ear can be rebuilt.

BUILDING NEW EARS

Ear reconstruction is one of the most complicated and difficult
procedures in plastic surgery. Even a sculptor working in clay
or wood finds it hard to duplicate the intricate folds and grooves
of the natural ear. Constructing an ear by reshaping living tissue
and cartilage requires the highest degree of skill, artistry, and
patience.

A deformity in the size and shape of the outer ear may be
inherited or it may occur spontaneously during development in
the mother's womb. A missing ear, called *microtia*, occurs spontaneously in one out of every 6,500 births in the Caucasian population, and in one out of every 4,000 births among the Japanese.
For unknown reasons, the incidence is as high as one in every
900 to 1,200 births among Navajo Indians. In the majority of
infants born with this defect, the ear is missing on one side only.
However, in one out of every nine cases, both ears are missing.
If you have a child born with a missing ear, your risk of having
a second child with the same ear deformity is one in twenty-five,
or 4 percent. Aside from the deformed ear, these children are
usually normal in every other way, although they may have some
bone and soft-tissue deficiencies in their jaw and cheek region.

Hearing and External Ear Development

When the external ear is missing, a child's hearing may be affected to some degree. The fully developed ear consists of three
parts: the inner ear, the middle ear, and the outer ear. The inner
ear relays messages to the brain for interpretation. The middle
ear is the actual hearing mechanism; it consists of the canal, ear-
drum, hammer, anvil, stirrup and air cells, and mastoid bone.
The outer ear is the little "trumpet" that gathers in sound and
protects the middle ear.

Although the complete ear has three distinct parts, it actually
develops in two phases. The inner ear develops from one block
of tissue very early in fetal growth, about week six. The middle
and external ear develop from a separate block of tissue and

are not fully shaped until about week thirteen. Eventually, the two blocks of tissue fuse together.

Because of this separate development, the inner ear may be normal, even when the outer ear is missing or deformed. However, when there is an external deformity, the middle ear is likely to be abnormal, with its conducting parts fused together. For this reason, a child born with a missing external ear will probably have a reduction in hearing of about 60 percent on the affected side. He will usually have normal hearing on the other side.

Reconstruction of the external ear alone will only improve appearance; it will not restore hearing. Except in a very few experienced hands, middle-ear surgery carries more risk than gain. Unless both ears are affected and hearing is impaired on both sides, corrective surgery to improve hearing is not usually attempted.

Ear reconstruction should be done by a specialist whose practice is largely devoted to ear surgery. Usually a medical center or plastic surgeon in your area can help you locate a physician who specializes in ear reconstruction.

Best Candidates

Parents often consult with a plastic surgeon when their child is still an infant, so that they can prepare for the time when he or she will be old enough for surgical reconstruction of the ear. Early medical consultation also means that parents will learn how to compensate for their child's probable hearing impairment.

A child born without an external ear will begin to notice the difference when he is about three and a half years old. He'll start referring to his ear as his "little ear," or his "closed ear." Parents can explain to their child that he was born with one small ear and that when he is older, if he wishes, he can have the ear fixed.

Ear reconstruction often cannot be done before age six or seven because younger children usually don't have enough tissue and rib cartilage to borrow for creation of a decent framework for the new ear. The plastic surgeon also must weigh the child's overall size against the size of the ear he's trying to match. For instance, if the child's normal ear is quite small, but he is big for his age, ear reconstruction may be possible at age five and a half. However, if the child's normal ear is large, and the child is small for his age, he may have to wait until he's seven or eight years old for there to be enough cartilage to fashion a framework.

When a child must wait, emotional trouble may begin when he starts school. Everyone is comparing body parts—ten fingers, ten toes, two ears—and teasing may occur just as a child's body image begins to form.

Most children are very aware of their problem before age six or seven and are capable of participating in the decision to have their ear reconstructed. The surgeon will need guidance from parents about the child's ability to understand and cooperate in the process. Ear reconstruction involves several procedures with long intervals of healing in-between and requires maximum co-operation from the patient. If a child wants the operation, and understands what is going to happen, he usually becomes fasci-nated with the process and very involved in it. Seeing the new ear appear in stages is like magic.

If the child and his parents do not choose plastic surgery at an early age, the next big emotional crunch is likely to come in adolescence. Perhaps the most pressing desire in a teenager's life is to be like his peers and conformity in appearance is most important of all.

For various reasons, including cost and availability, some peo-ple don't seek ear reconstruction until they are adults. Usually by adulthood they have been affected emotionally by this con-dition, but older adults also can have reconstruction.

The Consultation

Besides age and proper growth, the plastic surgeon will want to make certain that anyone choosing ear reconstruction is healthy enough to withstand multiple surgical procedures. The surgeon will also examine the skin. Sometimes when an ear is lost through injury, scarring is so severe that the skin cannot stretch over the rebuilt framework.

Once the plastic surgeon determines that it's technically fea-sible to reconstruct a good ear, the final step before going forward with surgery is to make sure that the individual under-stands what surgery can achieve and is sufficiently motivated. One of the best ways to do this is by showing photographs.

Doctors don't like to show pre- and postoperative photographs for many plastic surgery procedures because they are concerned that it implies a kind of guarantee. When it comes to ear reconstruction, however, photographs can be invaluable in helping the patient understand just what a reconstructed ear will look like. Even the best reconstructed ear will not look normal. Getting a feeling for what the results will be is especially important for ear reconstruction because it requires extensive involvement from patients and their families. If the potential result doesn't seem satisfactory to them, then they shouldn't go ahead with the procedure.

Costs

Ear reconstruction is very costly because it requires multiple surgical procedures and often involves travel and hotel expenses as well. You can expect to get some help from your insurance carrier for both the hospital costs and the surgeon's fee. However, unless you happen to live near one of the handful of specialists who perform ear reconstruction, you will have to pay travel and hotel expenses out of your own pocket.

The Procedure

The techniques involved in ear reconstruction are too extensive and complex for the scope of this book but, overall, reconstruction takes three or four surgical procedures, with intervals of several months in-between, to fully build a new ear. A framework for the ear is first sculpted from a piece of cartilage taken from the rib cage. If the patient has enough skin in the area planned for the new ear, this cartilage is then implanted beneath it. Otherwise, a skin graft must be used to cover the framework of the cartilage.

In the past, surgeons have tried to fashion a framework from silicone, rubber, plastics, and even metals, but none of these materials has been successful. A foreign body placed under thin skin tends to cause irritation and infection. Very few surgeons use these materials anymore.

Artificial Ears

For people whose skin is so heavily scarred that it cannot stretch over a new framework, an artificial ear may be the answer. Prostheses may be made of polyvinyl or other synthetic material. They are painted and tinted to match the individual's skin tone and then glued to the side of the head. It sounds easy, but in fact there are few artificial ears that look natural and the false ear must be reglued every morning. The glues are unreliable and sometimes irritating to the skin. Prostheses are also quite expensive and must be replaced periodically. For a child facing the prospect of a lifetime of wearing an ear prosthesis, reconstructive surgery would seem a better solution.

Success

Overall, while difficult and complex, ear reconstruction is successful and ultimately rewarding. It is truly one of the miracles of plastic surgery.

The Facial Skeleton: Chin, Jaw, Eyebrows, Cheekbones

A NEW WAY OF LOOKING AT THE FACE AS A WHOLE IS TO EVALUATE the skeleton underneath. If you look in the mirror at your own face, you can see how your facial bones harmonize with each other to form what science and artistry call a pleasing countenance. The bones of your face—the ridges above your eyebrows, the ledges formed by your cheekbones, and your lower jaw, which starts below your ears and extends forward to your chin—capture light and are called "highlight" zones. Between these bony ridges are "lowlight" zones, that is, your forehead, your eyes, the soft tissue of your cheeks, and the hollow of your neck.

The highlight zones that define the shape and balance of your entire face vary widely. You may have a pronounced ridge above your eyes, yet have flat cheekbones or a receding chin, or vice versa. The prominence of these ridges varies considerably from person to person. When one or more ridges are drastically over-sized or undersized, they seem to throw the face out of balance.

To adjust this imbalance is why facial skeletal surgery has been developed to adjust this imbalance. There are now plastic surgery procedures to correct problems in each of the highlight zones. The most common procedures are augmentation of the chin and cheekbones. Less commonly performed, but still possible, are procedures to build up or reduce the eyebrow ridges and jaw.

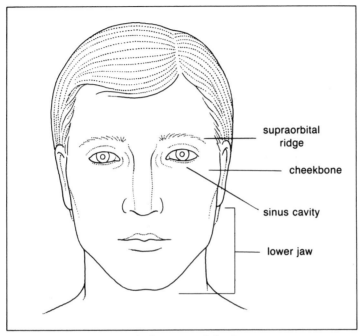

Highlight zones of the face.

LOWER-JAW IMPLANTS

The back of the lower jaw, whose wide, square shape is the hallmark of the model's look, is called the posterior mandible. New plastic surgery techniques now allow artificial implants to be placed along the jawline to create the clean, distinct definition that photographers love.

Implants placed along the posterior mandible can (1) help increase the definition between the jaw and neck, (2) increase the width of the jaw to make it more angular, or (3) improve the balance of the face if the jaw is asymmetrical. Posterior-mandible implants are usually inserted only in young people with one of these specific goals in mind. It is still not a common procedure, and it carries the same risks of infection and rejection as other implant procedures.

Before surgery, both photographs and x-rays of your jaw are

taken so the implant can be shaped precisely to fit your lower jawbone. The actual thickness of the implants is an aesthetic judgment based on your desires, as well as the degree of bone prominence and amount of soft tissue you have in your jaw. The implants are carved to the length, width, and angle of your jaw configuration and tapered so they have long thin tips at both ends. They sit precisely on the bone to assure a smooth fit.

Lower-jaw implants can be inserted by themselves or in conjunction with other plastic surgery procedures, including a facelift, facial liposuction, chin augmentation, or chinbone surgery. Either local anesthesia with sedation or general anesthesia can be used for lower-jaw implant procedures. The procedure takes one to two hours.

Before surgery, you will be given antibiotics to guard against infection. The incision is made inside your mouth and the jawbone is bared completely. The implant is then placed directly on the bone and the incision is closed. After one side of the jaw is augmented, the second side is done.

You will need to take oral antibiotics for about five days following surgery. Extensive swelling occurs immediately, so you will have to keep your jaw still to minimize swelling. You'll probably be advised to stick to a liquid diet for seven days, then soft foods for an additional week. You can gently brush your teeth the day after surgery and can also begin to use a mouthwash made of half-strength hydrogen peroxide several times a day.

The most visible swelling subsides within two to three weeks. You will not be able to open your mouth fully for several weeks following surgery. Don't force your mouth open for at least two weeks; at that time, your surgeon will give you a series of jaw exercises to practice. Within eight weeks after surgery, your jaws will open and close normally.

Jaw implants are new and long-term results are not yet known. To date, there have been no reports of infection or rejection of the implants, but there is always the possibility that either might occur over the long term. However, the risk of infection is less with implants in this area of the face because there is no involvement of the sinuses or other cavities that can harbor infection.

Facial skeletal surgery changes the basic structure of your face. Most candidates are younger people seeking a fundamental

change in their face—the creation of a more harmonious, attractive balance for their features.

In older patients, facial skeletal surgery is usually performed
in conjunction with other procedures such as a facelift to help
restore the face to a more youthful appearance. Although bone
shrinks only slightly as we grow older, the skin and other soft
tissues stretch and sag. Implants or other augmentation techniques can take up this slack. For example, if the ridge over the
eyes is built up, it elevates tissue hanging down over the upper
lids. Cheekbone augmentation takes up slack in the midface. But
the most dramatic result of facial skeleton augmentation is possible on the chin.

THE EYEBROW RIDGE

Protruding eyes can be set back by building up bones around
the eyes. Plastic surgeons use several different methods to
build up this ridge. In one method a piece of forehead muscle
is rolled down to add soft tissue. In another, pieces of bone
from the skull are used to create a more prominent ridge
above the eyes. Artificial material like silicone can also be
used to build up the ridge subtly. Overall, these are not frequently sought procedures, but they can be done for the individual who has a strong desire for this particular
improvement.

A chin implant or bone reshaping adds strength and definition to the jawline. The chin doesn't actually recede with age,
but the face does become slightly shorter and wider, as though
you pushed the top and bottom toward one another. Chin augmentation is a particularly effective procedure when done in an
older person in conjunction with a facelift.

IMPLANT MATERIALS

Implants may be fashioned from natural material from your own
body or from artificial substances made in a laboratory. How-

ever, no perfect implant material has yet been discovered. In fact, there is not even a "best" implant.

Natural Materials

Human cartilage, which is soft and can be carved to any shape, makes an excellent implant, except there's not much of it available in the body. Even when enough cartilage can be retrieved, say, from your ribs, it requires additional surgery and leaves a scar. More problematical is the fact that large pieces of cartilage tend to warp over time. Carved into one shape, a large implant made from cartilage will slowly shift into another shape.

Bone, which can be taken from the outer layer of the skull and carved into an implant, has the disadvantage of gradually dissolving. The rate of this absorption is unpredictable: Some people retain a lot of the bone, some people lose half of it, and others lose all of it. Bone also is difficult to shape into an implant with smooth, soft edges. As a consequence, you often can feel the edges of a bone implant. Given the options, most people choose implants made from artificial substances.

Artificial Materials

Various substances, primarily silicones or porous materials such as coral or plastic blends, are presently used to make implants. However, with all artificial implants, there is the risk of infection and capsular contracture, a condition in which the scar tissue holding the implant in place pulls tightly around it, sometimes making it feel unnaturally hard and making it look bunchy.

Advocates of the porous type of artificial implants like them because they can easily be carved to fit each individual and they are usually soft enough to mold to the curved bones in the face, which is critical with cheek and jaw implants. They are also light and easy to work with. In addition, the body's tissues grow into their surfaces so they stay fixed in position without causing capsular contracture.

However, this porous nature is also their main disadvantage; they are characterized by a slightly increased rate of infection. If infection occurs with any implant, the device may have to be removed and replaced (if desired).

Because of this problem, some doctors use smooth, nonporous silicone implants. Silicone is thought to be less prone to infection despite the lack of definitive studies comparing the incidence rate between the two types of implants. However, silicone devices are more likely to develop capsular contracture, and can't usually be carved to follow the dips and bulges of facial bone, although they are made in different sizes.

A silicone implant may be completely solid or solid on the outside with a gel core. Gel-filled implants are soft, but they can leak if hit hard. If you don't play arduous sports, and if you have thin skin through which an implant can be felt, your surgeon may recommend a gel implant.

Most physicians feel strongly about the implant material they use and your surgeon will tell you why he prefers the one he works with. So, when you and your surgeon plan your operation, you have to look at the trade-offs. New implant materials are being developed all the time.

Even more important than the type of implant used is your surgeon's evaluation of your face. The two zones most likely to be augmented—or reduced—are the chin and the cheekbones.

THE CHIN

The chin must be evaluated when looking at it both straight on and in profile. Straight on, the chin may appear square or pointed. In profile, it may jut or recede. Sometimes the chin itself isn't so bad, but drooping, aging skin gives the effect of a "witch's chin." An implant can help take up the slack without visible scarring.

Chinbone Surgery Versus Implants

Two highly successful plastic surgery procedures are used to augment the chin: insertion of a chin implant and chinbone surgery. The most commonly used is the chin implant, but some plastic surgeons believe that in the long run, bone surgery gives a better result.

A plastic surgeon who has experience with the technique may recommend bone surgery. The chin is an ideal area in which to cut the bone, sliding the bottom edge so that the chin can be lengthened or shortened, brought forward or back. Advocates of chinbone surgery believe that it is a superior procedure because it uses the patient's own bone. When you use the chin's existing tissue, the chance of success may be higher.

Most surgeons, however, use a chin implant—in a procedure called augmentation mentoplasty—rather than bone surgery because it is a less extensive operation and requires minimal recovery for the patient. Bone surgery is usually chosen only when an implant won't do the job.

For example, if you have a short chin (when there is very little distance from your lower lip to the bottom of your chin) an implant is usually not as effective as chinbone surgery. The most common way to lengthen a short chin is to slice the bone horizontally and wedge bone grafts or tiny blocks of silicone between the two layers. The same is true if your chin is a little asymmetrical, a fairly common problem.

It takes about thirty minutes to put in an implant and just slightly longer to do bone surgery. Both are outpatient procedures. However, chinbone reshaping may cost twice as much as an implant. Discuss the pros and cons for both options thoroughly with your plastic surgeon.

Best Candidates

Although your chin continues to grow until you are in your early twenties, you can have surgery earlier. If you are a teenager and are getting an implant to enlarge your chin, your surgeon will probably select a small- to medium-sized implant, which will continue to look good five or ten years hence, when your chin is fully grown. The recommended minimum age for implants is sixteen for girls, eighteen for boys. Chinbone surgery can be done at the same age. There is no upper age limit.

Perhaps more important than your age is the condition of your mouth. Because bone surgery and much of implant surgery is done through your mouth, your gums must be free of gingivitis and periodontal disease, and you should have no untreated cavities.

Costs

An implant costs approximately half as much as chinbone surgery. The surgeon's fee varies from $300 to $2,000 or more for a chin implant; chinbone surgery can cost from $600 to $3,000 or a little higher. Your choice of anesthesia and surgical facility will also add to the cost.

If your chin is malformed from a birth defect or from an accident, insurance may cover the surgery. Check with your surgeon and your insurance carrier.

Before Surgery

Chin surgery is often carried out through mouth incisions. If you smoke, it is critical to stop before and after surgery, at least until your mouth is completely healed, to reduce your risk of infection.

Chin Implant

Procedure

Both implant and chinbone surgery is usually done on an outpatient basis in your surgeon's office facility, a freestanding surgical center, or a hospital. If you have bone surgery, you may choose to stay overnight in a hospital.

For a chin implant, local anesthesia plus sedation is the usual practice. The procedure takes about thirty minutes to one hour. In the standard implant procedure, the surgeon makes an incision in the skin under the chin or inside your lower lip. He gently lifts the tissues off the bones to make a space large enough for the implant to fit—about one and a half to two inches long. He knows in advance the approximate size of the implant he will need, but during the surgery he uses several sample implants as "sizers" to determine the right dimensions for you.

The surgeon then places the selected implant in the pocket, stitches it into place, and sews up the incision. Tape is strapped across your chin to help control swelling and give your chin extra support when you talk and eat.

About 5 percent of the time, the chinbone must be surgically altered before the implant goes in. For example, if your chin is more prominent on one side, your surgeon may choose to shave down the bone. This problem may also be handled by inserting an implant that is slightly thicker on one side. Most surgeons choose the latter option. If you also are having a rhinoplasty, the nose surgery may be done at the same time as the chin enlargement.

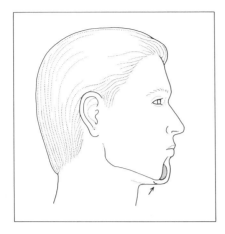

In the most common method of chin augmentation, a short incision is made underneath the chin or inside the mouth. An implant is inserted between the bone and tissue. The slight scar fades with time.

Recovery

There is minimal postoperative pain because your chin is not one of your moving parts. (Pain tends to be worse when motion interferes.) However, your chin will feel stiff and achy for two or three days. Your chin and your upper neck also may be bruised and you will have some swelling in the area. You may mistake this swelling for the implant, thinking that your new chin is much bigger than it actually is.

Your chin also will probably feel quite numb. If your implant was inserted through an incision inside your lower lip, your mouth won't open as fully as it usually does. Your doctor will give you detailed instructions on caring for it.

Numbness may last for the first two weeks and sometimes even longer. Visible swelling persists for about two weeks, then disappears over the next several months. If an incision was made inside your mouth, you will probably be asked to stick to liquids and soft foods for the first week. You can usually brush your teeth gently the day after surgery and will be advised to rinse your mouth several times a day with salt water, peroxide diluted with water, or an antibiotic mouthwash.

Stitches inside your mouth usually dissolve by themselves or your surgeon will remove them after the first week. If you have stitches under your chin, they are usually removed between the fifth and tenth day.

Some people are back at work as soon as the bandage is off, in about a week. Many people, however, don't feel comfortable going out socially until about two weeks after surgery. Most of the bruising and swelling are gone in about two to three weeks.

You should not have sex for at least a week and should avoid any facial contact during sex for at least two weeks. In addition, you will need to avoid any other activity that would result in an inadvertent bump or blow to the face, which might reopen your incisions or cause additional pain and swelling. You usually can start your regular exercise program at three weeks postop. However, for the next six weeks after surgery, avoid any sports in which you're likely to get hit in the face. It takes about that long for scar tissue to form around the implant and to hold it firmly in place.

Troubleshooting: What Can Go Wrong

Shifting Position. A shift in placement is the most likely thing to go wrong with a new implant. It doesn't happen often and it isn't dangerous, but if the implant shifts, the only way to correct it is to redo the operation.

Infection. The next most troublesome complication is infection. Infection around the implant may cause your body to reject it. In that case, the implant may have to be removed; it can be replaced after the infection clears, usually in several months.

Capsular Contracture. The body always forms a barrier around an artificial implant, but for most people this capsule of scar tissue is so subtle that it's unnoticeable. The capsule usually stabilizes one to two years after surgery. However, scar tissue sometimes contracts tightly around the implant, making it feel quite hard (capsular contracture). Capsular contracture is not as significant in a chin implant as it is in a breast implant, because the implant is supposed to simulate hard bone. However, if the capsule around the implant stands out noticeably from the natural line of the chin, you can have the implant replaced with a different one made of another material or can choose to have bone surgery to improve your chin.

Scars

If the implant was inserted through the mouth, there will be no visible scar. If an incision was made beneath the chin, the small scar will be out of direct sight.

Success

Chin implants are usually permanent. Probably about 5 percent of chin implants will have some kind of problem that causes them to be removed. That still produces a success rate of 95 percent.

Chinbone Surgery

The Procedure

Local anesthesia plus sedation or general anesthesia is used for this surgery. The procedure takes about one to one and a half hours. An incision about three to four inches long is made along the inside of your lower lip. The surgeon uses an electrical saw to cut the bone, then drills holes so that it can be wired into a better position.

Using this technique, a slice of bone can be brought forward. In rare instances, the chin may also be lengthened by wedging artificial material between the cut portions of bone. Once the bone is in its new place, the muscle and tissues inside the mouth are sewn up. An extensive elastic bandage is wrapped around your chin and head.

Recovery

Recovery is similar to that for implant surgery, but the ache will be more noticeable, and you are likely to have more bruising and swelling. Your chin may feel numb for at least two weeks and often for six weeks or longer. Lower-lip numbness may last up to several months before it gradually subsides.

If you had your chin reshaped with bone surgery, it's important to follow your surgeon's postoperative instructions carefully. You can usually brush your teeth the day after surgery, but you have to be careful because your mouth will be sore and your chin will hurt. You will probably be advised to stick to a liquid diet for seven days and a semisolid diet for another week after that.

Bandages are usually removed by day six following surgery.

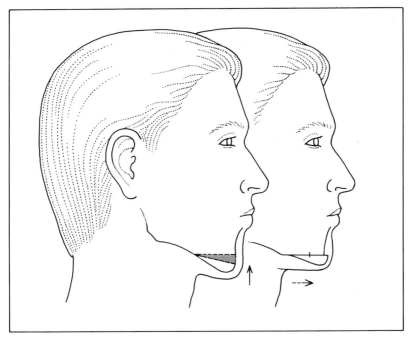

To shorten a long chin, an incision is made inside the mouth to provide access to the chinbone. A wedge-shaped piece of bone (shaded area) is removed. The lower segment of the chinbone is then shifted forward to give projection and is wired into place. There are no external scars.

As soon as the bandage comes off, men can shave and women can apply makeup, but everything must be done more gently than before. Besides feeling numb, your skin will be sensitive. Men should use an electric shaver for a few weeks after surgery.

Stitches in your mouth usually dissolve by themselves or your surgeon will remove them after the first week. To avoid an aching jaw, postpone dental work for at least a month following chin surgery. Most people can expect to recover by following the same program as recommended for chin implants. The improvement from chinbone surgery is permanent.

Troubleshooting: What Can Go Wrong

The most common side effects of chin surgery are numbness and swelling. Numbness is caused by nerves being bruised or stretched during surgery. Both eventually disappear, but it may take as long as six months.

You may think the feeling in your chin and lower front teeth will never come back, but nerves have been known to recover after a year or longer. Very rarely, a nerve is so damaged that it cannot recover, even if you have additional surgery to repair it. Your chin will still look good and your muscles will still give your face normal expression, but you won't feel much in the chin area.

Scars

Chinbone surgery is usually performed through incisions inside your mouth, which will leave no visible scars.

CHEEK IMPLANTS

Many people say, "I wish I had prominent cheekbones." Occasionally, however, someone is dissatisfied with the planes of her face, but can't define the problem. Something just looks out of balance. It's possible that this person has a well-defined eyebrow ridge and a prominent jaw, but a flat midface. The plastic surgeon will evaluate the harmony of her face and may suggest cheek implants. A dialogue is needed between patient and surgeon, because everyone's perception is different. Some people like prominent cheekbones and others don't.

People who have very high, very wide cheekbones sometimes want them to look less extreme in proportion to the rest of their face. For example, Asians and Native Americans tend to have very strong cheekbones. In Asia, cheekbone reduction is a more common procedure than it is in the United States. This is done by shaving the bone down.

Best Candidates

Infection is the critical risk of cheek implants, so you should start out with good dental work and a healthy mouth. You should be free of any sinus infection, which can spread to the area around the implant. You should have no untreated dental cavities or gingivitis (see your dentist first). Three years after surgery, one woman developed an infection around her cheek implant when having problems with a root canal. After the implant site has healed, you must take care of your teeth and gums to keep them healthy, and if you later require oral surgery, always follow your dentist's advice and take protective antibiotics.

Cheek implants can be inserted in anyone over the age of sixteen. Older women and men may have cheek-implant surgery at the same time as a facelift.

Costs

Surgical fees for cheek-implant surgery range from $600 to $4,000. Anesthesia and the surgical facility are additional costs.

Before Surgery

It is important to stop smoking before any cosmetic surgery and this is especially true for cheek implants. Implants are inserted through an incision in your mouth; smoking increases your risk of infection, which usually means the implants will have to be removed and replaced.

The Procedure

Cheek implants are inserted on an outpatient basis in a doctor's office, freestanding surgical center, or hospital. Cheek-implant surgery takes approximately one hour to perform. The usual anesthesia method is administration of a local anesthetic plus sedation, given either orally or intravenously.

Because the mouth is loaded with bacteria, your mouth will be rinsed before surgery with an antibacterial solution. You will also receive intravenous or oral antibiotics to flood the cheek area with antibiotics. Preoperative antibiotics cannot guarantee an infection-free procedure, but most surgeons feel it's impor-tant to make every effort.

If you are having a facelift or browlift at the same time, the cheek implants may be inserted through the external incision made for these procedures. If not, they will be inserted through an incision made inside your upper lip.

Whatever the approach, the surgeon lifts the tissue of your cheek away from the bone beneath and creates a tunnel that will hold the implant in place. This is a critical phase of the proce-dure. The implant rests directly on the bone, which must be completely bare of tissue before the device is inserted to provide a more stable "seal."

The surgeon usually performs the complete procedure on one

side of the face, closes it up, and then moves to the other side. This method ensures that the incisions are exposed only briefly to bacteria in the mouth.

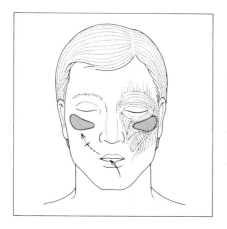

For cheek augmentation, implants are usually inserted through an incision made inside the mouth and they are placed on top of the cheekbone. There are no external scars left after this procedure.

Recovery

The surgeon will place a strip of tape across each cheek to keep the implants in place and to help reduce swelling. You can usually go home within two or three hours after surgery, depending on the kind of anesthesia you received. At home, you will want to rest with your head elevated by pillows and with a cold pack over your cheeks. You should keep your face as still as possible for the first forty-eight hours to speed healing.

Pain following implant surgery is minimal, but your cheeks will feel stiff and numb. You won't feel like talking or smiling for several days, and yawning and chewing will also make you feel uncomfortable. Numbness and swelling will usually begin to subside after four or five days.

Your surgeon will probably prescribe oral antibiotics after surgery to further protect you against infection. You can gently brush your lower teeth and rinse your mouth with salt water on the day after surgery, but your physician will probably advise you not to brush your upper teeth for about a week. If cheek implants were inserted through an incision inside your mouth, you will probably have to restrict yourself to a liquid diet for the first week and a semisolid diet for the following week.

Stitches inside your mouth usually dissolve by themselves; if not, your surgeon will remove them in about a week to ten days.

You can usually go back to work after a week. However, your cheeks may ache at the end of the day and you may not want to resume your full social schedule until later.

Bending over will make your cheeks swell and ache, so all exercise—including stretching—should be avoided for about two weeks. Sexual activity is off limits as well. Sports, particularly those that use balls, should be avoided for six weeks or more after surgery, until your cheeks are fully healed.

Troubleshooting: What Can Go Wrong

Infection is the greatest risk with cheek implants and usually that means the implants must be replaced. With any implant, there is a risk of capsular contracture. With cheek implants, however, as with a chin implant, the idea is to simulate hard bone and capsular contracture may not create any noticeable problem.

Because the incision underneath the upper lip tends to interfere with the nerves in the mouth, numbness is common. Although this may last for a few days to several months—typically about six weeks—it won't affect your facial expression or drag your mouth down. It just feels like you've been injected with novocaine. Very rarely, numbness is permanent. When an implant is inserted through a browlift incision, it doesn't affect the nerve and numbness is usually avoided.

Scars

There are no visible scars from cheek-implant surgery if the incisions are made inside your mouth. If implants are inserted through browlift or facelift incisions, you will have the slight scars associated with these procedures.

Success

Cheek implants are permanent. Some studies report that the incidence of infection with cheek implants is only 1 percent, but surgeons who regularly perform this procedure say it may be as high as 6 percent depending on the kind of implant used and where the incision is made. The incidence of infection tends to be slightly higher if surgery is done through the mouth and if a porous implant is used. Although no studies on the subject have ever been published, surgeons believe that the nonporous silicone implants probably have less risk of infection.

If infection occurs, the affected implant usually must be removed because antibiotics can't reach a concentration that is high enough around the device to kill the bacteria. However, the surgeon can put in a new implant later (usually after six months).

Sometimes an implant might also have to be replaced because it doesn't fit exactly to the bone and thus its position is slightly "off." This can be corrected through a second operation. A small percentage of patients may not like the implants because they appear either a little bit too big or too small. Cheek-implant surgery is an artistic endeavor, subject to imperfection and individual perception.

Overall, there is approximately a 15 percent chance that your cheek implants will have to be removed for one reason or another, which means that this procedure has an 85 percent success rate on the first attempt.

PART III

MINIMIZING
THE EFFECTS
OF AGING

Turning Back the Clock

HAS SHE OR HASN'T SHE HAD A FACELIFT? DID HE OR DIDN'T HE get his eyes done? Did the fifty-year-old rock star who looks twenty-five go to Brazil for surgery or is her medical file secreted in the plush office of a Beverly Hills plastic surgeon? Just how young can you look?

Our society is not forgiving of the inevitable aging of the face. In women, who tend to be more prone than men to loosening skin, the signs of aging may be more obvious. With pressure on women to be beautiful no matter what their age, it has primarily been females who seek plastic surgery for facial aging. Today, however, men also have a stake in a youthful appearance. Their profession may depend on it. Thirty years ago, a man didn't expect to get anywhere until he was over thirty-five or forty and had "paid his dues." Today, in many professions a man or woman past forty may be thought to be burned out and out of touch. In most professions, a vigorous, young image is a plus for both men and women.

Patricia described what happened to her as she approached and passed the age of fifty. She could see it in her face—the slight sags under the eyes, the heaviness in the jawline. She gained weight and felt age "weighing her down." These outward signs of aging coincided with a series of stressful life circumstances that included the death of her mother and a major professional setback. She gradually became more withdrawn. "If things had been going better," she said, "the bags and sags might not have bothered me so much. But as it was, it was very depressing and I hated the changes I saw in the mirror."

A facelift and eyelid surgery helped turn back the clock a little. Patricia said she looked more familiar to herself. As a result, she went on a diet, started a program of exercise, and bought new clothes. Her physical stamina and state of mind improved. The cosmetic surgery gave Patricia the boost she needed to start pursuing life with her customary zeal.

Each of us carries a mental image based on how we looked when we first reached full maturity. Even as we grow older, we still carry that self-image in our mind. Antiaging procedures bring us at least part way back to that image, creating the illusion that the years have literally dropped away.

It's not uncommon for a facelift or other antiaging procedure to give people a new lease on life. Some recently widowed women and men, for example, look to antiaging procedures to help refocus their life.

A widow in her early sixties said she felt that her badly wrinkled skin and sagging face reflected her feeling of sadness to the world. After a facelift and chemical peel she looked and felt refreshed. "It was like I had reentered the world, coming back from grief. People seemed to stop feeling sorry for me and treating me like I walked in the door with a load of troubles."

Each of us ages in a slightly different way, with some effects being more pronounced than others. As you grow older your skin begins to sag. The brow slides downward and little pads of fat collect underneath the eyes. Skin folds appear along the side of the nose. The chin appears to recede as the neck and jawline lose their sharp definition. The nose seems to grow longer. Fine wrinkling may appear across the surface of the skin, becoming particularly pronounced in people with thin skin and a history of heavy sun exposure.

Over the last several decades, plastic surgery techniques have been developed to counteract each one of these effects and may be done individually or in various combinations. In general, antiaging procedures today last longer and are more natural-looking than in the past. The emphasis is on recontouring as well as tightening. Contouring involves manipulating the under-lying fat and muscle in the face and neck. New methods have also been developed to smooth the surface of the skin by soft-ening fine wrinkling and acne scars or plumping out deep creases.

A total rejuvenation of the face might include a facelift and browlift, eyelid surgery, nose reshaping with a chin implant, and chemical peel or dermabrasion. How many and which proce-dures you choose will depend on the specific signs of aging that are visible in *your* face and which of them bother you. Cost may influence your choice. Although multiple procedures are less costly if done at the same time, they are still expensive.

Your choice may also depend to some extent on your age and whether you have had any previous plastic surgery. A person in her forties may choose only to have her eyelids done and may put off a facelift for another five or ten years. An older person who has already had a facelift, but whose skin is showing fine wrinkling, may choose to have a chemical peel only.

It's not always easy to know what procedure will work best. You may think your baggy eyes are the problem, but in fact you may need a facelift to achieve the look you desire. No one should undergo unwanted or unnecessary surgery. The key to selecting which rejuvenation procedures are right for you is the consul-tation with your plastic surgeon. In your consultation, it's prob-ably best to describe the signs of aging that bother you most. Then, let the surgeon advise you which procedures he thinks can best solve those problems.

How can you distinguish between a surgeon who is pushing you into surgery and one who is simply telling you what the possibilities are? During the consultation, your surgeon should try to help you pinpoint what bothers you the most. If you want a total facial rejuvenation, by all means ask for an evaluation of your face overall, with recommendations of what can be done to give you what you want. But if nothing bothers you except your baggy eyes, say so. You can always have additional proce-dures later if you choose.

One misconception about plastic surgery on the face is the amount of postoperative pain involved. Most popular proce-dures are not very painful for the majority of people. Pain is usually not a significant problem with facelift, eyelid surgery, or rhinoplasty, for example. One reason is that contemporary techniques cause very little bruising. Eyelid surgery and rhinoplasty require little, if any, pain medication. Any discomfort following facelifts can be controlled by oral medication.

The chapters that follow describe the ingenious plastic surgery techniques that have been developed to counteract the effects of aging. However, while all of these advances are effective—and in some cases results are dramatic—the best protection against wrinkling and other visible signs of aging is prevention through a healthy lifestyle. Don't stay out in the sun for long periods and always use sunscreens when you are out. After an antiaging procedure you are still the same person, and the same age, as you always were. A seventy-year-old who looks sixty is still, *physiologically* speaking, seventy. One seventy-four-year-old woman said that she couldn't understand why she felt so fatigued all the time after having a facelift. It turned out she was so enthusiastic about her revitalized appearance that she was staying out late every night going to parties and her facelift had not extended to boosting her energy levels!

Finally, remember that although the clock may be set back, it will continue to tick. After a while, wrinkles will begin to reappear and sags may show up again in response to gravity, and repeat surgery may be desired.

Surface Repairs: Chemical Peel, Dermabrasion, and Retin-A

OVER THE PAST THREE DECADES, PLASTIC SURGEONS HAVE DEVEL-oped and perfected techniques for smoothing out finely etched wrinkles, as well as refinishing scarred or blemished facial skin. Two of these procedures—chemical peel and dermabrasion—remove the damaged skin; as the skin regenerates itself, a fresh, new, smooth surface appears.

Some people think chemical peel and dermabrasion are mini-facelifts. They are not. Facelifts firm sagging jowls and tidy up double chins. In contrast, chemical peel and dermabrasion work only on the surface, without changing the actual architecture or contour of the face. They are often used in conjunction with a facelift, but they are not a substitute.

These procedures do not *prevent* aging. This belief is as mistaken as the notion that coloring the hair will keep it from turning gray. Both chemical peel and dermabrasion are treatments for specific conditions and are used only when there is an obvious need for them. They usually are used on the face, where the rich blood supply helps the skin heal with minimal risk of infection.

Both procedures are very popular and, when carried out by properly trained physicians, they are usually effective and safe.

However, neither should be considered on a par with losing weight or enrolling in an exercise class. Chemical peel and dermabrasion are serious procedures. If mishandled, they can result in devastating complications.

If you are considering surface repairs on your face, the two main considerations are choosing the best procedure for your needs and selecting a well-qualified surgeon. Similar results can be achieved with both procedures: Fine, cobwebby surface wrinkles are diminished, scars are softened, surface blemishes fade, and general skin texture becomes smoother and firmer. For most people, these results are usually permanent, although the procedures do not prevent the natural effects of aging from causing new wrinkles to form.

Both chemical peel and dermabrasion can be used on the entire face, or they can be limited to a specific area, such as the forehead or upper lip. Both operations are extremely delicate and require the skills of an experienced physician.

The two procedures are also similar in their depth of penetration. Both remove the top layer of skin, called the epidermis. Beneath that is the dermis, which contains connective fibrous tissue. Below *that* is a layer of fat.

The main differences between the two procedures lie in their method of removing marred skin. In a chemical peel, sometimes called chemosurgery, a caustic solution containing phenol or trichloracetic acid is applied. New skin forms underneath the treated tissue, which eventually sloughs off. In contrast, dermabrasion is a process in which the superficial, outer layer of skin is ground or scraped away using a hand-held machine. A new layer of skin then forms.

Many plastic surgeons perform both techniques, selecting one or the other, or a combination of the two, to solve a particular problem. As a general rule of thumb, chemical peel is the treatment of choice for fine wrinkles, and dermabrasion is preferred for deeper imperfections, such as acne scars.

Some plastic surgeons prescribe one technique or the other exclusively for all surface repairs. Physicians who favor dermabrasion say they like being able to perform such delicate work by hand. The ability to see immediately how much tissue they have removed gives them greater control of the process. They also feel that dermabrasion causes less postoperative discomfort and that patients recover more easily. Advocates of chemical peel admit that although there may be considerable discomfort during recovery, they can achieve better and more even results—a smoother skin—by using chemicals rather than a hand-held mechanical tool.

After either dermabrasion or phenol peel, your face becomes red, swollen, and painful. Your skin will tingle and throb, and you will need medication to alleviate the discomfort. Eating and talking will be difficult. You will begin to feel much better when the swelling subsides after a few days, but it takes two to three weeks before most people feel comfortable being seen in public.

In the case of the milder trichloracetic acid (TCA) peel, recovery time may be cut to just three or four days—although the results are not as dramatic and treatments may have to be repeated several times.

Your choice of procedure may depend on which doctor you consult and the procedure with which he has the most experience. Your choice may also involve personal feelings of your own. Some people simply do not like the idea of having their face treated with chemicals; others balk at having their skin scraped with a machine.

Age and sex usually are not important in determining your suitability for either chemical peel or dermabrasion. However, physicians do find that older patients tend to heal more slowly than younger ones, and that women generally heal more quickly than men. More important than age or sex, however, is your skin type and coloring.

After a phenol chemical peel, your new skin will be lighter than the area that was peeled away, and a line of demarcation between the treated and untreated areas may be noticeable. Often, this can be hidden with makeup, but some people don't want to use cosmetics. For these reasons, the best candidates for phenol chemical peel have fair, thin skin with a tendency toward fine wrinkles. If you have dark or sallow skin, dermabrasion may be a better choice for you, since it is less likely to change skin color.

People who tend to develop allergic rashes or other skin reactions, or who get frequent fever blisters or cold sores, run the risk of flare-ups after either procedure. Asian skin, black skin, and other dark complexions may become blotchy after either dermabrasion or a phenol peel, and they are not recommended for such highly pigmented skin.

If you have freckles, they may disappear after either chemical peel or dermabrasion. If only part of your face is treated, you may have patches of freckled and unfreckled skin. Unless a full-face chemical peel or dermabrasion is being considered, freckled people are unsuitable candidates.

Large, deeply pigmented birthmarks will not be improved by either procedure; nor is it likely that discoloration caused by birth-control pills or hormone therapy will respond well to these treatments. Certain health conditions may also preclude chemical peeling. If phenol acid is used, minute amounts can be absorbed by your body, where they are altered by the liver and excreted through the kidneys. This may prove harmful if you have chronic kidney or liver disease and your system is unable to handle the chemical. Phenol may also cause irregular heartbeats and can pose a special risk for a person with a history of heart disease. Your doctor should ask you about these possibilities when he takes your medical history.

THE CONSULTATION: CHEMICAL PEEL AND DERMABRASION

It is imperative to find a doctor who is experienced in providing dermabrasion and chemical peel, since these procedures have been offered by inadequately trained practitioners in the past and involve highly visible changes in the part of your body that plays the most significant role in self-image: your face.

During the consultation, the physician should explain the risks and benefits of the procedure you are interested in, and should especially describe in detail the length of the recovery period and the level of discomfort you can expect. If your surgeon prefers one procedure over the other, he should tell you why.

Costs: Chemical Peel and Dermabrasion

The costs and the time involved in both procedures are similar. Depending on the extent of treatment needed, the surgeon's fee may range from $100 for a small area to $3,000 or more for the full face.

These are both generally considered elective procedures that are not usually covered by insurance. However, health insurance coverage may be available if the procedure is performed to remove precancerous skin growths or extensive scars caused by acne or an accident. Check your policy and discuss the matter with your insurance carrier *before* the procedure is performed.

If need be, your surgeon can discuss your case directly with your insurance company.

Before the Procedures

If you smoke, you will be asked to stop one to two weeks before and after either chemical peel or dermabrasion. Smoking decreases blood circulation in the skin, reduces the amount of oxygen the blood can carry, and thus impedes healing.

CHEMICAL PEEL

The Procedure

The procedure can usually be performed within an hour to an hour and a half. Chemical peel can be performed in a hospital, a freestanding surgical facility, or—particularly in the case of a small, spot peel—the physician's office. A partial chemical peel is usually performed on an outpatient basis, where you arrive and leave on the same day. If you are having a full-face chemical peel or a peel in conjunction with other plastic surgery procedures, you may be admitted to a hospital as an inpatient, with the staff caring for you during the first two days after treatment.

Local anesthesia is not required for chemical peels because the chemical solution itself acts as an anesthetic. However, sedation before and during the procedure may help you remain relaxed and comfortable while the chemical is applied to your face.

Many people believe that chemical peel must be repeated at regular intervals, but if phenol is used, one treatment is usually sufficient. In the case of TCA, several treatments may be required to obtain the desired results; the mildest concentrations produce outcomes that may last only three to four months.

On the day of the procedure you will be asked to shampoo your hair and cleanse your face with antibacterial soap. Men are asked to shave closely. Chemical peel is performed by applying a chemical solution—usually phenol mixed with varying amounts of water, oil, and liquid soap—to peel away the top layers of skin. The depth of penetration is determined by the strength of the solution and the amount applied. During the healing process, a fresh, new skin surface develops.

Contrary to what you might expect, weakening the phenol

FACE-PEELING PARLORS

Chemical peeling is among the most delicate of procedures, and yet almost anyone with a little knowledge of chemistry who can read a book and follow directions may go into business as a chemical peel specialist. (These individuals may call the procedure endodermology or exodermology.)

This dangerous state of affairs has come about because peeling the skin with chemicals originated many years ago in Europe as a nonmedical treatment, performed by lay technicians. When the technique made its way to the United States shortly after World War II, the first clinics, which were set up in California and Florida, were never subjected to government or medical supervision. No licenses were needed then and, except in Nevada, no licenses are required now.

Numerous injuries and even deaths have occurred at the hands of such practitioners, but lawsuits brought by severely disfigured clients do not seem to affect business. Some owners of chemical-peel parlors are not physicians and therefore are not even required to carry malpractice insurance.

The most important fact that you need to know about chemical peel is that it is a serious procedure that may lead to serious consequences. In the wrong hands, it can cause mutilation; in the right hands, it can have wonderful results.

solution does not make it safer to use. A highly concentrated mixture is more easily controlled, quickly acting as a coagulant on the treated skin to create a barrier against deeper penetration. Since weak solutions do not cause coagulation, they may penetrate the skin over a longer period of time and could even seep into your system.

If your surgeon suggests a light chemical peel, he will not dilute the solution, but instead will choose a less caustic acid. Phenol acid is the usual choice for chemical peels, but for a light peel many doctors use TCA. In the latter case, many experienced plastic surgeons feel that pretreatment of the skin with Retin-A (see the last part of this chapter) for four to six weeks allows the solution to penetrate deeper, but in an even, controllable fashion.

Full-Face Chemical Peel

The surgeon cleanses your skin to remove all traces of oils or soap, then applies the chemical slowly and carefully to all areas of your face, except the brows, eyelids, and lips. You will feel a brief burning sensation when the solution is first applied; then the chemical itself acts as a local anesthetic and the rest of the procedure is pain-free.

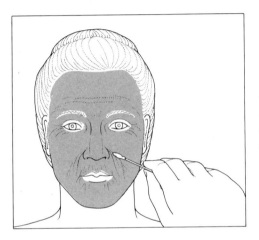

When the entire face is to be treated, a chemical solution is applied to "peel" off upper layers of skin in the shaded areas. In some cases, chemical peel is used only on limited areas of the face, such as around the mouth.

If you have a phenol peel, the surgeon will usually conclude by covering your face with petroleum jelly or a mask of water-proof adhesive tape, leaving openings for your eyes, nose, and mouth. This creates deeper penetration by preventing evaporation of the chemical. If deep penetration is not needed, some physicians elect to forego the tape and/or jelly, feeling that most patients get a good result with less discomfort.

Partial Chemical Peel

Not everyone wants or needs a full-face chemical peel. The most common partial or "spot" peels are performed to erase horizontal lines across the forehead, surface blemishes or age spots, fine wrinkling around the eyelids and cheeks and, most frequently, those vertical creases around the mouth that make a woman's lipstick "bleed" into her upper lip.

For partial peels, the doctor applies the caustic chemical solution only to the problem areas. The process and effect are the same as described for a full-face peel, but are limited to the treated areas. The new skin will eventually fade from red to pink and then—in the case of a phenol peel—to a permanently lighter skin tone.

Recovery

Shortly after the procedure, your face will begin to tingle and throb, but the discomfort is usually alleviated with medication. The recovery process is an integral part of the procedure. Every doctor asks his patients to follow a specific recovery routine, based on his own experience. It is essential that you stick to your physician's rules. Do not add any special routines of your own and do not follow a friend's advice who may have had the same procedure done by a different doctor.

In the case of a phenol peel, you may be limited to a liquid diet and cautioned not to talk for the next several days. Your face will be raw-looking and a bit swollen during this time. If tape was applied, it will be removed in about two days and your surgeon will dust the area of the peel with a medicated powder to help a crust—or scab—form. Your surgeon will caution you to keep your hands away from your face. It is essential that the skin heal cleanly. The crust is allowed to sit for two days; then ointment is applied to soften it. The crust will naturally flake away on its own in a day or so (if not, the surgeon will "help" it) and tender new skin will be revealed.

However, the new trend in postop treatment among some doctors is to avoid the formation of a hard crust over the face by applying antibiotic creams immediately to the treated skin. Many surgeons feel this is more comfortable for their patients and doesn't affect the final result. If your doctor prefers this method, he will give you very precise instructions for cleansing and applying the antibiotic creams.

By the third day, the swelling will have subsided. At first the new skin is a deep red color, not unlike a severe sunburn. With continued application of creams or moisturizers recommended by your doctor, the red gradually subsides to a pinkish color, usually over a period of three to four weeks.

The new skin is tight, smooth, and relatively free of wrinkles and blemishes, giving your face a younger, fresher, altogether brighter appearance. If you had freckles, they may be gone. Some fine lines may become slightly visible again when the swelling subsides, but they will be less prominent than before. Pores often are larger after a chemical peel, but they eventually shrink almost to their normal size.

Within about two weeks, you can begin to wear light makeup (see "Camouflage Cosmetics" in chapter 5). Your doctor will probably advise you to use liberal amounts of lubricating or heavy moisturizing cream for the next several months.

After several weeks, the pink hue fades away, leaving your skin lighter than it was before the procedure. This change in color is permanent. Because the tender, new skin has no protective pigmentation, it is essential that you protect yourself from direct sunlight for several months. Some doctors ask their patients to avoid sun exposure for as long as a year. After that, they prescribe sunblocks and sunscreens to use whenever you are outdoors. Sunbathing is forbidden forever because the peel interferes with your skin's ability to tan. These precautions are important. Sun exposure can lead to discolorations and blotchy skin.

You will be able to return to work within fourteen days or so, but since your skin will take about three months to lose its pinkness, you will probably want to wear nonallergenic makeup for appearance's sake (see "Camouflage Cosmetics" in chapter 5).

Exercise and sexual activities that could cause inadvertent injury to your face should be avoided for at least two weeks. After that, exercise should be restricted to relatively nonstrenuous activity for at least another two to four weeks. Shower immediately after exercising to keep your skin free of salty, stinging perspiration.

More active sports can be resumed after four to six weeks. Being hit in the face with a tennis ball or basketball would be painful and might leave a scar. Swimmers should stick to indoor pools, away from the sun and wind, and must keep their faces out of the water for four weeks (chlorine will dry the skin and new scabs may appear). Most people wait three or four weeks before they're comfortable going out socially and are able to drink alcoholic beverages without experiencing a flush of temporary redness.

While many of the recovery phases are similar for TCA peels, it is generally no longer than a week before you are back to normal. However, post-treatment skin care—such as the use of sunscreen—is essential.

Troubleshooting: What Can Go Wrong

No one can predict exactly how an individual will respond to a treatment. But the high percentage of successful chemical peelings makes this procedure a generally safe choice when performed by a qualified, experienced physician.

Infection is rare because of the rich blood supply that nourishes the face. The greatest danger is postoperative exposure to the sun—in summer *or* winter—which can permanently discolor the new skin. Any sun exposure should be avoided completely for three to six months; prolonged exposure should be avoided permanently. Scheduling the procedure for spring or fall avoids extreme weather that can burn or chap tender new skin.

Whiteheads, or milia, may appear in the treated area. They usually can be washed away using a rough buff pad or abrasive soap, such as those containing oatmeal. If the outbreak is particularly severe, your surgeon can treat them by "sanding" them away. There is no risk of scarring after these whiteheads are treated.

Severe scarring from chemical peel is extraordinarily rare if it is performed by a qualified physician. Occasionally, a slight scar may develop if one area of the skin has been burned more deeply than another.

DERMABRASION

The Procedure

The procedure can usually be performed within an hour to an hour and a half. Dermabrasion mechanically scrapes away the superficial layers of skin. The procedure is most often used to smooth away fine wrinkles, especially around the mouth, or to treat acne scars or other scars from accidents or previous surgery. It may also be used to remove precancerous growths on the face. Like chemical peel, dermabrasion is usually a one-time-only procedure. However, there are times when multiple procedures may be needed due to the size of the area requiring treatment.

Dermabrasion may have originated during World War II, when Army doctors used fine sandpaper, wrapped around an electrically driven cylinder, to remove metal fragments and particles of dirt that had become embedded in soldiers' skin. Later, the same process was used to erase tattoos.

Nowadays, a rough wire brush, or a burr impregnated with diamond particles, replaces the sandpaper. The surgeon, controlling the rate of revolution with a motorized handle, uses the brush or the burr to scrape away the top layers of skin. Skin abraded in this way forms a crust. Later, a smooth, tight, pink skin forms. Some surgeons apply ointment immediately after the dermabrasion and a crust is never allowed to form.

Dermabrasion is usually performed on an outpatient basis in a hospital, a freestanding surgical facility, or the physician's office. If you are undergoing extensive work you may have the procedure done as an inpatient in a hospital. Dermabrasion may be done in a single session or in stages.

You will be given a local anesthetic plus sedation. Sometimes your face is also numbed or "frozen" with a spray such as Freon or you may elect to have general anesthesia.

For a full-face dermabrasion, on the day of the procedure you will be asked to shampoo your hair and wash your face with an antibacterial soap; men will be told to shave closely.

Using a brush or diamond burr, the surgeon scrapes away the skin until he reaches the safest level that will make the scar or

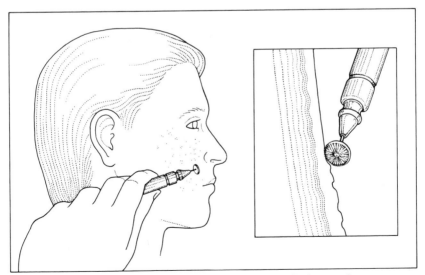

An electrically operated instrument with a burr attached is used to scrape away the outer layer of skin. The inset on the right shows how dermabrasion softens irregularities in the outermost layer of skin.

wrinkle less visible. As he proceeds, warm air from a hair dryer may be blown over your face to stop the bleeding and to help form a crust.

Partial Dermabrasion for Lip Lines and Acne Scars

Most people have partial dermabrasion to improve vertical lip lines and acne scars. Abrading the lip area rather than using chemical peel has the advantage of creating new skin that more closely matches the surrounding tissue in color. Dermabrasion is thus a boon for people who have sallow or darker-toned complexions.

Acne scars are like tiny craters in the skin. Dermabrasion sands away the raised edges so that the surface is smoother. Very deep craters cannot be completely eliminated. Any attempt to do so would risk the removal of too much skin and could result in additional scarring. To treat very deep craters, most surgeons will opt to perform the procedure in two stages: an initial dermabrasion to smooth the surface and then, after a year or more, when your face has healed, a second dermabrasion (or even a third) if you need further improvement.

Recovery

There are several ways to care for your face immediately after dermabrasion. Some doctors apply an ointment to the skin and cover it with a wet bandage or waxy gauze. Others prefer to leave the wound open, with no dressing at all. Still others rely solely on an ointment or use only the bandage.

Regardless of the dermabrasion method used, the amount of discomfort varies from person to person. Medication prescribed by your physician can provide relief. Unless your physician instructs you to immediately begin applying ointment, which keeps the surface soft, a crust will form soon after the procedure. This will flake off when the new skin underneath is ready. About a week later, swelling begins to subside. Your face may itch as new skin starts to grow, and some surgeons advise you to blow a warm hair dryer gently on your skin to keep it dry and to facilitate healing.

Your new skin will look a bit swollen and will be sensitive to the touch. It will be bright pink. The recovery process for dermabrasion is similar to that for phenol chemical peel. Again, the important thing is to follow to the letter the instructions your doctor provides for you.

As time passes, your new skin will lose its pinkness and match the surrounding tissue. This differs from a chemical peel, which results in new skin that is permanently lighter in tone.

You can expect to return to work within fourteen days, but since it will take about three months for the pinkness in your skin to fade, you will probably need to wear nonallergenic makeup (see "Camouflage Cosmetics" in chapter 5).

Exercise and sexual activity that could cause a bump to your face should be avoided for at least two weeks. After the second week, moderate activity is permitted. More active sports can be resumed after four to six weeks. Again, being hit in the face with a tennis ball or basketball would be painful and might leave a scar. Swimmers should stick to indoor pools to avoid sun and wind, and must keep their face out of the water for four weeks. The chlorine will dry the skin and new scabs may reappear.

For most people, it's three or four weeks before they feel comfortable going out socially and before they can drink alcoholic beverages without experiencing a flush of temporary redness.

Troubleshooting: What Can Go Wrong

Like chemical peel, the greatest risk after dermabrasion is exposure to the sun, which can lead to permanent discoloration of the new skin. Closely follow your physician's instructions about sun exposure and using sunblocks and sunscreens.

Tiny whiteheads sometimes appear. These usually can be washed away with an abrasive soap or sponge, or your body will eventually reabsorb them. Sometimes they are persistent and your physician may have to remove them. Your skin pores also may be larger after dermabrasion, although after the swelling subsides, they will shrink to near normal size.

Infection is rare with dermabrasion because of the rich blood supply to the face. However, if too much skin is removed, scars form. Again, the best protection against such damage is choosing an experienced, qualified plastic surgeon.

Rarely, an individual may develop keloids (excessive scar tissue), which can be treated with steroid injections. It is impossible to predict who will develop keloids (see "Predicting Scars" in chapter 3).

CHEMICAL PEEL AND DERMABRASION
COMBINED WITH OTHER PROCEDURES

Surface repairs are often carried out in conjunction with face-lifts. There are certain surface conditions, such as deep vertical lines around the mouth, that a facelift cannot solve. However, when a facelift is combined with a partial chemical peel or dermabrasion, the skin around the mouth will look as firm and smooth as the rest of your face.

A chemical peel to erase finely etched horizontal lines across the forehead may also be performed in conjunction with a face-lift. However, if the lines are actually deep furrows, the treatment of choice would be a browlift.

Chemical peel and dermabrasion can also be performed in combination with one another. For instance, dermabrasion may be used to treat acne scars, while chemical peel is performed on the surrounding areas to ensure a smooth, even look. In such instances, the chemical peel is done first, followed by dermabrasion in the same session. The procedure is then called chemabrasion. Overall, plastic surgeons report that chemical peel and dermabrasion are successful procedures that offer dramatic improvement in the surface of the skin.

ERASING BIRTHMARKS

Three out of every thousand people are born with a port-wine birthmark, a large purplish patch that often covers part of the face. New, advanced laser devices, specifically the pulsed tunable dye and copper vapor lasers, offer the best hope yet for removing these marks. These lasers eliminate the abnormal blood vessels, or at least lighten the birthmark to the point of being barely noticeable.

Until recently, birthmarks had been treated with the argon laser, which occasionally resulted in scarring, especially in young children. Whereas the argon laser relies on a continuous beam of light to obliterate the offending blood vessels, the tunable dye laser uses flashes that are just a few millionths of a second in duration. The light wavelength is absorbed only by hemoglobin—the substance that gives blood its red color—

so only abnormal blood vessels are destroyed; normal tissue is protected from the burning heat and healing occurs with no skin irregularity.

A treatment session takes between five and fifteen minutes, depending on the extent of the defect being treated. Patients usually need up to three or more treatments, depending on the size of the mark. The only pain is a stinging that for most patients feels no worse than a rubber band snapping against the skin.

This new laser treatment, which is also effective in eliminating cobwebs of blood vessels that can be seen just beneath the skin of the cheeks, can be done at any age, and most doctors feel the younger the patient, the better in terms of a child's developing self-image. Children also respond to the treatment much more quickly than adults.

Another kind of birthmark called a hemangioma can sometimes also be treated with lasers. A hemangioma is a tumorous collection of blood vessels that can cover half or all of the face, although it can also occur elsewhere on the body. Hemangioma occurs in 10 to 12 percent of all children, either at birth or within the first one to four weeks of life. The birthmark, which grows very fast initially, usually disappears by the time the child is five to seven years old and no treatment is needed. However, in a small percentage of children the hemangioma may overwhelm the nasal cartilage and partially or fully cover the eye, permanently robbing a child of his sight or distorting his facial features. Although the birthmark shrinks later, the damage done is permanent.

Another new technique that has been developed applies pressure to the affected area using a clear plastic facial mask, cutting the time it takes for the hemangioma to naturally disappear by 50 to 75 percent. With the use of the pressure mask, the hemangioma is often gone by the time children are two or three years old, before the birthmark has done irreparable damage.

REMOVING TATTOOS

Tattoos are made by using fine needles to pierce the skin and inject an indelible dye. Some people live happily ever after with their tattoos, but many others are eager to have them removed when their meaning fades or because they had the tattoo done on a whim or a dare. Many people have tattoos as a fashion statement, in a stupor, or for rebellion. The result remains on the chosen body part and it is no easy task to get rid of it. Some people choose to cover offensive tattoos with new ones that have a more appealing design. Others try to camouflage tattoos with cosmetics. Surgical solutions are more complicated and expensive.

Nearly all surgical methods to remove tattoos involve a scar or another kind of disfigurement, such as a white area or "ghost" where the tattoo has been, or the scraped outline of the original tattoo. The newest therapy, use of a Q-switch ruby laser to blast away the colors under the skin, is not yet widely available. It is also more expensive, and is most effective on black, brown, or blue pigments.

Which method is used to remove a tattoo depends on where the tattoo is located, the chemical composition of the pigments used, the condition of the skin at the tattoo site, and the size and age of the tattoo. (The longer a tattoo has been present, the further it will have spread into the deeper layers of the skin.) Some tattoos require multiple steps for removal. The most common methods of removal include:

Excision. If the tattoo is small enough, the surgeon can cut it out and close the wound, leaving a scar in place of the tattoo. When the tattoo is large or located in an area such as the shoulder that is difficult to close, a skin expansion technique may be used before cutting out the tattoo. Skin expanders—sacs filled with salt water—are placed on either side of the tattoo to expand the nonpigmented skin located there (see "Predicting Scars" in chapter 3). Once enough "new" skin is available, the tattoo is cut out and the edges of the wound are sutured together.

Dermabrasion. A wire brush or diamond burr can be used to abrade the skin down to the bottom of the pigment. A lighter tattoo may be nearly obliterated with this dermabrasion, but the shadow of a deeper tattoo will show through the healed layer of skin. Also, the procedure may result in white patching on dark-skinned individuals.

Chemical peel. Some doctors are now removing tattoos by applying trichloracetic acid. It is relatively inexpensive and quick, but like all the other techniques, it still leaves a mark (a patch of lighter- or darker-colored skin). It also requires a little more posttreatment care. The dressing must be changed two or three times a day for six to eight weeks.

Lasers. Removing tattoos with lasers has been practiced for some time; however, it is expensive and, in some cases, may not return the skin to a completely normal look. Although the carbon-dioxide laser is most often used for this purpose, a device called a Q-switch ruby laser is now being tested with very promising early results. This type of laser, however, is not yet widely available.

Although the end result of any method of tattoo removal is never perfectly normal-looking skin, most people unhappy with a tattoo are willing to make the trade. Plastic surgeons advise that if you are considering a tattoo you should think twice. A tattoo may cost only $30 or $40 to put on, but it will cost ten times as much to remove and considerably more discomfort.

RETIN-A FOR SUN-AGED SKIN

Doctors have stumbled upon a substance that seems effective in combating the signs of photoaging, or prolonged exposure to the sun. After collagen injections (see chapter 12), Retin-A is the most popular nonsurgical way to rid the face of fine wrinkles. (However, it is important to note that of this writing, it has not yet been approved by the Food and Drug Administration for this use.)

Also known as tretinoin or retinoic acid, Retin-A is a vitamin A derivative that has been prescribed for the past twenty years as a treatment for acne. Doctors noticed that the skin of young women using the treatment was notably smoother and free of surface wrinkles.

Most exciting to doctors and patients was the evidence that continuing, regular application of Retin-A can improve appearance regardless of the degree of damage. Physicians now often prescribe Retin-A for older patients who wish to soften the superficial signs of aging, such as fine wrinkles and uneven pigmentation. A few doctors also believe Retin-A is useful for younger patients who are eager to *prevent* lines and age spots.

Best Candidates

People who live in the Sun Belt states or lead an outdoor life are the most obvious candidates for use of Retin-A. Since the product is available in various strengths, age and skin type do not appear to be significant factors in limiting use. However, Retin-A may not be tolerated well by individuals with sensitive skin, and should not be used by pregnant women or nursing mothers. It is not currently known whether Retin-A causes any harm to a fetus or nursing infant, but since the form of the drug used for acne has been linked to birth defects, it is wise to be cautious.

The Routine

Retin-A is usually applied every night after you have removed all makeup and cleaned your face. You place a tiny amount of cream or gel, about the size of a pea, on each temple and rub it over your face and nose.

Retin-A is drying to the skin, so in the morning, after you wash your face, you will be asked to apply a moisturizer. If the weather is cold and dry, reapply the moisturizer in the afternoon. Because Retin-A also makes your skin more sensitive, only gentle soaps or cleansers should be used to clean your face.

This simple routine is repeated daily for eight months to a year. Your doctor will then switch you to a maintenance schedule, in which you use Retin-A twice a week. As you continue to use Retin-A, the outer layer of your skin becomes progressively thinner and more vulnerable to ultraviolet light. Your doctor will recommend that you use a sunscreen, usually a product with an SPF of at least 15. Fair-skinned people, as well as those who live in the Sun Belt or high altitudes, will probably be told to use a sunblock with an SPF of 29 or greater.

As mentioned, Retin-A comes in several strengths, and your physician will adjust the treatment to suit your age and skin type. Younger, fair-skinned patients may start with a low-strength dosage, which can be increased as the skin becomes accustomed to treatment. Older individuals, or those with darker complexions, may be able to increase the strength or frequency—applying the cream twice a day—to speed up their results.

The Results

During the first three to six months, most people notice a rosy glow and improved skin texture. Later on, fine lines become less noticeable and enlarged pores appear smaller.

However, you may also experience irritation or redness, itching, and stinging. These symptoms usually gradually disappear as the skin becomes acclimated to the treatment. If the itching persists, your physician may suggest that you apply the Retin-A only every other night until your skin adjusts. Within six weeks, most people become accustomed to the drug.

After about six months, wrinkles are usually noticeably smoother and age spots fade. There is also an increase in skin elasticity. However, the degree of improvement varies from person to person, and is often quite subtle. Some people with extensive wrinkling say they don't notice much difference at all.

Additional Benefits

Retin-A has been shown to be effective in inhibiting the development and growth of some skin cancers. Flaky red spots on your forehead or cheeks may actually be actinic keratoses, abnormalities caused by sun damage that, if untreated, can lead to skin cancers. It is hypothesized that continued use of Retin-A will prevent new keratoses from forming and will eliminate those in the microscopic stage.

Realistic Expectations

Doctors caution that Retin-A is not a magic potion. It does not give the dramatic results of a facelift, dermabrasion, chemical peel, or collagen injections, particularly when deep creases or sagging skin is involved. Further, lifelong use is necessary to maintain the benefits of Retin-A, which can add up to a significant expense over the years.

In the concentrations now being used, Retin-A appears to have no harmful side effects. But again, as with all medicines, we continue to learn new things about it all the time. Ultimately, its best use may be as a preventive measure. One day, Retin-A may be something that young people use to prevent wrinkling and development of skin cancer, just as we use fluoride in our toothpaste to protect against cavities. However, the greatest benefit of Retin-A may be that patients will be forced to moisturize their skin and use effective sunscreens.

The Injectables:
Silicone, Collagen, Fat

As WE AGE, MILLIONS OF FACIAL CONTRACTIONS—SMILING, WINK-
ing, squinting, frowning, chewing—cause a gradual breakdown
of the underlying tissues that keep our skin plumped up. Time
and gravity may reveal their effects through cheek wrinkles,
laugh lines, crow's feet, or a deeply furrowed brow. However,
some of these creases can appear in areas that don't lend themselves to surgery. Thus, another, less invasive kind of treatment
has been developed to cope with creases and lines.

While fine surface wrinkles are best treated by chemical peel
or dermabrasion, contour problems—creases and furrows—are
best battled with injectables: primarily collagen and, to a lesser
extent, fat.

Injectables work best in two kinds of wrinkles. The first kind
are caused by muscle movement when you frown or smile, and
the second are caused by gravity, such as sagging jowls and
grooves at the corners of the mouth. You can expect a *temporary*,
80 to 90 percent correction with injectables for frown lines; for
jowls and mouth grooves, it's more like 50 percent. Injectables
don't work on deep scars or craters left by acne, since they are
often bound tightly to the underlying tissue and are resistant to
"plumping."

Injectables are administered in a doctor's office by a physician or nurse specialist, generally without anesthesia. Even when anesthetic is mixed with the substance, these injections still may sting or burn, depending on your doctor's technique, your threshold for pain, and the area being worked on. Injections in the brow, crow's feet, and cheeks are generally less painful, while the area around your lips tends to be most sensitive. Injections are made into the upper layers of the skin, or dermis, instead of the underlying fat. Treatments take anywhere from fifteen to sixty minutes each, depending on the extent of correction needed.

Injectables can be used at any age, but they are not used on patients with active skin infections. You must wait six to twelve months before treating scars caused by injuries or infections.

If you have oily, thick skin you may not get good results with injectables because this skin type resists movement and stretches less than drier skin. Inflammation may occur in people with dark or sallow skin, resulting in permanent discoloration.

Doctors have long sought an injectable that won't be rejected or move away from the injected site. At the turn of the century, many thought the answer was liquid paraffin. These wax injections were in fashion until devastating side effects—including lumps, swelling, redness, and pain—became apparent. Nowadays, the use of paraffin is virtually unknown.

SILICONE

Silicone is a plastic with a wide range of medical uses. As a *solid*, it's the substance of choice for implants in the chin, nose, ears, and other areas, and it's used as a bone and cartilage substitute. As a gel, it is considered beneficial by most experts as a filler for breast implants. *Liquid* silicone, however, is more controversial.

Liquid silicone is an inert, nonbiodegradable, nonallergenic product. First used in the 1950s, it sprang to infamy in the 1960s as a popular injectable for breast augmentations. Massive quantities were pumped into breasts to create sometimes startling dimensions. But the sheer quantity needed resulted in hard, lumpy breasts that were painful, swollen, and covered by orange-peel skin caused by blocked lymph glands. Today, doctors in the United States don't use liquid silicone in breasts, and although some physicians use it in small quantities for facial contouring, that is controversial as well.

Liquid silicone's best feature is also its biggest problem: Because it's not metabolized by the body, liquid silicone retains its shape permanently. Only a small amount seeps into the surrounding tissues, lymph glands, liver, and other organs. If the results are good, they are permanent. If the results are poor, they are also irreversible.

There are no tests to predetermine who's the best candidate for silicone injections and there is no way to predict who will have an adverse reaction. There are no statistics on the frequency of complications, the most common being infection or a foreign-body reaction that can cause the substance to work its way out through the skin. Other possible complications include swelling, redness, pain, and loss of function. If you develop such adverse reactions—and they can happen years after your injections—the problem may last for life.

If an infection occurs, doctors may use antibiotics in an attempt to prevent its spread, as well as antihistamines and cortisone to alleviate symptoms. The only way to eradicate the infection permanently is by cutting out the silicone. (Since silicone disperses slightly in the skin around the injection site, it can't be suctioned out.) However, it may be impossible to cut out tissue in the areas where silicone is most often used, like laugh lines and eye creases. Removal leaves a scar. In the worst cases, patients' skin has actually died and sloughed off.

Doctors who favor the use of silicone say success or failure are factors of technique and prevention of contamination, not of the substance itself. Those opposed to silicone's use say that the body's foreign-body intolerance, which varies widely from person to person, makes silicone unsuitable.

Liquid silicone has not been approved for *sale* by the FDA (Food and Drug Administration), although it is legal for physicians to use it. For that reason, as well as the possible risks, most plastic surgeons do not recommend it despite the fact that, as of now, it is the only injectable material that offers permanent results.

COLLAGEN

Collagen is a natural protein produced by all animals to cushion and support the skin. When the collagen in and underneath your skin wears away—whether from disease, injury, exposure to the sun, or the passage of time—a scar or wrinkle results. Collagen holds us together, providing structural support for skin, cartilage, muscles, tendons, and bones.

Collagen injectables, made from natural protein derived from cow hides, are tremendously appealing. Collagen stays in place as well as or better than silicone. It's easy to administer and any allergic reactions, if they occur, usually last no more than six or eight months. (However, although it has not been proven, some health professionals believe it is possible for collagen injections to trigger or exacerbate certain rare connective-tissue diseases. Further research is being conducted.)

The biggest drawback of collagen injectables are their lack of staying power. Collagen is gradually absorbed by the body and its plumping effects may disappear within a year or less. However, it also means that you need repeat treatments. If, in fact, your body does react against the injected substance, it will build up scar tissue—your own collagen—at the site. Sometimes, this scar tissue acts as a filler and the results may be a better correction than the treatment itself.

Collagen is used primarily on the face, occasionally on the neck, and rarely on other parts of the body. Deep scars do not respond to collagen treatments. The substance cannot be ingested orally, and—advertising to the contrary—cannot be absorbed from lotions or salves.

Injectable collagen, approved by the FDA in 1981, is "packaged" in a saltwater solution. In the United States, only the Collagen Corporation holds a patent on its formula. It makes different formulations that use varying thicknesses of collagen mixed with lidocaine (a local anesthetic). The most liquified form of collagen is effective for smoothing shallow lines, like those around lips and at the corners of the eyes. Thicker concentrations are used for deeper hollows like smile furrows and forehead puckers.

However, roughly 3 percent of the population is *allergic* to the substance. Allergic reactions include a rash or hives, swelling, and flulike symptoms.

Your doctor should perform allergy tests before injecting collagen to determine whether or not you can tolerate the substance. The test involves injecting a tiny amount of collagen into your arm or some other spot and monitoring it for about a month. It's thought that some people are allergic to the traces of cattle protein remaining in the collagen. Some doctors prefer to run two tests, spaced over several months. If you're not allergic, you must wait one month between the test and treatment. (However, the allergy test is not totally error free. A small percentage of patients who do not react to the test have developed allergies during the course of treatment.)

If you are pregnant, suffer from connective-tissue disease such as lupus or rheumatoid arthritis, or have had a past allergic reaction to lidocaine, you should not have collagen treatments. (Make sure you tell your physician about any other drug allergies you have as well.) In addition, collagen injections are off limits for anyone receiving immunosuppressive therapy (like chemotherapy). Finally, if you've had facial herpes, be aware that the injection process could bring on a new eruption of herpes simplex.

Collagen allergy tests cost from $50 to $200. The price of the actual injection varies, depending on the type of collagen used (a greater thickness costs more), and ranges from $150 to $400 per visit. It takes fifteen to twenty minutes to treat two or three areas. Generally, the number of treatments corresponds to the size of your defect.

Collagen is injected using a delicate needle inserted along the wrinkle or scar. Since part of the substance is salt water that will be absorbed in a few days, your doctor will inject more collagen than is initially needed. The thicker the collagen used, the longer it takes to smooth out, and you may have lumps for several weeks.

Immediately following collagen injections, your skin may throb or sting for several hours. However, it's not necessary to bandage the treated area and you can return to work immediately if you like. If you're bruised, your doctor may apply ice or advise you to do so at home. Any faint redness should fade within twenty-four hours, though some individuals remain discolored for three to ten days, especially the fair-skinned.

Rarely, you may experience a temporary flush or itch in the treated area in the first twenty-four to forty-eight hours after surgery, possibly due to exercise, alcohol, or a mild allergic condition. These uncommon reactions will disappear on their own.

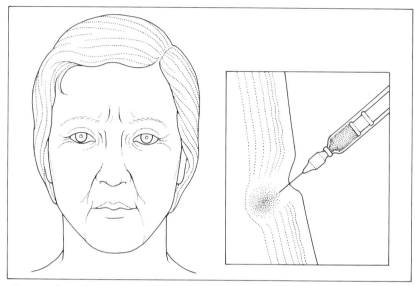

To smooth smile creases and forehead furrows, collagen is injected with a very fine needle just under the surface of the skin. The number of treatments needed and the thickness of the collagen preparation used depends on the size and type of the defect. The improvement will usually last six to nine months.

If you observe any symptoms such as prolonged redness and/ or swelling, inform your physician. You may be one of the very small number of people who experiences an allergic reaction to collagen. In that case, your symptoms will normally disappear as the collagen is absorbed by your body. No further injectable collagen is administered to someone who has experienced an allergic reaction.

The most important fact to remember about collagen is that it is not permanent. Collagen's longevity depends on the part of the body treated and the patient. How long you'll be able to go between treatments also depends on your tolerance for wrinkles. It usually takes about six months to lose 50 percent of the correction, and nine months to a year for it to dissipate 100 percent. Some patients insist on a 90 percent correction at all times and may return for injections every few months. There's no mandatory waiting period between injections.

LIP PLUMPING

A few years ago, using silicone injections to plump up thin lips was the rage. It has since fallen out of favor, because of the substance's tendency to become lumpy and to move around. However, for patients who want a sexier pout, lip plumping can be done using collagen or fat injections, although the results are temporary. (As of this writing, the use of collagen for lip plumping has yet to be approved by the Food and Drug Administration.)

Lip plumping was first requested by fashion models and actresses who wanted fuller, more sensuous lips. Today, older patients whose lips have shrunk with age may request lip plumping, as well as young women in their twenties who simply desire fuller lips. Like any procedure that makes a body part larger or smaller, the goal here is to make lips more proportionate to the face. Lip plumping may look good on a woman with a large head and high cheekbones, but it will look odd on a delicately proportioned woman.

The desired fullness can be achieved in one to three visits, but you'll have to return for touch-ups about every six months if you want to retain the effects. Plastic surgeons continue to search for a permanent alternative to injectables for lip plumping. The latest is surgical augmentation: cutting small flaps of skin from inside the mouth and lifting them forward to the lip line, stitching them into place. There is minimal visible scarring. An alternative surgical technique is called a dermal graft, in which small strips of tissue are taken from the groin and threaded through the lips. These surgical techniques are performed using local anesthetic, occasionally accompanied by a light sedative. They are expensive—about $2,000 to $3,000 for both lips—but the results are usually permanent.

FAT INJECTIONS

On paper, fat sounds like the ultimate injectable: Not only is it organic but it is harvested from your own body, eliminating the risk of allergic reaction. In reality, the use of fat is widely disputed, although scientists have experimented with fat transplants since the 1890s. Initially, it was hoped that fat transplants would prove effective for breast augmentation, but a large percentage of the fat dies, leaving scars and calcifications that can imitate or mask the presence of cancer on a mammogram.

With the advent of liposuction, fat transplants have become popular again, at least in theory. Fat is removed from one spot of the body, usually the abdomen, buttocks, or thighs, and is injected in another, usually the face. Some surgeons believe that inflammatory reactions to the transplant are reduced if the fat is centrifuged to remove fluid, blood, and cellular debris before injection, but this purification process hasn't yet been perfected.

The best sites for fat injections are the laugh lines between the nose and mouth, forehead wrinkles, and skin depressions such as scars and "dimples" left by liposuction. Most physicians consider the results of fat injections to be temporary. You will probably need repeated treatments since roughly 70 percent of the fat often is absorbed after only six months. As with collagen, so many fat cells are expected to die that your doctor will probably need to inject more than are actually needed during the initial treatment, leaving the area excessively plump for a while. Sometimes these contour irregularities do not correct themselves. Ultimately, most of the correction that remains is the result of the scar tissue that forms at the injection site.

Although allergic reaction is not a factor, fat transplants increase the incidence of infection because the body is invaded at two points: the site from which the fat is removed and the spot where it is reinjected. It's vital that your doctor perform both parts of the procedure in a sterile environment.

FIBREL

New injectables continue to be sought. The newest is Fibrel, a gelatin powder that is mixed with a component from your own blood, which turns it into a semiliquid glue. Results have been mixed to date, but some believe the results of Fibrel last longer than those of other substances. To date, there is a lack of evidence that Fibrel offers any clear advantage over collagen.

SPA SKIN TREATMENTS

America's fascination with spa vacations has as much to do with our passion for fitness as with an urge for sybaritic pleasures: Mud baths, seaweed wraps, mummification in soothing herbs, and a host of skin-care treatments are offered to eliminate poisons, tensions, acne, and other ailments of the modern age. These treatments may relax us, but experts have denounced most of their claims. Before undergoing any such treatments, consult the following list of caveats:

- If you have a heart ailment, avoid treatments that promote sweating and dilation of blood vessels, such as steam baths, saunas, and some wrap procedures.
- Cellulite, a particularly tenacious form of fat, can only be combated through rigorous diet and exercise. Wrapping the body in seaweed, plastic, and blankets will not smooth dimpled skin.
- Massages and electronic facial treatments can't turn back the hands of time. There is no such thing as a nonsurgical facelift.
- If you use Retin-A, avoid drying lotions, masks, and all treatments that tend to make the skin even thinner.
- If you have dry, sensitive skin, or if you are prone to acne, stay away from salt-glow treatments (a mixture of sea salt and oil), as well as therapies using stiff brushes or loofahs. Salt draws moisture *out* of the skin, making it even drier. And now dermatologists believe that abrading the skin with a hard brush may actually increase the spread of acne by contaminating the hair follicles with old skin.
- If you're acne-prone, avoid anything that stimulates oil glands, including steaming and facial massage.
- If thinning hair is a problem, shun treatments featuring massage or manipulation of the scalp. They can make delicate hair follicles shut down production.
- Asthma, eczema, hay fever, and allergy sufferers do well to use only fragrance-free products in their treatments.
- If you're pregnant, consult your doctor before having *any* body treatments.

The Eyes

OUR EYES RIDE IN FAT-CUSHIONED COMFORT IN THE BONY SOCKETS of the skull—pockets nature designed to protect them from harm. With age, the skin of the eyelids stretches, muscles weaken, and excess fat gathers over and under our eyelids, regardless of whether our bodies are thin or obese. Sagging eyebrows, drooping upper lids, and bags below can make the energetic appear perpetually sleepy, and the abstemious appear dissipated. Drooping upper eyelids may even interfere with vision.

If droopy, puffy lids run in your genes, you may want eyelid surgery—called blepharoplasty—as a teenager. However, many people begin to feel the desire for this rejuvenating surgery between the ages of thirty-five and fifty. Approximately half of those opting for eyelid surgery do so five to ten years before they need a facelift.

A delicate process requiring great surgical finesse, blepharoplasty is one of the oldest procedures in the cosmetic surgery repertoire. It removes fat from the upper and lower lids, often along with excess skin and muscle. After surgery, patients look refreshed, younger, and more alert. Eyelid surgery does not remove crow's feet or other wrinkles (unless they are located in the skin to be removed). It also won't lift your brow, though it's possible to perform a browlift simultaneously. (For more on browlifts, see chapter 14.) Eyelid surgery also will not eliminate the dark circles that many people complain about under their eyes, though it can remove some of the discolored skin.

Currently, about 16 percent of blepharoplasty patients are men and that proportion is growing. Most men who seek eyelid surgery—which is the second most popular procedure for males—are businessmen who look older and less energetic than they feel and who don't want their appearance to penalize them careerwise.

ASIAN EYES

A growing segment of patients seeking eyelid surgery are people of Asian ancestry who frequently choose the operation to "widen" the eyes. Most Asian-Americans who have eyelid surgery aren't trying to erase evidence of their Eastern heritage, only to modify it.

The Asian eyelid has no fold. Without a fold in the upper eyelids, the skin may droop, making the eyes appear small. Sometimes the eyelids appear large and flat, giving an appearance of exhaustion. A plastic surgeon will remove the excess skin and fat, then stitch the upper eyelids to create a fold.

THE CONSULTATION

It's vital to have realistic expectations about what eyelid surgery can and cannot do. You and your doctor should discuss your goals, determine whether to do all four lids (uppers and lowers) or just two, and whether to have this surgery alone or in conjunction with a facelift or browlift.

Health problems that rule out eyelid surgery include two thyroid disorders: hypothyroidism (low glandular activity) and hyperthyroidism (increased activity, called Graves' disease or thyrotoxicosis). The former causes eyelids to become waterlogged—a type of swelling that's not correctable with surgery. In the case of Graves' disease, the lids swell and the eyes may bulge. Attempting surgery would only worsen the bulging and aggravate the "dry-eye" symptoms these patients have. In addition, due to the sensitivity of blood vessels in the back of the eye, you should not have eyelid surgery if you have hypertension or other circulatory disorders, cardiovascular disease, or diabetes. Caution is also advised if you have an eye condition such as a detached retina or glaucoma. In these cases, you should consult with your ophthalmologist before having a blepharoplasty, since any irritation or pressure on the optic nerve can lead to complications.

Another condition that could preclude eyelid surgery is a lack of sufficient tears. The cornea (the eye's clear, outer covering) lacks its own blood supply and dries out easily, particularly after lid surgery. Without proper lubrication, the cornea can become ulcerated or permanently scarred.

Discuss your entire medical history with your plastic surgeon. If you're like most people, you'll be quite well suited to eyelid surgery.

COSTS

Surgeons' fees range from $1,000 to $3,500 for two lids (two uppers or two lowers), and from $1,500 to $5,000 for all four lids. Add to this the anesthesiologist's fee, if one is used. In addition, there may be an extra charge for the use of the operating facility.

Most insurance policies will not pay for eyelid surgery, unless you can prove—photographically and medically—that drooping upper lids interfere with your vision. You may need to have your plastic surgeon or ophthalmologist verify this in writing, and you'll usually have to have the surgery approved by your carrier before the operation is performed.

BEFORE SURGERY

Before scheduling surgery, your doctor or a nurse will test your vision and may measure your tear production by placing a small piece of specially treated paper inside your lower lids. If your tear production is low, your surgeon may send you to an ophthalmologist for additional tests. As with all cosmetic surgery procedures, you will be asked to stop smoking for one to two weeks before and after surgery.

THE PROCEDURE

Blepharoplasty is usually performed on an outpatient basis in your surgeon's office, a freestanding surgery center, or a hospital. Rarely, it is done as a hospital inpatient procedure.

The operation is sometimes performed using general anesthesia, but more often your surgeon will use a combination of local anesthesia and oral or intravenous sedatives. You may feel some tugging at your skin and occasional discomfort when the fat under your eyelids is removed. You and your surgeon should discuss your anesthesia options thoroughly, and he will make every effort to keep you comfortable and tension-free.

Your face is washed with a surgical cleansing solution and the eye not being operated on at the time may be covered with a sterile cloth or bandage. Using purple surgical ink, your doctor will mark the incision sites—a process that may scratch, but doesn't hurt.

Upper Lids

If you're having all four lids fixed, the uppers are usually done first, since lower lids require more time and finesse. An incision is made in the natural fold at the back of your lid. For minor corrections, this incision is roughly one inch long; however, if excess skin is being removed as well as fat (generally in middle-aged or older patients), it can extend as far as the crow's feet at the outer edge. The excess skin and some of the muscle beneath it are cut away, and then the surgeon removes the fat.

Not all of the fat will be removed, since cutting out too much would cause your eyes to appear sunken. The bulk of the excess fat is usually found near the outer edge of your upper lids. However, fat in the center, directly below the muscle, is easiest to remove. There's not as much fat near the inner edge of the upper lids, but it can also cause a noticeable bulge.

Once all bleeding has stopped, your surgeon closes the incision with fine sutures under the skin to leave a nearly invisible scar. A cold compress is then placed over your eye, while your physician begins surgery on the other side. All in all, the procedure takes about one to one and a half hours to complete.

Lower Lids

Lower-lid surgery removes less skin than upper-lid surgery; an incision is made just below the lashes in the eye's natural crease. The surgeon separates muscle fibers from fatty deposits and removes the fat. Here, most of the excess fat lies in the middle of the lid. Your surgeon will be cautious not to remove too much fat.

After removing the excess fat and trimming sagging skin and muscle, the surgeon pulls the lower-lid skin up and over to one side, being careful not to leave a pucker. Sutures follow the natural lid crease. Like the uppers, lower lids take one to one and a half hours to correct.

Some people, particularly in younger age groups, have a pocket of concentrated fat below their eyes, but don't need any skin removed. In this case, a transconjunctival blepharoplasty, which leaves no visible scar, can be performed. With this technique, a tiny incision is made on the inside of the lower eyelid and excess fat is gently teased out with fine forceps. The incision is closed with one dissolving suture. This technique is particularly good for young men, as well as Hispanics and blacks, who have a greater tendency to form raised scars in the thicker skin beyond the outer edge of the eyelid.

RECOVERY

After the operation, your surgeon will lubricate your eyes with ointment and may or may not apply a pressure bandage for several hours. Your lids will feel tight and may throb as the anesthesia wears off, but if you experience severe pain, call your doctor immediately.

Keep your head slightly elevated—above your heart—for several days, especially when sleeping. Cold packs in the first twenty-four hours following surgery will reduce bruising. Eyelid skin is quite thin and bruises easily. The severity of discoloration varies from individual to individual and can last anywhere from two weeks to a month. If a transconjunctival blepharoplasty was performed, bruising is usually very minimal.

If you are wearing a bandage, it will probably be removed in twenty-four hours. After two or three days, you should be ready to watch television or read for a while. However, contact lenses

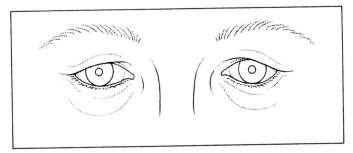

Before surgery, the patient has bags under the eyes and wrinkled folds of skin like hoods on the upper lids. Surgery on the upper and lower lids can be performed together or separately.

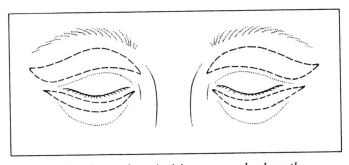

In a combined procedure, incisions are made along the natural contour lines just above the upper lids and beneath the lower lids. Skin and fatty tissue are removed. Sutures woven under the skin in the upper lid prevent visible marks; a straight line closes the incision in the lower lid.

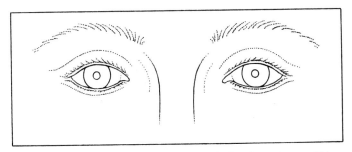

Hairline scars soon fade. Postoperatively, the upper eyelids are unobstructed and the skin under the eyes is firm and smooth.

cannot be worn for about fourteen days and may feel uncomfortable for some weeks after that.

If your doctor used an external incision to remove excess skin, your stitches will be taken out between the second and sixth day after surgery. However, your lids may remain swollen and sore for a day or two longer. You can wash your hair in the shower after several days and blow it dry on low heat, but avoid moving your head too much.

You may wake up with gummy eyes during the first week. Gently clean your eyes with a cotton swab soaked with plain water or a sterile eyewash. Your eyelids are bound to feel stiff and sore for about two weeks following the surgery. Most doctors recommend that their patients use eyedrops because lid surgery tends to make eyes dry and easily irritated. Artificial tears can be used several times daily to keep them moist. Also use drops if your eyes burn or itch.

You may feel ready to go out in public after a week to ten days. However, it's a good idea to stay out of the sun for extended periods. When you do go out, wear sunglasses or a sunblock made especially for eyelids. Tinted glasses can hide the signs of surgery and can also protect your temporarily sensitive eyes from light, dust, and other irritants.

You can generally return to work after a week, depending on how strenuous your job is. However, if you don't want your coworkers to see your bruising and other aftereffects of surgery, you may want to wait until you can wear makeup safely. That will depend on how quickly you heal and also on your physician's best judgment, but in general, you will be told to wait a week or two, which is usually several days after stitches are removed.

Avoid bending and lifting for two weeks, since such activity will make your eyes ache and swell. Alcohol is also off limits because it stimulates fluid retention in the tissues. Avoid sexual activity that might result in a bump to the face for at least ten days and strenuous sporting activities for three weeks.

TROUBLESHOOTING: WHAT CAN GO WRONG

The incidence of complications is relatively small. You may experience some double or blurred vision for several days, but your sight soon returns to normal. You may also experience swelling at the corner of your eyes. They will look slightly puffy and full. This disappears in three to four weeks.

The chances of infection are slim, unless you're lax about washing your hands before cleaning or touching your eyes. When your stitches are removed, harmless, tiny whiteheads may form, called milia. Your surgeon can remove them in a simple office visit using a very fine needle.

It's fairly common for one eye to heal faster than its mate. After surgery, your eyes' natural asymmetry may be more visible. Your scars may not be perfectly matched, either. This becomes less noticeable as the scars fade.

For several weeks after blepharoplasty, you may have difficulty shutting your eyes when you sleep. In about 2 to 5 percent of patients, this condition lasts for months. In very rare instances it's permanent.

One potentially serious complication is a pulldown of the lower lids that causes the "white" of your eye to show beneath the colored part. If this occurs, the problem may correct itself or may require further surgery. However, this complication is very rare.

SCARS

Plastic surgeons strive to leave their patients with nearly invisible scars. If you had only a pocket of fat removed through transconjunctival blepharoplasty, no scars will be visible. However, if excess skin was removed, you will have tiny scars that may be red, swollen, and lumpy for several weeks after the operation. This is normal and will clear up without medication or treatment. Scars may remain pink for six months to a year before fading to a fine white line that's virtually undetectable.

SUCCESS

The results of blepharoplasty last for five or more years, and many people enjoy permanent correction. For many, eyelid surgery takes years off their face, giving them an invaluable mental boost. This simple operation, more than any other, reverses a telltale sign of age and slows it for years to come.

PERMANENT EYEBROWS AND LID LINING

Cosmetic eye surgery involves getting rid of bags, droops, and wrinkles. But for some, the problem is filling in what's missing. Perhaps your eyes lack definition and you find the daily application of eyeliner tedious or unnatural-looking. For some individuals with arthritis, tasks that require hand coordination such as applying eyeliner are virtually impossible. Or, you may have lost your eyelashes after an infection, or your brows may have disappeared from overzealous plucking. Tattooing can add color permanently around the lids or in the eyebrows.

Unlike ordinary tattooing, permanent lid lining—technically called surgical skin pigmentation—is usually done by a physician using sterile nonallergenic pigment. It is performed in a doctor's office or hospital using local anesthesia and sedation.

Tattooing can be done on persons of any age, though it's wise to think twice about it since it's irreversible. What you like at fifteen, you may hate at twenty-five. On women over forty, the tattoo can look harsh. Your doctor may give you a scratch test before the operation to see if you are allergic to the pigment. In addition, the procedure should be delayed if you are experiencing any kind of infection or allergic reaction to makeup.

With your doctor, determine the color of your tattoo (mahogany is most common), whether you want it on both your upper and lower lids, and if it should extend past the outer corner of your eyes. The same procedure can be used for eyebrows. Up close, tattooed eyebrows will look like they are painted on your skin, just like eyebrow pencil; they will never look like natural eyebrows.

Tattooing costs between $1,000 and $2,000. The procedure takes roughly thirty to sixty minutes. Discuss anesthesia with your surgeon. Some doctors use only local anesthetic, whereas others prefer a combination of local and oral or intravenous sedatives. As the procedure begins, you'll receive a few anesthetic drops in each eye.

If you are having your eyes done, your eyelids are cleaned with an antibacterial solution; then the lid being colored is pulled over your eye to protect the sensitive organ from damage. The special tattoo needle is nearly microscopic and makes a low humming noise. Your surgeon will work on one eye at a time, keeping the other under ice to prevent swelling from the anesthesia injections.

For lower lids, pigment is applied in tiny dots between the

lashes to create a realistic darker lash line. On the larger upper lids, an arc of up to three rows of dots is used, placed just above the lashes and narrowing into one line as they approach the inside corner.

Tattooing will make your eyes burn, possibly for several days, but you shouldn't be in pain. Your eyes may tear and remain swollen for up to five days. Your surgeon will give you an antibiotic ointment to keep crusts from forming on your lids. There are no bandages, stitches, or scars from this procedure. At home, keep ice compresses over your eyes for twenty-four hours. You can use a commercial cold pack, gauze soaked in ice water, or any similar alternative. Most people feel able to return to work in three days to a week, but you may want to wait until the bruising or swelling fades or eye makeup can be worn, which is usually a week.

Eyelid or eyebrow tattooing will *not* make you look like Elizabeth Taylor in *Cleopatra,* but it will add definition where it's lacking. At first the tattooing will look quite dark, but after several weeks it fades to a more natural look.

On the down side, your surgeon may skip a spot that will need to be retattooed, usually after several weeks have passed. If the tattoo is put in the wrong place entirely, your surgeon must scrape it out of the tissue. This is easily done during the operation, but more difficult after your skin has had time to heal over the pigment. In a worst-case scenario, the pigment could show up as a dark line and not blend with your eyelashes. The only solution is to remove the pigmented skin, which may leave a scar. In rare cases, patients develop a foreign-body reaction signaled by redness and swelling.

Finally, remember that *any* treatment around your eyes may damage eyelashes and cause them to fall out; however, this is very rare and the lashes usually grow back.

Reversing Tattooing

Lid lining by tattoo has been something of a craze recently, and like all trends, a lot of people change their minds afterward. There are now several techniques to remove tattooed lines. They include surgical removal and bleaching the pigment with alcohol. However, they are extremely difficult to perform and do not consistently produce good results. (For more on removing old tattoos, see "Removing Tattoos" in chapter 11.)

The Brow

THE TOP PART OF YOUR FACE ISN'T IMMUNE TO THE EFFECTS OF aging. As you age, your eyebrows may seem to fall lower on your face and the outer sides of your upper eyelids may start to sag. Creases can develop on your forehead and at the top of your nose. To minimize these changes, a browlift, also called a forehead lift, is the surgery of choice.

Lifting the brow and slightly smoothing the forehead can make you look younger and more alert. Because a browlift can raise the upper lids as well, it replaces upper eyelid surgery for some patients. It also softens frown lines above your nose and, by actually removing the muscles that cause these furrows, may prevent them from recurring.

A decade or so ago, the results of a browlift were short-lived. At that time the skin was merely lifted; today, the muscles that cause the problems are removed or altered in some way, with far more dramatic and long-lasting results.

Best Candidates

Men and women of any age may be good candidates for a browlift. A browlift is most commonly performed to stave off the effects of aging in people forty-five to sixty-five years old, often at the same time as a facelift. However, a droopy brow or furrowed lines above the nose can also be inherited. This can create an appearance of being perpetually sad or angry.

Jennifer, a bright and charismatic woman of thirty-six, was an anchorwoman at a local television station in the South. A visible local personality, her stories often generated a big response. In one letter to the station, a fan who lauded her reporting style said he wanted her to answer one question: Why was she always sad?

Jennifer knew her brows sagged, particularly at the outer edges, but hadn't realized just how pronounced it was. She started to wonder if her facial features could have an effect on her career. Were her looks undermining her credibility? Her assignments tended toward offbeat features. How could she talk about the Thanksgiving Day parade, when to her audience she looked like she was about to cry?

Jennifer decided to have a browlift, and within a few months after surgery she began to get a new crop of letters, many commenting on how her appearance had improved and how much happier she looked. "What did you do, take a vacation?" one viewer asked.

To see if a browlift might enhance your appearance, stand in front of a mirror and place your fingers at the outer edge of your eyes, above your eyebrows. Then gently draw the skin upward to raise the whole brow area. More or less, that is the effect a browlift would have.

If you have already had plastic surgery on your upper eyelids, your plastic surgeon should make sure that enough skin remains to allow you to close your eyes after a browlift. A more conservative browlift may be in order, or your surgeon may recommend against surgery altogether.

Another point to consider is the type of hairline you have and the height of your forehead. Usually, the incision is made *behind* your hairline. If you have a high forehead, you may do better with an incision just in *front* of your hairline to avoid making it appear even higher. Individuals in this situation usually wear their hair down on their forehead and their hairstyle hides their scar.

Other factors such as the extensiveness of surgery needed, the condition of your skin, and your overall health determine whether a browlift is for you. For example, someone with a skin condition like acne rosacea, a type of acne that affects older people, or someone with a scalp infection might run a higher risk of contracting an infection during the operation.

Attitude is also very important. A browlift will probably leave you looking younger and more animated, but it will not radically change your life. It will not change your basic expressions, nor will it erase all the lines on your forehead.

Costs

Count on a surgeon's fee of $1,000 to $4,000 or more. The use of an anesthesiologist or a hospital room will add to the cost. A browlift would be covered by insurance only if the brow droops so much that vision is impaired. Check your policy beforehand.

Before Surgery

The preoperative preparation for a browlift is similar to that for a facelift (see chapter 15), including the recommendation not to smoke for at least one to two weeks before and after surgery. If you have very short hair, it's not a bad idea to let it grow longer before the browlift so that it will cover the scars before they heal and fade.

The Procedure

The surgery will either be done in a freestanding surgery center, your surgeon's office-based facility, or the hospital, where you may either stay overnight or leave the same day. A browlift usually takes no more than an hour or two. Local anesthesia with sedation is generally used, although general anesthesia is an option.

Your hair is tied with rubber bands in front of and behind the incision area. Your head does not have to be shaved, but hair immediately in front of the incision line may need to be trimmed. If local anesthesia is used, it is injected into the area above your eyebrows.

The surgeon makes an incision along premarked lines, starting at about the level of your ears and running along the top of your forehead, usually well behind your hairline so that the scar won't show. For those with a receding or high hairline, the incision is made along the hairline.

The scalp is rich with blood vessels and has a tendency to bleed heavily. The surgeon, however, immediately stops the bleeding with a cautery or clamps. After the incision has been made, the forehead skin is carefully lifted up. The broad band of tissue that causes creases in the forehead is called the frontalis muscle. The vertical muscles that lie between the eyebrows and cause furrowed lines are called the corrugators. Portions of these muscles are removed during surgery, depending on which areas are being treated. Excess tissue is then trimmed and the surgeon closes the incision with either stitches or metal clips.

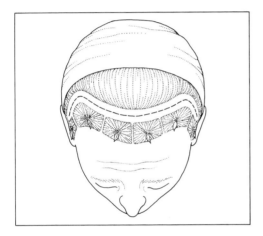

The browlift raises drooping eyebrows and erases horizontal wrinkles across the forehead and top of the nose. In preparation, the hair is tied with rubber bands in front of and behind the incision area. An incision is usually made across the top of the head a few inches behind the hairline.

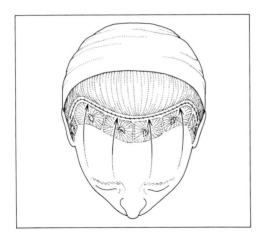

The forehead skin is gently pulled upward and excess skin is removed, sometimes with part or all of the muscles. The incision is then closed with stitches.

After surgery, your face and hair are cleansed. The incision is covered with a gauze padding and your head is wrapped with bandages. A drainage tube may be placed beneath your scalp to collect excess blood.

Recovery

You are likely to have some pain around the incision area and will sometimes experience headaches. If you have a tendency toward headaches, alert your doctor. He may recommend an additional local anesthetic during surgery as a preventive measure.

You will be advised to keep your head elevated for the first forty-eight to seventy-two hours. Some swelling is inevitable and don't be alarmed if bruising occurs around your eyes or cheeks as well. Gravity often pulls discoloration downward. Bruising and swelling should fade after two weeks or so.

Following a browlift, all patients experience some numbness on the top of their scalp. The skin may also feel tingly or itchy. That's because some nerves are severed in that area and these sensations may take as long as six months to disappear.

The bandages will be taken off a day or two after surgery, with stitches or clips removed within two weeks. Your doctor may remove them in two stages, particularly if there is any scalp irritation.

You will probably be allowed to shower and to shampoo your hair the day the bandages are removed. Hair growth may be inhibited for up to six months, since the follicles can be affected by the trauma of surgery. As a result, you may notice that your hair falls out or becomes thin. Normal growth will usually return; permanent bald patches occur only if there are rare complications such as infection or excessive scarring.

As a general rule, you can expect to be back at work in about a week to ten days, if the browlift was the only type of surgery you had. Plan to take it easy, however. Vigorous physical activity, including anything from jogging to having sex, should be avoided for at least ten days. Standing for long periods of time or any strong physical exertion may cause your head to throb. It's also advisable to stay out of the sun for at least six weeks.

You can face the world as soon as you feel comfortable with the prospect. The visible signs of the surgery should fade completely within two to three weeks. Before that, makeup can cover any minor swelling or bruising that makes you self-conscious (see "Camouflage Cosmetics" in chapter 5).

Troubleshooting: What Can Go Wrong

Complications after browlift surgery are rare, but the possibility must always be considered.

Bleeding. Even though the scalp bleeds easily, the chances of excessive bleeding are remote. Also rare is a collection of blood underneath your skin (hematoma) that may have to be drained.

Nerve Damage. Some nerves are cut during the operation, but in the vast majority of cases, sensation rapidly returns. In rare instances, an injury to the nerve that controls eyebrow movement can be permanent. In this case, only one eyebrow is affected and your appearance is made more normal by severing the equivalent nerve on the other side of your face. Symmetry is then restored.

Infection. Infection after a browlift is extremely rare, due to the excellent blood supply in the forehead.

Poor Healing. If the skin has been drawn too tight, or if there's a great deal of swelling, the incision may pull and cause a broad scar to form. Treatment is relatively easy by surgically removing the scar tissue. A new, thinner scar will then form.

Scars

You can expect some scarring, although most of the time it will be hidden by your hair. Some scars may spread, possibly to the width of half an inch. No hair will grow along this scar tissue. If you have extremely fine hair, a broad scar may show through. For most people, however, the browlift scar is unnoticeable.

Satisfaction

Browlift can seem like a miraculous procedure for those patients with deep forehead furrows. Many people, however, don't even realize that their foreheads showed aging signs like the rest of their face until after the lift. They are surprised and usually very happy with the results, which provide a distinctly younger appearance.

The Face

NONE OF THE ANTIAGING PROCEDURES DESCRIBED EARLIER CAN IM-
prove loose skin and sagging muscles around the face, jaws, and
neck. Enter the facelift, known as rhytidectomy. It can lessen and
even reverse these signs of aging.

Facelifts have been done for about seventy years, but the last
fifteen years or so have brought great improvements in the procedure. In the early days of the operation, a facelift was merely
a skin lift. All too often, women emerged from surgery with a
higher hairline—nothing more. Their neck continued to sag and
their cheeks looked pulled up at the corners, giving a stretched,
unnatural look to their face.

Today's facelift is a much more involved procedure that offers
better, more long-term results. Plastic surgeons' ability to manip-
ulate the deeper facial tissues now enables them to "clean up"
the neck and jaw more effectively. The emphasis is on contouring by suctioning away excess fat, particularly under the chin;
tightening underlying muscles; and redraping the skin.

There are three basic problem areas that a facelift can improve: (1) the nasolabial fold, or deep crease between the nose
and mouth; (2) a slack, jowly jawline; and (3) folds and fatty
deposits around the neck. A facelift may be performed alone or

in conjunction with other procedures, such as a browlift, eyelid surgery, nose reshaping, and chin or cheek implants.

Best Candidates

The best candidate for a facelift is a woman or man who has developed a saggy face or neck and has realistic expectations. There are no strict age limitations. Although it's fairly uncommon for persons in their thirties to show signs of an aging face, occasionally the skin is so fragile or sun damaged that premature sagging occurs. (Note that facelifts should not be used as a preventive tactic.) Octogenarians can be fine candidates as well. Most often, however, a facelift patient is in his or her forties, fifties, or sixties.

More important than chronological age is the condition of your skin and underlying bone structure. Your skin should still have some spring in it, and your bone structure should be strong and well-defined. Because of its thinness and excellent blood supply, facial skin tends to heal well with almost invisible scars. But certain medical conditions—such as the tendency to form excessive scars, uncontrolled high blood pressure, or blood clotting problems—could rule out surgery.

Both men and women can be good candidates. Men now constitute about 9 percent of all facelift patients. George, a senior executive in finance, chose a facelift because he was worried about his job. Rumors that his company was about to be purchased were starting to fly and there had already been cutbacks. "They'll probably lay off those who have recently come aboard or those close to retirement," he shrewdly guessed.

At fifty-eight, George was edging toward retirement, but he felt he had many years left as a productive employee. His cheeks and jowls sagged, making him look tired. He was beginning to look like his father. So, George decided to have a facelift. As it turned out, his insurance policy, one specially drafted for the top managers in the company, covered *all* medical expenses, even elective surgery. George kept his job. Whether the lift had anything to do with it, he never knew. Nevertheless, he was satisfied with his decision and no longer worried about being pushed out by younger men.

ELECTRIC FACIAL TONING

Known as facial toning, myotonology, or electrical muscle stimulation (EMS), this salon beauty treatment has been billed as the "nonsurgical facelift," promising rejuvenated skin tone and a sleeker, tauter complexion. However, the actual results are subtle and temporary.

A low-current machine is used to administer the treatment that is similar to the electrical muscle stimulators used by sports medicine specialists to rehabilitate athletes' injured or inactive muscles. The FDA approves the machines only for such medical uses as relieving muscle spasms or increasing blood circulation and has given no clearance for cosmetic purposes.

Facial toning devices feature two stems tipped by large cotton swabs that are dipped in water, aloe vera gel, collagen, elastin, or royal jelly. The cosmetician massages your face with the probes, which generate microcurrents of electricity. The current is so low that you can't feel it. However, makers say that circulation is revved up, making complexions glow and giving the face's thirty-odd muscles a vigorous workout.

Facial toning is a long-range treatment program: ten to fifteen one-hour treatments at $45 to $150 a session (two to three times a week), followed by once-a-week maintenance visits for life. (There is a home model of the muscle stimulator that sells for about $150.)

Plastic surgeons and many dermatologists say that electricity will not lift the face or do anything more than a good facial massage will do. Further, the current used in facial toning isn't strong enough to make the muscles respond and you feel no contractions. (The current used by sports doctors in electromuscle therapy is a thousand times stronger than what the salons use on the face.) Even if it were possible for electricity to improve muscle sag, it will not tighten slack skin or get rid of excess fat, which are the primary facial problems.

Doctors do concede that facial toning may yield immediate, pleasing results in the same way that a good facial will by plumping up skin. For some women, this is enough and they swear by facial toning. But when the skin relaxes again, the effects are gone.

The Consultation

Your plastic surgeon will evaluate your face as a harmonious whole, including your eyelids and brow. The extent and type of facelift he recommends will depend on your unique anatomy and the particular changes aging has wrought.

To a certain extent, a rhytidectomy can give you back your former face by reversing some of the changes brought on by age. However, the aging process is only set back, not stopped altogether. In addition, physically, you will still be the same age, subject to the same health conditions and other limitations.

If you're counting on having a totally different look, you're setting yourself up for disappointment. If you're hoping to give yourself a psychological boost by looking younger, a facelift may help. Discuss your goals with your surgeon so that your expectations are in line with the surgical reality.

Plastic surgeons hesitate to use words like *younger* when they describe the results of a facelift. They prefer the word *fresher*. In fact, a good facelift, along with stylish makeup and hairstyling, *will* make you look younger. If you understand the goals, accept the risks, and appreciate the fact that recovery will be necessary before you see the final results, you're likely to get what you expect: a healthy, psychological boost. A facelift may give you the confidence to make other positive changes in your life, like improving your diet, starting an exercise routine, or getting out more socially.

Costs

Surgical fees start at $1,200 and go as high as $8,000 or more. Doctors' fees in large cities are generally higher. Having general anesthesia and staying in the hospital for a couple of days also will boost the price. Facelifts are almost never covered by insurance plans, so be prepared to shoulder the financial burden yourself.

Before Surgery

If you have very short hair, it's not a bad idea to let it grow longer before your facelift so that you can use it to hide the scars that will be visible immediately following surgery. To ensure the smoothest, safest operation possible, smoking is definitely out. Smoking inhibits the flow of oxygen and blood to the skin, which particularly affects how well the incision area heals behind the ears. Most surgeons recommend that smokers put their habit on hold for at least one to two weeks before and after surgery.

Immediately before the surgery your hair is pulled back or trimmed and the surgeon or nurse marks the incision sites. Your face is washed with an antibacterial solution and a bit of gauze is placed in each ear to keep out fluids.

The Procedure

A facelift may be performed in your plastic surgeon's office, in a freestanding surgery center, or in a hospital as an inpatient or outpatient. If you have any conditions that will need to be monitored after surgery, such as diabetes or high blood pressure, you may be advised to have the procedure done as a hospital inpatient.

Most facelifts today are performed using a local anesthesia, which numbs only the face, as well as sedatives to make you drowsy. Some plastic surgeons prefer to use general anesthesia, which will put you to sleep during the entire procedure.

Facelift surgery can usually be completed in less than five hours. A patient who needs significant amounts of fat removed will require more time, as will someone who bleeds more than usual. Surgery may also take longer when more than one procedure is being performed.

If several extensive procedures are scheduled, surgery may be divided into two separate sessions. If you are having local anesthesia plus sedation, surgery may be done on consecutive days; if you choose general anesthesia, the second session may be delayed for a couple of days.

A facelift is highly individualized. For some, most of the work is focused on the neck; for others, the cheeks or jawline are altered most dramatically. Your surgeon pays close attention to two important structures in the face and neck: in the face, the membrane called the SMAS (superficial musculoaponeurotic system); in the neck, the thin sheet of muscle extending from your collarbone up your neck, called the platysma. When loose, it is the SMAS that gives a jowly look to the face. The platysma is the culprit behind the "cords" that may show up in the neck and may give the Adam's apple a pronounced prominence.

The operation is performed on one side of the face at a time. The goal is to leave a nearly invisible scar and a natural-looking hairline. Every surgeon has his own special techniques for accomplishing these two goals and your physician will explain his preference during your consultation.

Typically, the incision begins inside your hairline, at the temples. It then slopes down just inside (or in front of) your ear and around the earlobe, until it reaches the nape of your neck in the back of the scalp. It may or may not be necessary to shave or clip your hair around the incision lines.

Retaining a natural-looking hairline requires surgical artistry. For instance, to avoid losing the hair that naturally grows along the front of your ear, some surgeons make a short, horizontal incision below your "sideburns." The skin is lifted back, but not up, leaving a natural-looking hairline. The trade-off is the little horizontal scar, which can usually be hidden by your hair.

The plastic surgeon first lifts up the skin at the temples and around the ears, and separates it from underlying fat and muscle. The surgeon then tightens the SMAS and the muscles, pulling the layers of underlying tissue up and back. The layers are then secured with stitches behind and above the ears, and the excess is cut off.

The skin is drawn over this tightened layer of muscle and membrane, and it too is then carefully trimmed. Stitches are used to close the incisions and are usually placed just inside (or in front of) the ear, and behind the ear, as well as in the hairline. Metal clips may be used in the scalp area, where the skin is thick.

One side of the face is done at a time. If local anesthesia is used, it is administered twice—once for each half of the face. For neck improvements, an incision is made under the chin, excess fat is trimmed or suctioned out, and the bands of platysma muscles are tightened.

If any blood begins to collect under the skin, a small tube may be temporarily inserted in the back of the ear for drainage. Most surgeons will then wrap your head in bandages with an opening that exposes most of your face. This minimizes bruising and swelling, and keeps your head fairly immobile.

Recovery

There is usually little pain following facelift surgery. Any discomfort can be alleviated with oral medication prescribed by your doctor. Severe or persistent pain may be a sign of complications: Let your physician know immediately.

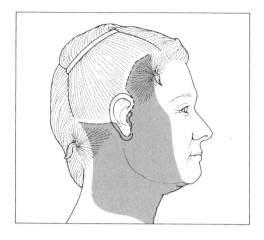

Before a facelift, the face shows sagging jowls and neck, along with deep cheek folds. Incisions are made on both sides of the face, starting inside the hairline at the temples and extending down the front of (or just inside of) the ear, around the earlobe, to the lower scalp. An incision may also be made under the chin to provide access to the neck. The shaded area is the skin that will usually be separated from the underlying tissues.

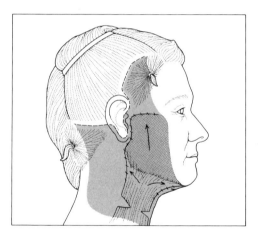

The underlying facial tissue and neck muscle are sometimes divided, then pulled up and sutured into place.

Most facelift patients experience numbness in the cheeks or ears. Some numbness is unavoidable, since the small nerve endings in the muscles are disturbed. However, it usually disappears in a few weeks to a few months.

Many doctors recommend keeping your head elevated for the first two days after surgery. If you bend over or even let your head drop forward, the force of gravity may aggravate swelling, so keep your head up as much as possible. Keeping your head fairly immobile is also helpful. Eating lightly for the first couple

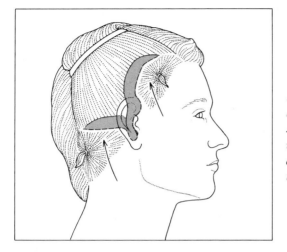

The loosened skin is then pulled up and backward. The excess skin in the shaded area is trimmed, and sutures are placed evenly along the incision lines.

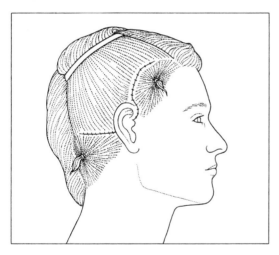

Scars are hidden in the hairline and in normal skin creases down the front of, or just inside of, the ear.

of days, and perhaps sticking to a liquid or soft-food diet, will help you keep your face still.

Bandages are typically removed after one to five days. You will look pale, slightly bruised, puffy, and tired. The skin on your neck may be bruised or discolored. Bruising in the middle to lower neck will last longer than in the face, since gravity pulls the discoloration downward. The more extensive the surgery, the more evident and lasting the bruises. Given time, bruising fades and improvements begin to emerge.

After the bandage is off, you may take a shower. (If any drainage tubes have been put in, it's best to wait until they are taken out, which is usually between twenty-four hours and four to five days after surgery.) Many surgeons also will permit you to shampoo your hair at this time. Mild, nonirritating shampoo like baby formula is best to use at first.

The stitches around your ears and any under your chin will be removed about five days after surgery. The stitches or metal clips within your hairline may be left in for a week or two, since this area takes longer to heal. For a while, your facial skin will not feel heat the way it did in the past. For this reason, be careful with hot blow dryers or curling irons. You should also avoid scrubbing your face for a week or two after surgery, since your skin will be tender.

You can promote healing and minimize the chances of complications by taking good care of yourself after the operation. Don't overestimate your ability to bounce back. Make up your mind ahead of time to be patient and take it easy for the first week.

A facelift needn't keep you off your feet very long, but you don't want to rush things either. You may be particularly aware of your facial movements in the beginning as a result of the swelling, which may also distort your features a bit. Your eyes, for example, may assume something of an almond shape until the swelling recedes. You may feel disappointed and self-conscious about the swelling and fresh scars. To avoid a letdown, it's good to visit with friends or go to the movies. But keep socializing simple and nonstrenuous.

Most people are back to work about nine days after surgery, or even sooner if they don't mind their bruises showing. Special postoperative camouflage makeup that uses different colors to mask the blues and yellows of bruises allows some people to feel comfortable going back to work after a week (see "Camouflage Cosmetics" in chapter 5). You will probably be more easily fatigued than usual and the visual signs of surgery may be evident until the third week.

As for sports, beyond mild stretching and a bit of walking, hold off for at least two weeks. Even heavy housework will deprive you of the rest you need to fully recover. Exertion also aggravates facial swelling that may pull on the stitches or scars. Since sex, like exercise, can raise the blood pressure in your face, you should avoid it as well for at least two weeks after the operation. Other activities to put off for several weeks are drinking alcoholic beverages (alcohol increases swelling and the possibility of bleeding) and taking a steam bath or sauna.

After two weeks most people look pretty good and after three weeks even better. Mild swelling can camouflage imperfections in the surface of the skin, and some people are disappointed when fine lines or wrinkles reappear as swelling disappears, usually after the second week. In addition, your facial movements may be slightly stiff and the area around your neck may feel tight, especially when you move those muscles to talk or eat. This, too, will disappear after the second week.

There are other side effects. The hair around your temples may be thinner and it may take several months for it to grow back to its normal thickness. Your skin may feel drier, particularly during the winter or in dry climates, but a good moisturizing regimen will compensate. Its texture may feel rougher, but its natural texture should return within a few months.

In men, the beard-growing skin on the upper neck is drawn back behind the ears, so they must shave behind the ears after surgery. Men may also need to shave the back of their neck, if hair-bearing skin has been drawn back there as well. During the operation, the surgeon can try to destroy these hair follicles using electrolysis, but men are still likely to have to shave behind their ears after a facelift. Because some areas of skin will be numb for a time, an electric razor will minimize the chances of nicks.

Troubleshooting: What Can Go Wrong

This operation is generally quite safe. The more skilled your surgeon, the lower the likelihood of complications. However, the human body is a highly unpredictable machine and physical variations—where a nerve lies, how an incision heals—are tremendous.

Bleeding. Blood loss during surgery is usually insignificant. After surgery, some blood may collect beneath the skin—a condition called hematoma. This is usually discovered within a day or two after surgery. However, your surgeon will normally wait until a follow-up visit a week or so later to draw off the collected blood. This aspiration is painless because your skin is usually fairly numb at this stage.

Nerve Damage. Temporary nerve damage may range from a partial lower-lip paralysis to a more severe situation in which larger muscles, such as in your forehead, lose their ability to respond.

Rarely is this effect permanent. Numbness may also occur around or behind the ears, but is usually tempora

Poor Healing. The face normally heals rapidly because ot its good blood supply. However, some people heal more slowly than others. If a large spot of skin—perhaps a square inch or more— refuses to heal, you may be a candidate for minor, corrective surgery, in which the section is cut out and sutured closed.

Infection. Infection is rare, but it can happen if bacteria are inadvertently introduced into the incision area. Sometimes the infection is already present, say, in the ear canal, before the operation is performed and it travels during surgery. Or infection may occur during the healing process if you scratch your skin under the bandage. Depending on its severity, antibiotics may be administered intravenously in the hospital or by mouth at home.

Scars

Scarring is inevitable, but a facelift is designed so that most scars will be covered by your hair or hidden in the creases of your ears. If an incision was made in front of your ears, the scar will fade until it is virtually invisible. Many surgeons make their incision just *inside* the ears, so the scar is out of sight.

Although it is unlikely, a scar may sometimes "spread." The most stubborn scars are usually behind the ears. Don't be alarmed if a sore, crusty, or discolored area appears there for a few weeks. All scars should fade with time, but the timing and final result cannot be predicted. The scar should fade to a fine white or pinkish line, but in someone with a ruddy complexion, even this might be visible. The scars behind your ears may also shift or broaden.

These aftereffects are most visible to *you*. Others probably won't notice them at all. Scars can usually be camouflaged with ordinary light makeup, or you may decide to modify your hairstyle, perhaps letting your hair fall forward instead of pulling it back. If your scars don't fade, you should talk to your doctor about minor surgical treatment that may improve them (see "Predicting Scars" in chapter 3).

LASERS FOR COSMETIC SURGERY

Some people have the idea that a facelift or eyelid lift is some-how less like surgery if it is performed with a laser rather than a scalpel. Claims have been made that using a laser for this type of cosmetic surgery eliminates or greatly reduces pain, swelling, bruising, and other side effects.

However, *no* surgery—no matter what technology is used—can eliminate all side effects and possible complications. In fact, one scientifically controlled study on the use of lasers for eyelid surgery indicates that patients are subject to an extra risk poten-tial and additional cost, *without* any significant benefits.

A laser is basically a tube that contains carbon dioxide, ar-gon gas, or another active medium that is energized by a power source such as electricity. The resulting beam of light is up to 10 million times more powerful than the sun and is absorbed by different substances depending on its wavelength. For ex-ample, the invisible light produced by the carbon-dioxide la-ser is absorbed by water, the prime ingredient in human skin. In contrast, the blue-green light of the argon laser is heavily absorbed by substances that are red, such as the hemoglobin in blood. Laser light can be used to vaporize tissue or to si-multaneously cut and seal blood vessels.

Specific types of lasers have been shown to be the treatment of choice for treating defects such as port-wine stains and spi-derlike blood vessels on the cheeks and nose. They can also be effective in removing tattoos and recurrent warts. How-ever, the same cannot yet be said for such cosmetic problems as aging faces and eyes.

Unless they are in very experienced hands, lasers can be extremely dangerous when used around the eyes. A stray beam can hit the cornea and blind the patient. No matter what area of the body is being operated on, a beam that is just off the mark or allowed to penetrate too deeply can do damage.

In addition, contrary to common belief, laser surgery re-quires up to 25 percent more time than operations using con-ventional scalpels. It's also more expensive. A laser costs anywhere from $20,000 to $150,000. That cost, along with the expense of regular equipment maintenance and the advertis-ing that many doctors use to promote their new service, is passed on to patients.

Perhaps the best way for consumers to protect themselves when a physician proposes to use lasers for plastic surgery—or for any operation—is to find out whether he has privileges to use that particular type of laser at an accredited hospital.

Satisfaction

The overwhelming majority of patients are happy with their facelift. However, because the expectations for a facelift can be high and the immediate reality of the process—surgical trauma, bruises, fatigue—can be less than exhilarating, it's not unusual to feel mildly depressed afterward. This is normal and usually passes soon.

Jean, a recently divorced woman in her late forties, was surprised at her postsurgical emotions. Her surgery had gone well and she was healing nicely. Within a few weeks of surgery she was up and going to parties, but she still felt depressed. She had been hoping for something exciting to happen after the facelift; specifically, she wanted to meet someone new. She wanted people to notice how her face had improved, yet at the same time she didn't want them to notice.

After a couple of months, Jean hashed out her feelings with a friend who had had a facelift the previous year. The friend told her that she too had suffered the same ambivalence. She urged Jean to get on with her life and to stop waiting for the facelift to change it. Once she realized that she was not alone in her experience and that the adjustment—and the enhancement— took time, Jean's mood swings ceased.

A dip in your mood after surgery most probably will pass as soon as you start resuming your normal activities. If your depression lingers, like Jean's did, talk it over with a friend. You may be expecting too much from the facelift and may need to put things in perspective.

A facelift doesn't "freeze" time. Your face will continue to age and you may well want to repeat the procedure at some time in the future. Most people who have a facelift, in fact, do come back for a second one.

Many people wait five to ten years before coming back for a renewal operation, if they do at all. However, for some individuals who want to look the very best they can, a second operation just one to three years later may not be out of order. If you don't wait too long in-between, the results of each renewal tend to be maintained for a longer period than those from the previous surgery. How soon you decide to have another facelift will depend on how fast you age and how comfortable you are with those changes.

Hair-Replacement Surgery

THE POLKA-DOTTED LOOK OF THE PUNCH GRAFT IS NO LONGER THE inevitable signature of hair-replacement surgery. Using several different procedures, it is now possible to shrink wide, bald spots on the crown; blend in thin spots; and create new, natural-looking hairlines. The surgeon may use scalp reduction; skin expansion; strip grafts; scalp flaps; or clusters of plugs, mini-plugs, or even microplugs.

The results of hair-replacement surgery are permanent and can be remarkable. The biggest drawback is the time they take. Natural-looking hair replacement usually requires multiple surgical procedures, with extended intervals in-between to establish hair growth and to allow full recovery of blood circulation to the scalp. The typical treatment regimen lasts eighteen months. Correcting extensive baldness may take even longer.

Hair-replacement surgery is used to correct hair loss caused by male-pattern baldness, an inherited trait. Some men start losing hair at seventeen, some in their twenties, and some in their thirties and forties. A number of factors have been blamed for premature baldness, including poor circulation to the scalp, vitamin deficiencies, dandruff, and even wearing hats. All have been disproved.

HAIR-REPLACEMENT TECHNIQUES

The different techniques can be used individually or in various combinations. Your physician will design a plan that incorporates the best procedures for your problem.

Punch grafts, also called plugs. This is the most common hair-replacement procedure. A round graft measuring one-eighth inch across is "punched" out of a donor site at the back of the scalp. Each graft contains about fifteen hairs, plus skin and fatty tissue that hold the follicles. The grafts are fitted into punched-out holes made in the bald area. About fifty grafts can be used in one session. Usually several sessions, spaced several months apart, are required to fill in a bald area.

Miniplugs are about half the size of a normal plug and are used to fill in spaces between larger plugs.

Microplugs are made by splitting a plug into four segments. These fill in little spaces and also add some irregularity, which gives a natural look to the hairline.

Strip grafts are based on the same principle as punch grafts, except that the graft is long and thin rather than round. A strip graft measures about one-quarter of an inch in width and may be one or two inches long. Strip grafts are most often used to finish the hairline after plugs have filled in the bald spot.

Flaps give an immediate, dramatic improvement to large areas of baldness at the front of the head. Large segments of hair-bearing scalp are removed from the donor site at the side or back of the head, but remain tethered to their original location at one end. The flap is swiveled into the bald spot. (The edges of the donor site are pulled together and sutured close.) Flaps can survive because circulation is maintained from the original donor site.

Scalp reduction is the quickest way to reduce large areas of baldness on the crown. An ellipsis of bald skin measuring approximately one to two inches wide by six to seven inches long is cut out of the scalp. The two sides of the scalp are then brought together and sutured closed, leaving a thin line down the middle. A series of scalp reductions can be carried out over many months, reducing large bald spots.

Tissue expansion is performed using a balloon inserted under hair-bearing scalp on the sides of the head that is gradually inflated with a saltwater solution. When the skin has been stretched enough, the adjacent bald area is removed and the expanded tissue is brought over to cover it.

(Vitamin deficiency would have to be severe and prolonged to induce hair loss, an unlikely event in American society.)

Hair loss is sometimes associated with illness, hormonal shifts, chemotherapy, or severe emotional stress (although the stress typically occurs two to three months *before* hair suddenly begins to fall out). However, hair loss in these cases is usually transient.

In the 1940s, it was conclusively shown that male-pattern baldness is primarily genetic and that no amount of massage or scalp tonics could reverse it. That finding didn't dampen sales of magic hair-growing scams to the 40 million American men frantic over their hair loss. (Note that there is one cream sold under the name Rogaine that *can* stimulate hair growth in some people. See end of this chapter.)

Although hair does thin with age, aging plays a minor part in male-pattern baldness. Secondary to the role of genetics, but still important, is the male hormone testosterone. Myth has it that a man who becomes bald has an excessively high level of this male hormone. While the presence of testosterone does play a part in baldness, the *quantity* of the hormone doesn't seem to matter—at least in the case of men.

Testosterone may increase hair growth on the face, back, and chest, but it has the *opposite* effect on the top of the scalp. This is due to the fact that there are different types of hair follicles, whose distribution is determined by genetics. Each hair follicle on the body is genetically programmed to live a certain number of years.

BALDNESS IN WOMEN

Women can inherit the gene for male-pattern baldness, but only rarely will a woman actually become bald. This is either because in women the baldness gene is recessive, or because women have only minimal levels of the male hormone circulating in their blood. Occasionally, a woman will experience some baldness, perhaps because of illness or because her hormone level is a little higher than is usual. If a woman has a history of baldness in her family, a slight excess of male hormone could cause some baldness to occur.

The average woman *does* tend to lose hair with age, probably because of hormonal changes after menopause. However, it shows up as a subtle thinning all over the scalp and body, rather than as the dramatic patches typical of male-pattern baldness.

BEST CANDIDATES

The ideal candidate for hair-replacement surgery is a healthy male who has been losing hair for several years and who has an obvious area of baldness on the front or crown of his head. The hair at the back and sides of the head should be dense and of good quality.

The back and sides of your scalp maintain their hair growth for your lifetime, which makes them ideal donor sites. After a graft or flap is transplanted, it will continue to grow for the rest of your life.

The best candidate has reached a standstill in his hair loss. Most men with male-pattern baldness reach this plateau by the time they are in their late thirties or early forties, so the average hair-replacement patient is about thirty-five. (Older men in their sixties and seventies, whose hair grows thinner as a result of age rather than genetic predisposition, are not good candidates for hair replacement.)

If your hair is thinning, but you don't have any actual bald spots, it is probably too early for surgery. Plastic surgeons estimate that 50 percent of men ask too early for hair transplants and must postpone surgery for two or three years. At age twenty-seven, for example, Ken's hairline was starting to recede. He knew it would worsen because his father was completely bald. Could he have surgery "in advance," he asked, "so I don't ever have to see myself completely bald?"

Ken's plastic surgeon suggested he wait another year or so, until his baldness became more obvious. Ken could then have the procedure, with the understanding that although his "new" hair would grow, his overall hair loss would continue unabated and he would need additional surgery later on.

Finally, the ideal candidate is someone who is highly motivated as well as patient. The surgeon also must feel that surgery can make a big difference. That's the perfect combination.

POOR CANDIDATES

Men who have lost just a little hair are not good candidates for hair replacement because the effort isn't worth the difference it will make. Further, they are likely to lose more hair over the next few years. (However, they may be good candidates for minoxidil therapy. See end of this chapter.)

Men with poor-quality hair at the sides and back of their heads also are not good candidates. Some people are born with thin hair all over the scalp and don't have any good donor sites.

If you have only a thin rim of hair left, hair-replacement techniques usually cannot accomplish enough to make it worth the effort and expense. However, there are exceptions: Sam, age fifty, was severely bald. His surgeon explained that punch grafts on his scalp would look very obvious to others. Sam said, "I don't care; I can't stand this cue-ball look." He had a series of five surgical procedures involving a total of 250 punch grafts. The grafts grew well and he now has a new line of hair in the front, which he combs back. People tell him he looks younger. Sam is satisfied with the result because he knew what he wanted and he knew what to expect.

A candidate for hair replacement must be in good general health because most such procedures require several sessions to complete. Anyone with severe or uncontrolled medical problems would not be considered suitable for a hair transplant.

THE CONSULTATION

Your surgeon will document your family history carefully to establish the cause of your baldness. How old were you when you first started losing your hair? Has it been a gradual or a precipitous loss? Has hair loss reached a plateau? Are you losing hair, stabilizing, then losing it again? Your answers give the surgeon an idea of whether it's wise to attempt replacement at this time.

Your plastic surgeon will also ask whether other males on either side of your family were bald. If no one else in your family is bald, it suggests that something other than genetics may be involved. Your doctor will ask you about stress and various other problems you may have. If other causes for your baldness are identified, your hair loss may reverse itself with time.

If you are an appropriate candidate, your surgeon will ask what kind of result you're hoping for. Do you want a dense growth or only some hair to counteract the appearance of baldness? This will influence the choice of procedures. For just a little more hair, the answer may be plugs. For a dense growth,

WHO DOES HAIR-REPLACEMENT SURGERY?

The physician you choose should be someone who can evaluate your scalp, design an overall plan for you, and be involved with you on a long-term basis. Treatment may go on for two or three years, so a critical aspect is a good working relationship with your surgeon.

You want to choose someone who has the ability to do *all* hair-replacement procedures, so that the best one for you can be selected. Many physicians limit themselves to punch grafts. However, most plastic surgeons who perform hair replacement offer every technique: punch grafts, strip grafts, scalp reduction, flaps, and even tissue expansion.

Hair-transplant "clinics" usually offer the punch-graft, or "plug," method only. With the advent of hair clinics, punch-graft procedures have become an assembly-line type of operation. Clinics advertise hair transplants on television and in magazines and newspapers. These clinics will accept almost anyone, whether or not a person is a good candidate for surgery. So, a prospective patient rejected by a plastic surgeon may well go to a hair clinic and may be immediately accepted. An inadequately trained practitioner may accept a new patient before he is ready for surgery, or may do too many transplants at one time, which ultimately can lead to loss of the hair and severe scarring.

At a hair-transplant clinic, you usually will meet with a nonmedical staff person who will explain the procedure to you and set up an appointment. You often don't see the doctor until you go into the operating room for the procedure. When multiple procedures are involved, you might not see the same doctor twice. In addition, doctors at hair clinics may not be certified in *any* medical specialty.

the best solution may be a combination of procedures. Your surgeon's plan will lay out which procedures will be used in your treatment, the sequence in which they will be carried out, and how long each will take.

Your surgeon will explain what you probably will look like immediately after the first treatment. At the beginning, other people will most likely notice you are being treated, with some techniques being more visible than others.

Some men drop out after the first treatment because they are unprepared for the initial discomfort (although it is relatively mild) and for the time it takes to see new hair growth. Sometimes a patient has one or two operations, stops for a while, then comes back a few years later. Money may also be a factor. It's not always easy to project your financial circumstances a year or more into the future.

COSTS

Plugs, or punch grafts, cost $15 to $60 each. An average transplant of fifty plugs, then, will cost between $750 and $3,000. There may also be an additional charge for use of the facility and the services of an anesthesiologist.

A strip graft costs an average of $400, depending on its size. Scalp reduction and flaps vary in cost from $1,000 to $3,000, exclusive of the anesthesiologist's fee and the operating facility fees. The cost of tissue expansion may range from $1,000 to $5,000. The total cost of hair-replacement surgery can only be determined after your individualized plan has been designed by your surgeon.

BEFORE SURGERY

Most plastic surgeons recommend that aspirin, which thins the blood, be avoided for at least two weeks before and after any cosmetic surgery procedure. This is particularly important with hair-replacement surgery because the scalp has a rich blood supply and tends to bleed easily.

Smoking may drastically affect the success of some hair-replacement procedures. Since it causes blood vessels to constrict, depressing circulation, smoking can cause transplanted skin to die. Plastic surgeons will not usually perform a flap or a strip-graft procedure on someone who has not stopped smoking, at least temporarily. Smoking does not appear to pose the same risk to those who have plugs or scalp reduction, although surgeons prefer that these patients, too, stop smoking until they are healed.

THE PROCEDURE

Most hair-replacement procedures—plugs, strip grafts, and scalp reduction—are done on an outpatient basis, usually in your doctor's office. Hair-replacement techniques that use skin flaps or tissue expansion are more complex and usually require more sedation. In these cases, surgery is likely to be performed on an outpatient basis in a hospital or freestanding surgical facility.

Plugs, strip grafts, and scalp reductions are done using local anesthesia, usually combined with sedation. Flaps and tissue expansion are performed either with local anesthesia plus sedation, or with general anesthesia.

Punch Grafts

Punch grafts, or plugs, in which small plugs of hair and skin are punched out of a hair-bearing donor site and inserted into a bald spot, were the first hair-replacement technique and remain the procedure most commonly done today. If you let your hair grow before surgery, your surgeon can trim a section very short, from which the donor plugs will be taken. The surrounding long hair can then be combed over to cover the area after surgery.

The number of plugs removed and transplanted in each procedure depends on the size of the bald area. The average number of plugs used in one session is fifty, although for larger areas of baldness as many as seventy-five plugs may be used. The plugs must be spaced at least an eighth of an inch apart so that enough skin surrounds each one to maintain healthy blood circulation.

Because plugs cannot be transplanted too close together in one session, one procedure is not enough to densely cover any area of baldness. After the scalp recovers its normal circulation, additional plugs can be placed in-between the original transplants.

First, your surgeon injects local anesthetic into both the donor and the recipient sites. These injections are likely to sting, which bothers some men more than others.

Using a tubelike instrument, the surgeon literally punches out a small portion of the bald site. Then, he punches out the hair graft from a donor site at the back of the scalp, with each small plug comprised of about fifteen hairs and the skin and fatty tissue that hold the follicles. The grafts are gently fitted into their recipient holes and arranged so that the hair will grow in the right direction. Depending on his technique, your surgeon may or may not close each donor site with a tiny suture. Your scalp is then cleansed and a layer of gauze is applied, followed by a pressure bandage to hold the plugs in place. A session of fifty plugs may be completed in about two hours.

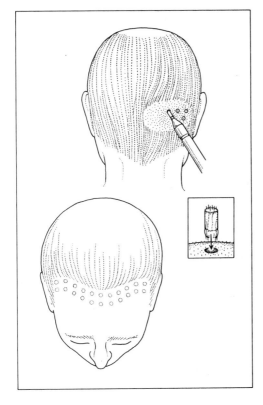

For punch grafts, small plugs of hair and skin are punched out of a hair-bearing spot at the back of the head and transplanted into a bald area. The plugs are spaced at least an eighth of an inch apart.

Recovery

Recovery after punch grafts is relatively easy, although men have varying reactions to postoperative discomfort. Some say they hardly notice any discomfort; others feel it is moderately painful. Your surgeon will probably give you a two-day supply of pain medication, although most men are not in much pain after the first day.

Two days after surgery, the bandage comes off. By this time the plugs are usually well set. Occasionally, a plug will stick to the bandage when it is removed; the physician will reinsert it, and the piece of hair and tissue will soon settle in place. Plugs will not usually fall out unless they are combed or pulled too quickly after surgery (within the first week or so).

A week after surgery, any stitches will be removed and you can wash your scalp and hair. (Your doctor will probably permit water-rinsing of your hair even earlier.) You will probably see your physician again in two weeks. Some plastic surgeons will recommend applying a topical cream to your scalp during the healing process. Some also like to use minoxidil after transplants in the hope that it will stimulate better hair growth, even though its effectiveness after replacement surgery has not yet been proved. You probably will not see your physician again for three or four months, when you will be ready for your next transplant.

Troubleshooting: What Can Go Wrong

The most common problem with plugs is their placement. If a plug is too big or the opening in the scalp is too small, the transplant will sit on top of the scalp and form a little bump, creating a "cobblestone" effect. If the physician takes too many plugs from one small area, you may develop some scarring at the donor site.

The most serious problem arises if too many plugs are put into one area at one time. Circulation to the scalp will decrease, hair growth will become sparse, and sometimes scarring and loss of scalp tissue occurs. Trying to do too much too fast inevitably backfires.

Bleeding may sometimes be a problem, but since most physicians suture closed any donor sites that begin to ooze during surgery, it is rare. Any bleeding that does occur can be treated with a pressure bandage. Bleeding is not usually a problem at the recipient sites, because the plugs themselves prevent it. Occasionally, however, some bleeding occurs during the procedure. Physicians cope with this on the spot by administering adrenaline to constrict the blood vessels, using a cautery to coagulate the blood or, if the punch instrument hits a tiny artery, closing the vessel with a suture. In general, however, bleeding is minor and is kept in check with a pressure dressing.

Infection also is rare with plugs because of the good circulation to the scalp. Rarely, one or two plugs are lost due to infection. It takes three months after the operation before the scalp fully recovers its normal circulation. Some physicians prefer to wait four months between operations. Allowing full recovery of circulation assures that subsequent operations will succeed as well as the first. Speeding things up or transplanting too many plugs at one time depresses blood circulation and risks loss of *all* the plugs.

Hair Growth from Transplants

You will have to wait several months before you can tell for sure if your transplants "took." (This is true for strip grafts and flaps as well.) Immediately after transplant, hair follicles go into a resting phase. In about a week, you may think you see a little hair growth in the plug, but this is misleading. What you are actually seeing is the hair shaft getting ready to shed. In many cases, some of the hair in the transplanted grafts will fall out in three or four weeks.

It takes another two months (three months from the time of the operation) before new hair starts to grow in the plug. Men often want to know if they can wear a hairpiece during this phase of hair replacement. Unfortunately, the answer is no, as this may cause the new hairs to break. Take heart; after a number of grafts have been done, the plugs begin to blend in, and your hairline begins to look natural.

Your new hair will grow at a rate of about one-half inch a month. At the end of four months, then, your surgeon can evaluate the transplants. Did they grow enough new hair or did they produce only sparse hair? Are you a good candidate for more transplants?

Out of fifty plugs, forty-eight should have a good growth of hair, with an average of fifteen strands each. Occasionally, one or two grafts do not survive. Most of the time, however, all survive, although some may not have a full growth of hair. At this point, the transplants have established their own blood supply and your physician can begin to insert additional plugs in-between. It usually takes about four sessions to completely fill out an area of scalp, spanning a total of eighteen months. A variety of new procedures may be used in conjunction with plugs, often to create a natural-looking hairline.

Finishing the Hairline

How skillfully the hairline is handled determines the whole look and success of hair replacement. *Miniplugs,* about half the size of a normal plug, can fill spaces between larger plugs. *Microplugs* can be made by splitting a plug into four segments and inserting the segments into little stab incisions between standard plugs. These smaller grafts also add some irregularity, which gives a natural look to the hairline. An alternative to mini- and micro-plugs is the strip graft.

Strip Grafts

Long, narrow strips of hair-bearing scalp removed for use as transplants were first invented to create new eyebrows for burn victims. The same technique was then found to be effective in evening out the hairline in front of punch grafts. Thin strips of skin and hair are taken from the side or back of the head and moved to the problem spots.

Strip grafts cannot be laid one behind the other because doing so would interfere with blood circulation and endanger the grafts. The usual plan is to start off with plugs, then to add strip grafts to complete the hairline. About one out of four patients who have plugs also have a strip graft.

The Procedure

The strip-graft procedure is similar to the punch-graft technique. A local anesthetic is injected into the donor site as well as the front part of the hairline. The bald area is cut out, creating a bed for the graft. The strip graft—approximately one-quarter inch wide—is then removed from the donor site and gently stitched into the bald area. The donor site is sutured closed, forming a fine, almost invisible line. The scalp is cleansed and a gauze dressing is applied, followed by a pressure bandage.

One or sometimes two strips are done per session. An additional graft or two to finish the hairline is often transplanted one to two months later. The entire procedure takes about one hour. Because the strip graft is so much larger than a plug, and because it takes some time for it to develop circulation of its own, a course of antibiotics will usually be prescribed to guard against infection.

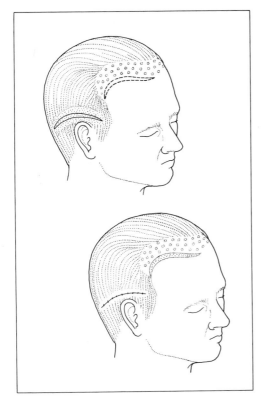

Long, thin strips of skin and hair can be used to complete the hairline. Here a strip graft is taken from the side of the head and transplanted to the hairline in front of the punch grafts.

Recovery

Your scalp will ache and your physician will prescribe pain medication for the first two days. The bandage is removed in about five days. Stitches come out within five to ten days. You can rinse your scalp after the bandage comes off, but avoid shampooing for a week to ten days. Follow your doctor's instructions for postoperative care until your scalp is fully healed.

Flaps

A dramatic result can often be achieved with another new hair-replacement procedure called flap surgery. In flap surgery, the hairline is restored in one step by rotating large sections of hair-bearing skin from the side or back of the head to the front. The difference between a flap and a strip graft is that a flap allows a larger segment of scalp to be moved, with a greater chance for survival, because it remains tethered to the donor site for circulation.

There are several types of flaps. The typical flap gives you a dense growth of hair measuring one to two inches wide and about five inches long, tapered at the ends. One flap spans half the hairline. A second flap, from the other side, spans the other half. A flap may be the best choice if hair in the donor sites is thin. A plug taken from a sparse donor site might have only five or six hairs, but a flap will provide an even covering of hair.

The Procedure

Flap surgery is often a hospital procedure, with antibiotics given to protect against infection. The surgeon injects anesthetic into the donor and the replacement site. The bald area is then cut out, and the flap of hair-bearing skin is loosened and lifted from your scalp, but left attached at one end.

The flap is then *rotated* to the front of the scalp and sewn into its new position. The "tether" that connects the flap to its orig-

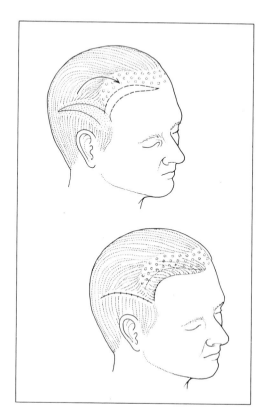

A hair-bearing flap of scalp lifted away from the side of the head remains tethered just above the ear. The flap is swiveled up and across the hairline, and sewn into place. Plugs can be used to fill in the area behind the flap if necessary. A second flap procedure is performed on the other side.

inal site contains an artery that provides a nourishing blood supply.

One problem with the flap technique is that hair growth is oriented upward, or away from the face. (The natural orientation of the hair is down, toward the face.) Nevertheless, if the flap is set into position properly, the hair will grow to the very edge of the incision and the scar will not be visible.

After the flap is positioned, the donor site is closed up. Your scalp is washed and a layer of gauze is placed over the incision sites, followed by a pressure bandage around your head. A flap procedure may take two or more hours to complete. Occasionally, an additional procedure may be needed before or after the main operation to prepare the skin or touch up the results; however, it is often a one-step surgery.

Recovery

The bandage will remain for at least five days; the stitches will be removed in about ten days. Your surgeon will probably want to see you several times during the first three weeks after surgery to make sure the flap is healing properly.

Scalp Reduction

Scalp reduction has become very popular because it also offers a dramatic result quickly. One scalp-reduction operation can take the place of one hundred plugs.

Scalp reduction is used on a bald crown. The surgeon first tests the scalp to determine the looseness of its skin. Generally, the older the man, the looser the skin. In young men, the scalp may be too tight for successful scalp reduction. Sometimes the skin-expansion technique is used before scalp reduction to increase the amount of skin that can be removed.

The Procedure

Your scalp is injected with local anesthetic. An ellipsis of bald skin, measuring approximately one to two inches wide by six to seven inches long, is then cut out of the scalp. This takes only a few minutes. The remaining scalp is loosened all the way to the sides of the head; the two sections are then brought together and sutured closed, leaving a thin line down the middle. You will feel a pulling sensation, but no pain. Your scalp is cleansed and gauze is placed over the sutures, followed by a pressure bandage.

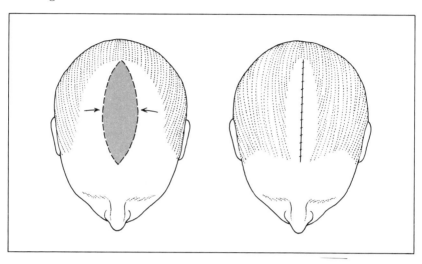

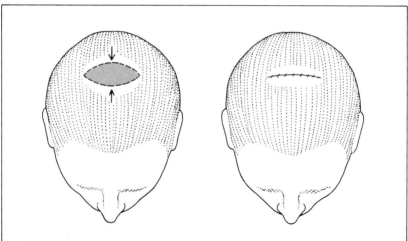

To quickly reduce large areas of baldness on the crown, a horizontal or vertical ellipsis of hairless skin is removed. The remaining scalp is loosened all the way to the sides of the head; then the two sections are brought together and sutured closed. The remaining baldness can then be filled in with plugs.

Scalp reduction does not raise your eyebrows or elevate your ears; nor will it preclude you from having other plastic surgery procedures, such as a facelift, in the future. If your bald spot is very wide, a series of scalp reductions can be done, with four to five months in-between each procedure. With three scalp reductions, for example, a bald crown that is four to five inches wide can be narrowed to less than one inch. The remaining baldness can then be filled in with plugs. The end result is a full, natural-looking head of hair.

Recovery

Your scalp will feel tight from the sutures, but you will have minimal pain because there are few nerve endings in the crown of your head. The scalp quickly reattaches to the skull.

You will probably visit your physician a few times in the first two weeks after the operation to make sure the incision is healing properly. The bandage can be removed in about five days; stitches usually come out in about ten days. The incision heals nicely if not too much skin is removed at one time. Two weeks after the operation, the scar will be hardly visible. Occasionally, the scar will widen because the scalp is tight. Again, the best hope for a good scar is a good surgeon who carefully evaluates the resiliency of your scalp before the operation. After two months, you can return for a follow-up visit, if necessary, and plan the next step.

PICKING UP YOUR LIFE AGAIN

Resuming normal activity after any hair-replacement procedure is a gradual process. Most men are ready to go back to work when the bandages are removed, usually in two to five days. You can resume your social life whenever you feel up to it, although most men prefer to wait another five to ten days, when all the stitches are removed.

Sexual activity will greatly increase blood flow to your scalp and bleeding around the donor or transplant site may result. In addition, a bump to your head during the healing period may dislodge the grafts or flap. Complications such as these could lead to larger scars or loss of the grafts, so it is best to avoid sex for at least ten days after surgery.

For the same reasons, exercise should be avoided for two to three weeks and contact sports for at least three weeks. Exercise stimulates blood flow to the scalp, which may lead to bleeding around the transplants. And there is always the possibility that the grafts or stitches will be damaged by a blow. So, take it easy when you resume your regular exercise and follow your surgeon's advice carefully.

TISSUE EXPANSION AND HAIR REPLACEMENT

A few plastic surgeons are using a new skin-expansion technique to take hair-replacement procedures one step further. Tissue expansion originally was developed to cover burn scars. By using a "balloon" that is placed under the skin and is gradually filled, normal, healthy tissue adjacent to a wound can be induced to grow. The scar, such as a burn scar, is then cut out and the new, expanded skin is stretched over the site and stitched into position.

To use this technique in hair replacement, a balloon is inserted under hair-bearing scalp on the sides of the head and gradually inflated with a saltwater solution. When the skin has been stretched enough, the adjacent bald area is removed and the expanded tissue is brought over to cover it.

The advantage of the skin-expansion technique is that a dramatic, natural-looking improvement is achieved and only two surgeries are required. The drawback is that it takes two months for the skin to expand enough to do the job. Not only does a man have to walk around with the gradually expanding balloon under his scalp for that length of time but he will have to visit his plastic surgeon once a week so the balloon can be filled with the saline solution. For this reason, as well as the high cost (up to $5,000 or more), tissue expansion is not a popular option. However, when used, the results can be dramatic and very satisfying.

MINOXIDIL: TOPICAL AGENTS THAT GROW HAIR

Although hair-replacement surgery has come a long way, most plastic surgeons believe that the ultimate solution for hair loss will be a medical, rather than a surgical, treatment. Minoxidil, a drug originally developed to treat high blood pressure, is a step forward. Sold under the trade name of Rogaine, it has been tested in controlled studies conducted in dermatology clinics throughout the country on thousands of patients and has been shown to slow hair loss in 40 to 50 percent of young males who have recently lost hair. New growth appears in a small percentage of men.

Hair follicles must still be alive for minoxidil to work. It has no effect when hair loss is severe and long established: Once dead, hair follicles cannot regenerate. The best candidate is a young man who has recently lost hair. The rate at which he loses his hair should slow down with minoxidil therapy, but he will have to use the topical agent for the rest of his life. Once minoxidil is stopped, hair loss resumes.

Widely advertised tonics and conditioners that allegedly grow hair or prevent loss are the oldest scams in the business. To date, minoxidil is the only medical treatment that has been shown to have any effect on hair growth.

No one knows why minoxidil, which dilates the blood vessels, works to slow down hair loss. Some say that increased circulation to the scalp is the reason. However, since loss of circulation does not cause baldness, increased blood flow is unlikely to be the cure. Further, the diluted form of minoxidil used on the scalp does not penetrate the skin deeply enough to affect circulation. Others believe that minoxidil may have some direct effect on hair follicles.

The full answer to minoxidil is still to come. The search continues for better drugs that might work for everyone. The final solution to baldness may eventually lie in gene research.

PART IV

RECONTOURING
THE BODY

17

Body Contouring

BEFORE THE MODERN SURGICAL ERA BEGAN IN THE 1890S, CHANGES
in body shape were attempted with external methods. Depending on the fashions of the time, girdles and other tight bindings
were used to cinch waists and bosoms, shoulder pads were employed to dramatize the shoulders, and bustles were attached to
accentuate the bottom.

However, at the turn of the century, surgeons first began to
cut out excess skin and fat at the same time that they repaired
hernias. This technique eventually developed into the modern
abdominoplasty or tummy tuck.

Until very recently, there was no way to surgically alter body
shape without creating massive scars. In the last ten years, however, a new technique called liposuction has been developed to
remove fat without making large incisions (see chapter 23). A
long, narrow tube called a cannula is inserted through a small
stablike incision. The cannula is attached to a machine similar
to a vacuum cleaner and fat is literally sucked out of the body.
Originally, liposuction was limited to the outer thighs (saddlebags), buttocks, and abdomen, but today the technique may be
used for many types of body contouring.

No one has yet devised a way to surgically make you taller or shorter, but almost anything else can be done. Body contouring is achieved in one of four ways: surgical reduction, in which excess fat and skin is cut out; liposuction; a combination of the two; or the insertion of implants to enlarge or emphasize.

Which technique is selected depends on the nature of the problem being corrected and the condition of your skin. Skin that has lost its elasticity will be unable to "bounce back" if the underlying fat is removed by suction alone; surgical removal of sagging folds of skin may be required.

Your physical self-image is an important consideration when it comes to having an operation that changes the size and shape of your body. After surgery, your body will look different; this shape is likely to require an emotional adjustment.

In particular, many women who have had breast reduction or reconstruction describe feeling anxious or upset after surgery. The uneasiness persists until they have incorporated their new size and shape as part of their body image. It may take six months or longer to get used to being a different size and shape. It helps to be aware of this, to realize that it is a natural reaction to change, and to remember that in time it will pass.

Considering
Cosmetic Surgery
on the Breasts

THE BREAST CONSISTS OF THREE PARTS: THE INNER CUSHION OF milk-producing glands and fatty tissue, an outer envelope of skin, and the nipple/areola. However, this clinical description doesn't begin to define the infinite varieties of breast shape and size; nor does it capture the complex relationship between a woman and the most visible symbol of her femininity.

Breasts begin to develop during puberty in response to a flood of estrogen from the ovaries. The inside of the breast is composed of fifteen to twenty lobes of milk-secreting glands embedded in fatty tissue. The glands have their outlet in the nipple, which is surrounded by the areola, a circular area of pigmented skin. Although the breasts rest atop the pectoral muscle that crosses the chest, they contain no muscle themselves. Fine ligaments attached to the skin weave between the fat and glands to determine the breasts' height, shape, and projection.

All women have approximately the same amount of glandular tissue in their breasts. It is most concentrated beneath the nipple, but a portion swings up and under the arm. The amount of fatty tissue that accumulates during puberty, however, varies widely depending primarily on the response of each woman's body to estrogen. Sometimes the breasts respond very little and the amount of fatty tissue remains small; other times the breasts are overly sensitive to the hormone and an excessive accumulation of fat forms. The degree to which breast tissue reacts to hormones is an inherited trait. The fact that the amount of fatty tissue primarily determines breast size explains why size is not related to sexual responsiveness or to the amount of milk produced after a woman gives birth.

There is also a wide variation in the shape and position of the breasts and nipples. Breasts may be positioned high or low on the chest wall. These also are characteristics that may be passed down by either parent. All configurations are normal and none affect the function or responsiveness of the breasts.

Breast growth is often erratic during puberty. Rapid growth may be followed by a period when no change is evident. Sometimes one breast grows faster than the other. For most women the breasts eventually become similar in size, although they are seldom identical. In rare instances, only one breast develops fully. A woman may choose to have the underdeveloped breast surgically enlarged with an implant after she reaches full maturity. (Sometimes, the reverse occurs and one breast overdevelops, requiring reduction.) During childbearing, a woman's breasts swell and often sag, particularly if they're large to begin with. After birth, when a woman is no longer nursing, the breasts may shrink again, but still sag. In this case, a lift might be helpful or, if the woman liked her new size during pregnancy, enlargement may be favored.

Occasionally a woman or a man may be born with extra nipples. Other mammals are always born with two parallel rows of nipples. Since humans usually produce only one baby at a time, our bodies have efficiently reduced the number of nipples to two. However, we still have a pair of milk lines running from the underarms, down the chest, and into the groin. One or more extra nipples occasionally appear along these lines, usually as a result of an inherited trait. Sometimes the extra nipple is no more than a small mole, but if the growth is pronounced, it can be surgically removed.

Today, there are a range of surgical options for women unhappy with their breasts, including breast lift (mastopexy), enlargement, reduction, and reconstruction. The most common and simplest procedure is enlargement (augmentation). At the opposite end, reduction surgery is lengthy and complicated. However, perhaps more than any other, this procedure satisfies its recipients, who may be in physical agony because of large, pendulous breasts. (Men also can benefit from breast reduction surgery: It is estimated that 40 percent to 60 percent of men have overly developed breasts and there are procedures available for them.)

The consultation for breast surgery is as vital as the operation itself. You want to make sure that you and your surgeon are on the same wavelength. When it comes to body shape—particularly breast size and shape—different people have decidedly different perceptions of what they consider large, small, beautiful, or sagging. This is as true of surgeons as it is of patients.

The initial portion of the consultation should be spent just talking things over. Tell your surgeon what you consider troublesome and the degree to which you would like it corrected. Then listen to your physician's view of your problem and what he believes can be accomplished with surgery.

A good rapport is especially important for the physical examination that always accompanies a consultation for breast surgery. Perhaps more than any other type of plastic surgery, breast procedures require a bond of trust and understanding between surgeon and patient.

Most plastic surgeons prefer that the husbands or life partners of prospective patients also attend the consultation. Both you and your mate must understand the benefits and risks of the operation. If your spouse is against surgery, let your doctor know ahead of time; no physician wants to be caught in the middle of a marital battle. If your partner is adamantly opposed to the operation that you adamantly want, there may be some underlying problem with your relationship that needs to be talked out between the two of you before you proceed.

The flip side of this coin is when a woman's partner wants her to have her breasts changed in some way, but she is ambivalent. If you are considering breast surgery, be certain that *you* personally want it and that you're not doing it to satisfy someone else.

Above all, make sure you understand the procedure and have realistic expectations about the results. Some patients don't clearly understand just how extensive scarring may be following some types of breast surgery. Not every plastic surgeon shows photographs of postsurgical results, because no two operations are alike and it is impossible to give every woman the same outcome. However, when it comes to breast operations, it may be a good idea to ask to see some of your surgeon's "after" pictures to give you a more realistic idea of the kind of scars that will accompany the procedure you have chosen. Some women decide that the trade-off isn't worth it. Others think it over, opt for surgery, and are usually happy with the results because they are well prepared.

It is virtually impossible for a plastic surgeon to make both breasts identical. Perhaps one breast is small, pointed, and droopy, while the other is large; or the nipples and areolas may be different sizes. It is possible to make the breasts more similar, but they will never be exactly the same. If you want perfectly matched breasts, you may never be satisfied with breast surgery.

Surgery to increase or reduce breast size requires you to adapt to a new body image. This is something you have to experience; you really cannot work it out ahead of time. However, it helps if you can anticipate this and allow yourself time to get used to your new body. The next four chapters describe in detail the four breast procedures: enlargement, lift, reduction, and reconstruction.

```
┌─────────────┐
│ ┌─────────┐ │
│ │   19    │ │
│ └─────────┘ │
└─────────────┘
```

Breast Enlargement

ALTHOUGH IT'S EASIER TO DISGUISE SMALL BREASTS THAN OVERLY large ones, being small-breasted is quite traumatic for some women. For example, one young woman had never worn a bathing suit or gone swimming until after she had her breasts enlarged (called augmentation mammaplasty).

Not every woman who chooses augmentation is completely flat-chested. Some have small or average-sized breasts and choose augmentation because they want to be a little (or a lot) bigger than they are. Often, small-bosomed women experience having larger breasts for the first time during pregnancy and want to keep that fullness permanently. Still others lose some of their natural breast volume after pregnancy and simply seek to regain their former size.

Augmentation is the second most popular cosmetic procedure for women after liposuction, yet the procedure remains somewhat controversial. Doctors continue to debate implant types and where these should be placed in the chest. Consumers worry that the implants could cause cancer or arthritislike diseases.

Like every other plastic surgery procedure, breast augmentation involves trade-offs. On the plus side, you will have larger breasts that often look natural and feel soft, that allow you to

---

As this book was going to press, the FDA called for a moratorium on the sale and use of silicone gel–filled breast implants pending further review by the Agency of the safety of these devices. In light of this development, any person considering breast implants should discuss the contents of this chapter with his or her physician.

wear a wider variety of fashionable clothes, and that enhance your self-image. On the down side, there is a chance that your breasts may begin to feel unnaturally firm and there may be a change in the sensitivity of your nipples and breast skin. In addition, when your breasts are examined by x-ray as part of your regular health-maintenance program, you will require the services of a radiologist with the special skills needed to examine augmented breasts. Even with this special care, tissue may not be seen clearly when examined for cancer. (For this reason, a woman who has a personal or family history of breast cancer may want to carefully consider whether implants are worth any extra risk.) However, the FDA has found no evidence that the silicone in implants increases a woman's risk of developing breast cancer, nor is there any conclusive evidence that implants can cause arthritislike diseases such as scleroderma (see "Implants and Health Problems").

Despite the potential for problems, the vast majority of women who choose augmentation say they are happy with the results. In fact, in the first national study of 592 breast implant patients conducted in 1990, 95 percent of the women who had had augmentation said they were satisfied with the results. The same number said they would definitely or probably choose surgery again.

Augmentation will increase your breasts by one or more cup sizes. The basic shape of your breasts will not change, although augmented breasts are slightly lifted. Almost all implants retain their size over time, so even if your breast tissue shrinks somewhat following menopause, pregnancy, or weight loss, your breasts will always appear larger than they were before surgery.

As breast tissue sags with age, the implant may remain in its original position, while the breast tissue and nipple droop. If this is severe enough to be bothersome, it can be surgically corrected with a breast lift.

THE CONSULTATION

Be candid about your expectations. Sometimes the biggest disagreement women have with their plastic surgeons centers on the size of the implants used. Doctors would rather discuss options with you before surgery—obtaining an understanding of what you hope for and giving you a clear picture of what can be achieved—than have you be unhappy with the results. Some doctors may ask you to bring in a photograph of a woman with breasts you like, as long as you understand that a perfect match is impossible. If your doctor feels that your breasts sag too much, he may suggest a breast lift in conjunction with augmentation. Be aware, however, that a lift is a completely different procedure, with different trade-offs involved (see chapter 20).

Thoroughly discuss the different types of implants and surgical techniques available. There are three main choices that must be made: the kind of implant used, the location of the incisions, and the placement of the implant. Plastic surgeons are constantly conducting research to determine the most effective combination, but to date there is no one right way to do the operation. Each has its own advantages and disadvantages.

IMPLANTS: THE OPTIONS

There is no perfect implant. The search continues for an implant that is safe, is easy to insert, will hold its position, and feels soft and natural over the long term.

The most common implant problem is a condition called capsular contracture. A capsule of scar tissue forms around any object implanted in the body—a natural reaction that helps keep the device in place. In some women, this capsule contracts, squeezing the implant until the breast feels unnaturally firm. This can occur immediately following surgery or years later. It can affect both breasts or just one, and can vary from slight firmness to being quite hard and uncomfortable.

Physicians aren't sure why capsular contracture affects some breasts and not others, but some types of implants appear to minimize the problem. (Varying the placement of the implant may also reduce capsular contracture. See the later discussion of this issue under "Troubleshooting.")

Types of Implants

The outer envelope of all implants is made of silicone rubber and the devices are filled with silicone gel, salt water, or a combination of the two. In addition, new, alternative filler materials are being developed.

Traditional implants have a smooth outer surface, but the newest types have textured surfaces, created by roughening or otherwise altering the silicone casing, or by covering it with polyurethane foam. Textured implants are believed by many to reduce the incidence of capsular contracture, but statistics are still being collected and experience has varied from surgeon to surgeon.

The "fuzzy," polyurethane-surfaced implant—which as of this writing is no longer available—has the longest track record of the textured types and has been shown to reduce the incidence of capsular contracture to 5 percent or less, although no one knows for certain why this benefit occurs. It may be because the body's tissues grow into the porous foam and form a firm bond. Other research theorizes that as the foam gradually dissolves, a chemical reaction occurs that keeps the surrounding tissue soft. However, some physicians feel that this apparent tendency of the polyurethane foam to dissolve is also its greatest disadvantage. (See "Implants and Health Problems.")

The most common implant in use today—introduced more than twenty-five years ago and still popular—uses silicone gel (which feels like soft gelatin, very similar to breast tissue) as the filler. If the outer shell should ever break, the thick gel usually remains within the capsule of scar tissue, causing little or no change in breast shape.

Surgeons may use two other types of breast implants: the inflatable, saltwater type and the double-lumen, combination variety. The inflatable implant is a silicone-rubber balloon that is filled at the time of surgery with a saltwater solution, similar to the body's natural fluids. This allows your surgeon to adjust the size of the implant, depending on what looks best in you.

The biggest drawback of this type of implant in the past has been leakage. Although small folds in the covering or normal wear-and-tear can sometimes cause a small hole in any type of breast implant, silicone gel will usually remain in place. In contrast, salt water will spill out and the body rapidly absorbs it. While this is harmless, the breast will lose its added size within hours. The implant must then be replaced. (It is very unusual for a blow or other trauma to cause the implant to rupture.) Users of modern saline implants report a deflation rate of about 1 percent. Some women also say that saltwater implants do not feel as much like natural breast tissue as those with silicone gel do.

The double-lumen implant attempts to combine the best characteristics of silicone gel and saline: It consists of a balloon within a balloon, with the outer sac containing a small amount of salt water and the inner sac filled with silicone gel. (A "reverse" double-lumen has the gel in the outer sac.) This permits slight size adjustment during surgery, but if the saline envelope leaks, the amount of fluid lost is so small that the breast "deflates" only slightly. Whether this type of implant actually provides better protection against leakage is not yet known. New implants continue to be researched, developed, and tested. The goal is to develop an implant that does not cause capsular contracture, that is easy to see through on a mammogram, and that offers an alternative to silicone gel.

Fat Transplants

Enlarging breasts using your own body fat—suctioned from one part of your body (usually the abdomen or thighs) and injected into your breasts—has been tried. However, after extensive study of fat transplants used in various parts of the body, the ASPRS Ad Hoc Committee on New Procedures was unanimous in warning against the use of fat injections for breast augmentation. Much of the injected fat dies, leaving scar tissue and calcification. These irregularities may mask the presence of early breast cancer, or—at the other extreme—mimic the disease and result in unnecessary breast biopsies.

COSTS

Surgical fees range from $1,000 to $5,500, depending to some extent on the type of implant selected. Additional fees may be charged for the operating room and anesthesia. *(Note:* Although such practices are not encouraged by the ASPRS, most insurance carriers will not pay for treatment needed to correct complications that occur after breast implants are inserted. Check with your plan to be sure.)

THE PROCEDURE

The method of inserting and positioning the breast implants are two other important choices that must be made. To insert the implant, your surgeon makes an incision either in the armpit (axilla), in the crease where the breast meets the chest, or around the lower or upper half of the areola.

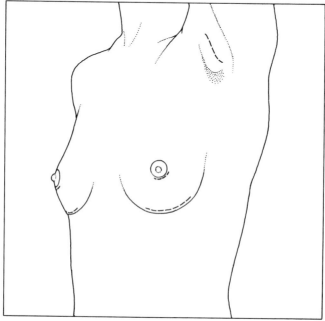

An incision is made in the crease of the breast where it meets the chest, around the border of the areola, or in the armpit.

An armpit incision reduces the risk of losing nipple sensation and hides the scar. However, because this incision is furthest from the breast, a surgeon may have trouble manipulating the implant into position, sometimes leaving it too high in the chest. Surgical skill is extremely important in this case.

Polyurethane or other types of textured implants are not used with an armpit incision because their roughened surface makes it almost impossible to slide them down through the breast tissue.

Breast-crease incisions are the most common and offer the surgeon more options in terms of implant types and positioning. Although scars in this location can be up to two and a half inches long, they are hard to see when you're standing. An incision just under or over the areola is also frequently used. In this case, the scar usually blends in well with the areola if the pigmented skin is dark.

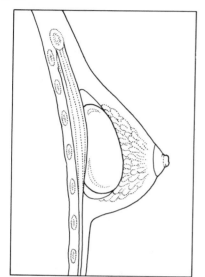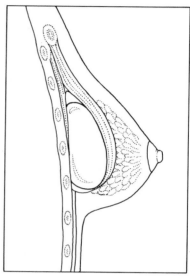

Implants are positioned directly behind the breast tissue (LEFT) or underneath the chest muscle.

Once inserted, implants are centered beneath your nipples, either directly behind the soft breast tissue or underneath the chest muscle. Placement behind the muscle may reduce the occurrence of capsular contracture; there is also some evidence that this positioning enhances the ability to examine the breasts for cancer using mammography. However, some plastic surgeons feel it requires more postoperative discomfort for the patient and does not produce as good a cosmetic result; specifically, when you exercise, the muscles will flex over the implants and make them more visible. In addition, if you exercise heavily it's possible for the implant to be pushed out of position. Should that occur, it can't be corrected without another operation to reposition the implant.

Discuss all of these options during your consultation. Ask more questions later if necessary. It's important for you to fully understand what's involved and the results you can expect.

IMPLANTS AND HEALTH PROBLEMS

SILICONE

Over time, all silicone breast implants leak or "bleed" minute amounts of the substance into the surrounding capsule of scar tissue—an amount estimated at less than a few drops. Even smaller traces are thought to move to other parts of the body, where they are picked up by scavenger white blood cells and filtered by the lymph glands in the armpits. Concerns have been raised about two potential health problems:

Cancer. Most scientists believe there is no evidence of any causal relationship between silicone breast implants and cancer. Pacemakers and artificial joints are made from silicone, and diabetics use silicone-tipped needles because they slide into the skin easily.

Controversy occurred when a study of rats injected with the silicone gel showed a 25 percent incidence of fibrosarcoma, a rare cancer of the connective tissue. However, the ASPRS points out that the strains of laboratory mice and rats used in the study are known to develop this disease in response to almost *any* type of smooth implant, including cellophane, metals, and various plastics.

Meanwhile, a study of more than 3,000 breast augmentation patients whose implants have been in place an average of eleven years indicates that the incidence of breast cancer is no greater than in women who do not have implants. A more comprehensive study is now being conducted to provide more conclusive evidence of whether or not a link exists between cancer and breast implants.

Connective-Tissue Disorders. In a small number of instances, breast-implant patients have exhibited symptoms suggesting an allergic sensitivity or a disease of the immune system such as scleroderma and other arthritislike conditions. It is not known whether these reactions were triggered by the implants. True allergic reactions to implants are unusual.

Autoimmune diseases occur when your immune system, which attacks foreign elements in the body, begins to work against your own tissues. This reaction is not fully understood, but it's thought that bacteria, viruses, and drugs may play a role in triggering an autoimmune process in someone who already has a genetic predisposition to it.

There are a wide variety of autoimmune disorders, but the ones charged with being triggered by silicone are called connective-tissue disorders. Connective tissue is an essential component of every body structure. Its major ingredient is a protein called collagen. If the connective tissue becomes inflamed, virtually all body systems can be affected, including joints, bones, cartilage, and skin. Scleroderma—a hardening and thickening of the skin and internal organs—is an autoimmune disorder caused by excessive fibrous-tissue growth. Scleroderma occurs most frequently in Japan, where liquid injectable silicone is still used in large quantities for procedures such as breast augmentations. Liquid silicone is chemically different than gel; further, because it is not held by a capsule of scar tissue it is free to move into other areas of the body.

Most scientists say there is no clear link between silicone breast implants and the onset of connective-tissue disorders, nor is it known how much silicone would have to leak from the implants to affect the immune system. Further studies are being conducted.

POLYURETHANE

Recently, the "fuzzy" polyurethane implants have been the center of attention from the FDA. Concerns have been raised that the gradual breakdown of the foam covering the implant over time may produce a compound called 2,4-diaminotoluene (TDA) that has caused liver cancer in laboratory animals. However, as of this writing, the FDA has said that if the polyurethane foam coating were to break down in the body at the same rate as in laboratory experiments, the lifetime cancer risk for a woman with two implants would probably be less than one in a million, assuming she had the implants in place for thirty-five years. If the polyurethane were to *completely* break down—which is unlikely to occur—the risk would be about one in twelve thousand.

As of this writing, the manufacturer has withdrawn the implant from the market. According to the FDA, the cancer risk is too small to warrant advising women who have them to remove the implants. In fact, the agency has said that the risk of removal could outweigh the risk of keeping the implant. Ask your plastic surgeon about the current status of this implant.

Most surgeons perform the operation in their in-office facilities, a freestanding surgery center, or a hospital outpatient facility. You may also choose to have the surgery performed as a hospital inpatient, in which case you can expect to stay for one or two days.

Surgery usually takes one to two hours. Breast enlargement may be performed under general anesthesia or, more commonly, local anesthesia with sedation. After the initial incision is made, the tissues are separated to create a pocket for the implant. This may be rinsed with an antibiotic solution to reduce the risk of infection. Some surgeons tilt the surgical table to observe the position of the breasts.

The implant is placed in position and multiple layers of sutures are used to close the incisions. Your surgeon may then tape the incisions to give them support. Finally, a gauze bandage may be applied over the breasts and you may be dressed in a surgical bra.

BREAST IMPLANTS AND STEROIDS

Steroids have received a lot of bad press in conjunction with their use by athletes, but a different form of these compounds may have a role in breast-implant surgery. Here, too, their use is controversial.

Steroids are used to improve the appearance and feel of implanted breasts. Some physicians put steroids in or around the implants during surgery to reduce the likelihood of capsular contracture. Because steroids are antiinflammatory, they may inhibit the growth of scar tissue and keep the implant feeling soft. Although the steroids disappear from the body in six months to a year, the scar tissue has been made less "contracted," so the effects of steroids may be considered permanent.

However, steroids may also suppress the immune system, slow the healing process, and soften tissue, increasing the chance that breasts will sag. Although advocates say these dangers are minimal if the quantity of steroids used is minute and carefully controlled, other physicians are waiting for long-term proof of their safety. Discuss this option with your physician.

Recovery

Immediate postoperative discomfort is easily controlled with medication. Pain usually subsides within a day or two. In a few days the gauze dressing, if you have one, will be replaced with a surgical bra. The bra helps relieve soreness and aching, and you'll want to wear it twenty-four hours a day for about two to four weeks. A few women experience an intense burning sensation in their nipples for about two weeks, but this subsides as bruising fades.

You'll probably feel like moving around after forty-eight hours or so. You can bathe, but some surgeons may want you to avoid wetting the stitches. In about a week, you should be able to bathe and shower normally.

The sutures are removed about a week after surgery, but your breasts will be swollen and appear overly large for another couple of weeks. Each breast may heal at varying rates. After six weeks, most of the swelling should be gone from both breasts. Your scars will be firm and pink for at least six weeks; after that time, they may remain the same size or widen. After six months, the scars will begin to fade.

You may be able to return to work after a week; however, if you have had general anesthesia, you may want to allow yourself two weeks at home. Wait about two weeks to resume an active social life and wait a month before dancing.

Your breasts will be sensitive to stimulation for two weeks or so, so you should avoid sexual arousal. After that, gentle sex without breast contact is all right, until your breasts no longer feel sore (usually another two to four weeks).

For the first six months after surgery, your physician may recommend daily breast massage to promote softness, as well as exercise such as swimming, rowing, or light weight lifting. This will revitalize your chest muscles. Carefully follow your plastic surgeon's instructions for the best way to get back into shape following breast surgery.

Troubleshooting: What Can Go Wrong

Breast enlargement is a relatively straightforward operation, but it can cause some significant complications. It's estimated that one out of every five patients will require additional surgery for reasons as diverse as capsular contracture, asymmetry, infection, bleeding, or implant rupture.

Capsular Contracture. As mentioned earlier, capsular contracture is the most common problem. This condition may occur to a noticeable degree (moderately firm to hard) in about one out of every eleven implanted women. Its frequency varies widely, depending on the type of implant used, where it is placed in the chest, and other unknown factors. Some surgeons believe that regular breast massage helps prevent capsular contracture.

Many women who have this condition aren't bothered by the firmness in their breasts, whereas others find it uncomfortable and unattractive. You may feel the implant when you hug someone, you may have difficulty sleeping on your stomach, or you may find that your arm movements are restricted.

Although doctors don't know what causes capsular contracture, there are three theories: Some believe the scar tissue may contract because of undetected internal bleeding. Others say it could result from infection. Finally, it is speculated that tight scar tissue may be caused when minute amounts of silicone leak out of the implant and into the surrounding membrane. Since doctors don't know *why* it happens, they can't predict *who* is likely to develop capsular contracture.

Capsular contracture can be treated in several ways. Your surgeon may perform a closed capsulotomy, in which the breast is squeezed vigorously to break up the underlying scar tissue. It's like popping the clear plastic bubble wrap used to pack fragile purchases. However, closed capsulotomy is not always successful or may be only partially effective. Occasionally, it can cause bruising, bleeding, or implant rupture.

Another common treatment for capsular contracture is an "open" capsulotomy, in which the surgeon reopens the incision and cuts into the capsule to relieve pressure. Less often, the implant and surrounding scar tissue are removed. This can be a painstaking procedure, particularly if a polyurethane-covered implant has been used. A new implant can then be inserted, but the same problem may recur.

Infection. A less frequent complication is infection around the implant, estimated to occur in less than 1 percent of cases. (Infection, should it arise, usually occurs between seventy-two hours and two weeks postop; rarely infection arises months or years after the implants are in place.) The implant usually must be removed and the pocket cleaned out. Sometimes it is also necessary to remove the capsule of scar tissue. When the infection has cleared, and about three to six months have been allowed for the tissue to completely heal, a new implant can be inserted.

Other Problems. As with any operation, bleeding, fluid collection, excess scar tissue, or difficulties with anesthesia can occur. Fortunately, such complications are uncommon. Although they may need treatment, they are rarely severe enough to require even temporary removal of the implant. If you develop a collection of blood under the skin (hematoma), your surgeon will drain it. Untreated hematomas result in capsular contracture.

It is also possible for your nipples to become oversensitive, undersensitive, or even numb. You may notice small patches of numbness near the incision site as well. However, these symptoms usually disappear with time.

Infrequently, an implant is damaged from a sharp blow to the chest or it leaks for no apparent reason. The result of a breakage or leak depends on the type of implant. The capsule of tissue surrounding a gel-filled implant will usually keep the gel contained. You may not even know the implant is damaged. If a break is discovered, your physician will probably recommend replacing the implant. (Symptoms *may* be a breast that feels suddenly softer or you may feel a small lump away from the implant.) If the capsule of tissue is also torn, the gel may spread into other areas such as the armpit or stomach wall. Although it can leave some unsightly lumps that are hard to remove, there is no conclusive evidence that the loose silicone is a health risk.

However, these lumps or "granulomas," which are formed when droplets of silicone are surrounded by cells in the body, can make it difficult to differentiate them from other masses in the breast. As a result, your doctor may recommend a surgical exam, or biopsy, to rule out cancer.

If a saline-filled implant leaks or breaks, your body will easily and safely absorb the salt water within a few hours. Your breast will lose its added size and the implant must be replaced. In a double-lumen implant, a leak or break in the saline portion of the balloon will have little noticeable effect. Nevertheless, your physician may suggest replacement.

BREAST-FEEDING

There is no evidence that implants affect fertility or pregnancy, the ability to nurse is unpredictable with or without implants. Many women have successfully nursed after their breasts have been enlarged and there is no evidence that implants have any effect.

Current studies also suggest that you do not have to worry about silicone seeping into your milk, since the implant is placed *behind* your breast tissue. The ASPRS says that even if silicone was found in breast milk, it is generally considered safe and points out that it is added to many nonprescription medicines pediatricians recommend for infants.

If you nursed a baby less than one year before augmentation, lactation may occur for a few days after surgery. This may be painful, but can be treated with medication.

CANCER DETECTION AFTER IMPLANTS

One of the greatest concerns of women and their doctors is whether implants make it more difficult to detect breast cancer in its critical early stages. One in nine women develops breast cancer. This statistic is the same whether or not a woman has breast implants. To detect cancer early, women with implants should follow these three steps:

Self-Examination. All women over the age of twenty should examine their breasts monthly. After augmentation, self-examination is particularly important so that you can familiarize yourself with the new shape and feel of your breasts. If you notice any unusual lump or other change, contact your physician immediately.

Physician Examination. Your breasts should be evaluated by your personal doctor during regular, annual examinations. For a doctor experienced in examining implanted breasts, conducting an accurate evaluation should not be a problem. However, if anything abnormal is noticed, consult your plastic surgeon as well before proceeding with a biopsy. Breast implants may develop folds or "knuckles" in their coverings and harmless little lumps called granulomas may form nearby. They can cause confusion or unnecessary concern when felt by a physician who is inexperienced in this type of exam.

Mammography. All women should have a baseline mammogram (breast x-ray) between the ages of thirty-five and forty, as well as one every year or two between forty and fifty. After age fifty, mammograms should be performed annually. (Women who have an increased risk of breast cancer should follow a special schedule set up by their physicians.)

Once implants are in place, mammograms may be more difficult to read, depending on the size and fat content of your breasts, the extent of capsular contracture, and whether the implants are placed behind or in front of the chest muscle.

Skilled radiologists and technicians have learned special techniques for examining augmented women. It is helpful to have a mammogram before your operation; after surgery, consult a radiologist who has been recommended by your plastic surgeon and has the special skill needed for proper pictures of augmented breasts. He or she can use a special technique to push the implants back against the chest wall while pulling breast tissue forward. Additional x-rays may also be taken from different angles. These procedures may cost more, but routine mammograms may be unreliable for augmented breasts.

SATISFACTION

Breast enlargement is permanent, unless the implants have to be removed for reasons described earlier. Many of the first recipients of silicone implants remain satisfied with the results after more than twenty-five years. However, although plastic surgeons say they hear few complaints, they also admit that it's difficult to follow up with augmentation patients. Many are young women who change their residence as they marry or progress in their careers. Others don't return to their plastic surgeon for their breast exams. It's also possible that some women who experience complications feel embarrassed for having had "frivolous" surgery and hesitate to come forward to express concerns. This difficulty in accurately tracking patients' problems may be alleviated by the Safe Devices Act of 1990, which requires manufacturers and distributors of such devices as pacemakers, heart valves, and also breast implants to monitor and report related deaths and injuries.

Nevertheless, published studies and anecdotal evidence indicate that the vast majority of women with implants are happy with the results of their surgery and would do it over again.

Breast Lift

A BREAST "LIFT," OR MASTOPEXY, IS NOT A SIMPLE OPERATION. SAG-ging breasts are probably the most common breast "deformity" among women, yet mastopexy—a removal of excess skin akin to putting darts in a dress—is not as popular as other breast pro-cedures because even today's modern techniques leave notice-able scars for what may be a temporary result. Sooner or later, gravity prevails and breasts may begin to sag again. For women whose breasts are very heavy, the sagging may begin soon after the operation. To offset this, in women whose breasts are also smaller than desired, implants are often inserted during the lift procedure for better, longer-lasting projection.

BEST CANDIDATES

A mastopexy is often sought by women who have had children, since pregnancy and nursing leave a stretched outer skin enve-lope with less volume inside. (However, if you plan to become pregnant again, it's best to postpone surgery.)

The best candidates for mastopexy are women with small, sagging breasts, especially since they're also likely candidates for implants. However, breasts of any size can be lifted.

THE CONSULTATION

Your surgeon will examine and measure your breasts while you are sitting or standing (never when you're lying down). In a mastopexy, the nipple and areola will be moved higher. Generally, your nipples should rest about eight and one-half to ten inches below the notch in your collarbone, roughly even with the crease beneath your breasts. Let your surgeon know exactly what results you would like to see. Moving the nipple again later would cause additional scarring—you want to get it right the first time.

COSTS

The surgeon's fee for mastopexy ranges from $1,000 to about $6,000 or more, with additional costs depending on the type of facility used for the operation and the kind of anesthesia used.

Insurance carriers usually will not pay for a breast lift, except in very unusual circumstances. Occasionally extreme breast sagging can cause serious irritation or infection in the breast crease. In that case, insurance might cover the operation. Check with your insurance company beforehand. Your physician will have to document your case.

THE PROCEDURE

Mastopexy is often performed on an outpatient basis in a hospital, a freestanding surgical center, or a surgeon's in-office facility. It may also be performed as an inpatient hospital procedure, in which case you should expect to stay one to two days.

The operation takes one and a half to three and a half hours. Mastopexy may be performed using local anesthesia plus sedation, or general anesthesia.

During the operation, the plastic surgeon usually makes an anchor-shaped incision that encircles the areola and extends downward to the crease below the breast. Excess skin above and

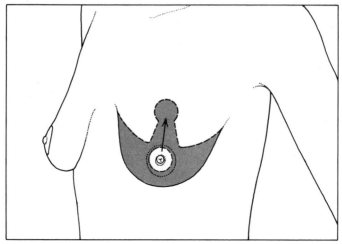

Incisions are made that outline the area from which skin will be removed, as well as the new position for the nipple. Breast skin in the shaded area is removed and the nipple is moved to a higher position.

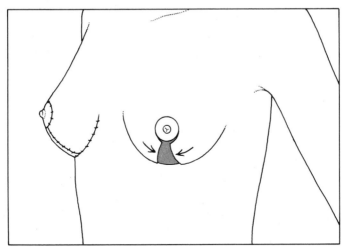

The skin formerly located above the nipple is brought down and together to reshape the breast (right side of illustration). Sutures close the incisions, restoring breast contour (left side of illustration).

next to the nipple is removed, and the nipple and areola are moved to a higher spot. The skin surrounding the areola is brought down and together to reshape the breast, and stitched into place. The surgeon may work on one breast at a time, or both simultaneously to ensure a more even match.

In most cases, you will have stitches around the areola, in a vertical line extending down the breast, and along the lower fold. However, in some cases, techniques can be used to eliminate the vertical part of the scar.

If an implant is used, it will be placed in a pocket beneath the breast tissue or under the muscle of the chest wall. Some doctors favor implants with textured surfaces because they believe this helps the devices stay firmly in position. (For a complete discussion of implants see chapter 19.)

RECOVERY

Expect considerable bruising following surgery. Your breasts also will be swollen and uncomfortable for a day or two, but pain is not severe. Wear a support bra around the clock to support your breasts for three to four weeks, along with a layer of gauze to protect your stitches from rubbing. If you have had a lift *without* implants, you shouldn't need a bigger bra size.

Surgery can leave breast skin excessively dry and you may want to apply a light moisturizer several times a day. Be careful to avoid pulling at your skin and don't apply lotions to the area near the stitches or to the sutures themselves.

Expect some loss of sensation in the nipples and breast skin, caused by postsurgical swelling. Although this numbness generally fades as swelling subsides, it may be permanent in some areas. Your stitches are removed after one or two weeks.

Avoid lifting anything over your head for three to four weeks. Your physician will give you detailed instructions for resuming normal activities. In general, don't plan to return to work for at least a week and be prepared to allow yourself more time if you need it. You may resume sports and other strenuous activities after about four weeks, but start slowly.

Avoid sex for at least a week. (Sexual arousal can cause incisions to swell and breasts to ache.) In a week or two, you may gently resume sex if you keep your bra on and avoid breast contact. After a month you can have sex with your bra off. Your breasts may be somewhat less—or more—responsive to sexual stimulation for several months after surgery.

Bleeding and infection rarely follow a breast lift. Should infection occur, however, it may cause scars to widen. Don't underestimate the scarring left by a traditional breast lift. The keyhole-shaped scar may be lumpy and red for months and may take a year or longer to fade. Your scars can be covered with a bra or bathing suit. Most doctors try to place scars so you can wear low-cut tops.

Mastopexy should not affect your ability to breast-feed, since the milk ducts and nipple are left intact.

SATISFACTION

Women who have implants along with mastopexy may find that the lift lasts longer, since the increased projection is permanent. Otherwise, the length of time your lift will last depends on the variables of pregnancy, weight fluctuation, and gravity.

Women whose breasts droop only slightly usually feel that the scars from a breast lift aren't worth the improvement gained. Women who have severely sagging breasts are usually quite satisfied with the operation, even though it leaves visible scars. For many women the scars fade to thin white lines. Lois, age thirty-two, had long, pendulous breasts that sagged almost to her navel. Having her breasts lifted gave Lois a whole new image of her body. Her comment: "I wish I had had it done years ago."

Breast Reduction

BREAST REDUCTION—CALLED REDUCTION MAMMAPLASTY—REMOVES fat and glandular tissue from oversized breasts and sometimes reduces the size of the areola, the dark area around the nipple. Breast reduction is designed for women with excessively large breasts, which often cause medical problems like back pain, skeletal deformities, breathing difficulties, skin irritation, restricted motion, and numbness in the hands. Many women with oversized breasts also develop indentations in their shoulders where their bra straps press into their flesh. For these reasons, breast reduction is usually considered a reconstructive procedure.

Overly large breasts may cause emotional problems for young women. For example, psychologists believe that it is more emotionally charged to have big breasts than to have a nose that isn't quite what you want. Excessive breast development usually begins at age ten or eleven, a time when a girl is especially self-conscious about her body. Developing enormous breasts at such a young age can cause severe emotional distress. Those who continue to feel self-conscious about their breasts after they grow up often choose to have them surgically reduced.

Women who seek reduction usually have extremely large, pendulous breasts that cause considerable physical discomfort and functional problems, as well as embarrassment. Most will say they want reduction for physical relief rather than for cosmetic improvement.

BEST CANDIDATES

Breast reduction can be performed at any age after puberty. The best candidates are those who have a clear understanding of the procedure and what results can be expected.

In breast reduction, the degree of scarring is unpredictable and it may take a year or more for scars to fade. However, if a woman is well-informed, if her surgeon has shown her photos of the usually expected results, and if reduction will provide physical relief, she is likely to be very happy with breast-reduction surgery.

THE CONSULTATION

The surgeon will perform a breast examination. You should discuss both the potential positive and negative effects of reduction surgery. After breast reduction, you may lose sensation in your nipples and breast skin. Because both glandular and fatty tissue are removed, you probably will be unable to breast-feed. Your scar, which is similar to the anchor-shape mark left by a breast lift, is permanent and may vary from being relatively inconspicuous to very prominent depending on how your tissues respond to surgery. On the plus side, the physical discomfort caused by overly large breasts will disappear. Your body will look more in proportion and your clothes will fit better. Women often buy dresses for the first time (instead of separately sized sportswear), wear a bathing suit without embarrassment, and participate in sports comfortably.

COSTS

Surgical fees range from $1,500 to $8,000, with additional costs for the hospital and services of an anesthesiologist. Insurance companies will pay for this procedure, since it is often performed to correct physical and health problems. However, others refuse to pay, or pay only if the doctor removes at least 500 grams (about one pound) of tissue. Be sure to check before you undergo the surgery.

BEFORE SURGERY

If you are overweight, try dieting before surgery. This enables the surgeon to best judge the extent of the surgical correction needed. Smokers should plan to stop one to two weeks before and after surgery.

If you take birth-control pills, hormone replacement therapy, or any other medication that affects blood coagulation, you may be asked to discontinue taking it for six weeks to three months before surgery.

Reduction mammaplasty usually does not require a blood transfusion. However, discuss this with your physician. If he feels it would be in your best interests, it is advised to have a unit of your own blood taken well in advance of your surgery, then held for your use.

Before surgery, your doctor measures and marks your breasts to determine where the nipple and areola will be placed. This is an important step in which you should participate, since moving a nipple later is difficult and creates more scars. Your nipples should fall about eight and a half to ten inches below the notch in your collarbone, level with your breast crease. Marks are made while you sit or stand, never when you're lying down. Placement should be discussed well in advance of surgery, although you will not actually be marked until just before the operation.

THE PROCEDURE

The operation usually takes place in a hospital; you may stay two to three days. Breast reduction can take from two to five or six hours to complete depending on the size of your breasts and the method used. Breast reduction is performed under general anesthesia.

Your surgeon will work on one breast at a time. Typically, he creates a key-hole–shaped cut that circles the areola and extends down to the crease so that the nipple can be moved into its new position. In most cases, the nipple remains attached to its blood vessels and nerves. Occasionally, however, a woman's breasts are so large or pendulous that her nipples and areolas must be completely removed and grafted into a higher position.

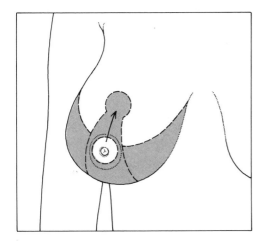

To reduce oversized, heavy breasts, incisions are made that outline the area of skin to be removed and the new location of the nipple. Breast tissue, fat, and skin in the shaded area are removed, and the nipple is relocated to a higher position.

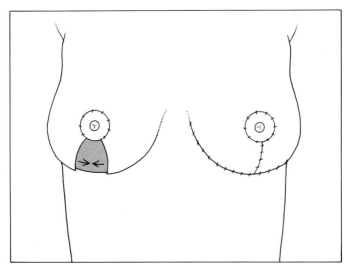

Skin formerly located above the nipple is brought down and together to reshape the breast (left side of illustration). Sutures close the incisions, leaving scars that are concealed by a bra or bathing suit (right side of illustration).

Excess glandular tissue, skin, and fat are cut away from around the areola and from the sides and bottom of the breast. The plastic surgeon then uses single stitches to "tack" the nipple and areola into their new location and to pull together the skin below. Liposuction is sometimes also used to remove excess fat from the armpit area.

When the surgeon is satisfied with the new shape and size of the breast he will close the incisions with stitches that surround the areola, come down in a straight line, and follow the curve of the breast crease. When both breasts are complete, the incisions will be bandaged and you will be dressed in a surgical bra.

In some cases, techniques can be used to eliminate the vertical party of the anchor-shaped scar. In a few cases, when a woman's nipples are already at a "normal" level and her breasts are composed of a high percentage of fat, liposuction alone can be used to reduce breast size. In this instance, scarring is minimized.

RECOVERY

You will feel pain for the first twenty-four to forty-eight hours after reduction surgery and you may find it difficult to move; even sitting up or coughing may make your chest hurt. Some discomfort may continue for several days after that. Medication will be prescribed to lessen discomfort for the next ten days.

After ten days or so the pain should lessen, although your breasts may start to ache by the end of the day. You may bathe or shower after the first week, but at all other times you must wear a bra to protect your breasts and the dressing over your stitches. After several weeks, when the swelling and bruising subside, you will no longer have to wear a bra around the clock.

Stitches are removed in one to three weeks. Your first menstruation following surgery may cause your breasts to hurt because the hormonal stimulation will cause them to swell, pulling on the incisions. You may also experience numbness in your breasts and random, shooting pains for several months. Don't buy a complete set of new bras until the swelling in your breasts has subsided, about six weeks after surgery.

When to resume your normal routine depends on how you feel and how quickly you heal. Your surgeon will explain how and when to begin stretching exercises. Avoid excessive movement immediately after surgery and don't do any overhead lifting for three to four weeks.

Most women can resume work, social activities, and some

exercise in about two weeks. At first, you'll notice a sharp decrease in your stamina. This is due to the combined effects of anesthesia, blood loss, and inactivity. Limit exertion to stretching and swimming until your energy level returns. Once vigorous exercise is resumed (no sooner than three weeks after surgery), be sure to wear a good athletic bra for support.

Since sexual arousal can cause incisions to swell and can make your breasts ache, avoid sex for about three weeks. After that time, you can have sex if you are careful to prevent contact with your breasts; after six weeks, depending on your comfort level, your regular sexual activities can be resumed.

TROUBLESHOOTING: WHAT CAN GO WRONG

Many women experience a loss in nipple sensation and breast sensitivity. This is usually temporary, but feeling may return so slowly that you begin to think sensation is permanently lost.

Don't count on being able to breast-feed. The odds are against it since milk ducts are usually damaged and some milk-producing glands are removed during surgery.

The area beneath your nipples will heal less rapidly than the rest of the breasts and you may develop small sores. These can be treated with antibiotics. The skin over your breasts will be unusually dry after surgery; you can use a light moisturizing cream to counteract this problem, but be sure to avoid the area of the stitches.

SCARS

Reduction surgery leaves prominent scars. They may remain red and lumpy for several weeks or they may begin to fade immediately. It usually takes a year to eighteen months for scars to fade to pale pink, brown, or white. They will be thickest in the creases beneath your breasts. On the plus side, you may find that when excess skin is removed, old stretch marks are eliminated.

SATISFACTION

Though reduction surgery is permanent, your breast size may still fluctuate in response to hormonal shifts, weight gain or loss, and pregnancy.

By and large, women who have had breast reduction are enormously relieved to be free of the physical and emotional discomfort of having too-large breasts. Nonetheless, adjustment after surgery is not always easy.

Of all plastic surgery operations, breast reduction results in the quickest body-image changes. Many women would like the change to go unnoticed by others. Chances are they have felt self-conscious about their breasts for most of their life and don't want any more attention drawn to them. However, the alteration in their body shape may be difficult for women to accept.

Psychologists conducting postsurgical interviews with breast-reduction patients have discovered that although all of the women were happy with the result, a significant percentage also experienced underlying emotional difficulties. Some felt depressed, experiencing a loss similar to that felt by mastectomy patients. After surgery, if they saw a woman with large breasts, they felt grief for loss of part of their body. It is also not uncommon for breast-reduction patients to fear that they've lost a characteristic that made them unique.

Still other women reported feeling a general uneasiness. One woman said that a few weeks after breast-reduction surgery she began to feel very anxious whenever she left the house. Had she turned off the stove? Was she wearing her new bra? She realized finally that she was uneasy because she was going out and she was a whole new size and shape. Some said they felt like they were going to fall over. They could see their toes for the first time since they were kids and couldn't get used to this new perspective. One woman feared that her nipples—which had been down at the bottom of her breasts and now were front and center—were going to fall off when she took a shower and go down the drain.

A few women feel no anxieties because they had never incorporated large breasts into their body image and smaller breasts are consistent with the way they have always viewed themselves.

BREAST REDUCTION IN MEN

Enlarged breasts are not a problem exclusive to women. A condition known as *gynecomastia* is characterized by womanly looking breasts in men. In fact, some estimates indicate that gynecomastia exists to some degree in 40 to 60 percent of men.

Liposuction or reduction surgery can create a flatter, more masculine chest. However, correction is often not recommended for teenage boys, since the problem may be caused by baby fat that will disappear on its own. Surgery also may not be appropriate for obese men or for those who drink heavily or smoke marijuana frequently. These drugs may *cause* gynecomastia and may also interfere with anesthesia and/or healing. Stopping the use of alcohol or marijuana may reverse breast development without surgery.

Breast reduction in men is often performed as an outpatient procedure in a hospital, a freestanding surgery center, or a physician's in-office operating facility. Small corrections can be done under local anesthesia plus sedation. More extensive surgery is usually done under general anesthesia. Costs run between $1,000 to $4,000 or more depending on the severity of the condition, and the type of surgery performed. The operation will take from one and a half to two hours.

Some physicians recommend that gynecomastia patients have their breasts x-rayed before surgery, since excess breast tissue may predispose men to developing cancer in that area. Sometimes gynecomastia is caused primarily by fat and can be corrected with liposuction alone. However, if glandular tissue must be removed, the surgeon makes an incision below the nipple and cuts away the excess. At this point, fat also may be suctioned out to further recontour the chest.

A drain may be inserted to draw off excess fluids, and the incisions are stitched closed and covered with a dressing. The chest will be wrapped with a bulky bandage to keep the skin firmly in place.

If a man is an outpatient, he may be able to go home within two hours after the operation, but will need to rest in bed. The chest will be sore, but not painful. If pain, fever, or swelling does occur, it may be a symptom of a problem such as bleeding, infection, or a troublesome dressing. Bleeding is the most common complication with this operation.

Men who have only a slight correction usually begin to feel

better after about five days. For older men, or for those who have had general anesthesia, it may take longer. The bandage is removed after a week and stitches are removed after eight to eleven days.

Most men return to work in seven to ten days, although they may still feel tired at the end of the day. Social engagements and walking as exercise usually can be resumed after ten to fourteen days. Sports, dancing, and other strenuous activities should be avoided for three to four weeks. The more the chest skin moves, the longer it will take to heal. Any activity that risks a blow to the chest should be avoided for at least a month. Sexual activities should be avoided for one week if surgery was minor and for at least two weeks if the procedure was more complicated.

A ridge may form under the chest skin at the outer edge of the treated area. Eventually, it will go away, but it may take as long as a year. The chest also may feel numb for almost a year after surgery, but this, too, disappears with time.

Scars trace the outer edge of the areola. If they pucker, they can be surgically improved about six months later. Avoid exposing the scar to sun for at least six months or use a strong sunblock. Sunlight can permanently affect the skin's pigmentation, causing it to turn dark or pink.

This operation is permanent and it's currently the only way to eliminate larger-than-normal breasts in men.

Breast
Reconstruction

Breast reconstruction is one of the most rewarding procedures in plastic surgery. Today, most cancer specialists agree
that every woman is a candidate for breast reconstruction after
mastectomy, regardless of the extent of her disease. This is a
fairly recent consensus. According to a survey conducted by the
ASPRS, since 1981 the number of mastectomy patients seeking
reconstruction has jumped by 114 percent.

At one time, doctors strove only to create a nonprosthetic
breast that looked normal under clothes. Now, new techniques
have enabled plastic surgeons to create a breast that comes close
to matching the opposite, natural one (if only one breast was
removed).

Cancer surgeons have become more supportive of this option
and often team up with plastic surgeons to achieve the best results. Experts now agree that in most cases, reconstruction does
not interfere with chemotherapy and other types of cancer treatment, or with the physician's ability to detect any recurrence of
the disease. Further, there is no evidence that breast reconstruction promotes cancer development.

It is estimated that about 38 percent of breast reconstructions
are performed when the mastectomy is done, rather than months

or years later, and that figure is expected to grow. Most patients are probably better off emotionally if they can have reconstruction immediately. It also eliminates the need for another major operation. However, some women don't feel comfortable weighing all the options while they are struggling to cope with the cancer diagnosis and prefer to postpone reconstruction.

Other women—more than one-half of all mastectomy patients—elect to forego reconstruction. Some women simply don't want to go through any further surgery; others harbor misconceptions about the risks involved. Still others are unaware of the options available to them or of the increasingly natural-looking results many surgeons are achieving. Even if your mastectomy was performed years ago, it is never too late to consult with a plastic surgeon. Just because a woman is older doesn't mean she doesn't care about her appearance; what's important is what matters to *her*.

Jane, a grandmother in her late sixties, had had a mastectomy ten years earlier. She thought she was now too old to have reconstruction. But then her daughter-in-law Beth also had to undergo mastectomy at age forty-nine. Beth elected to have reconstruction, which gave her a natural-looking breast. Beth was so happy with the results that Jane, with Beth's help and support, decided to have her breast reconstructed as well. The procedure she chose was relatively simple and Jane was glad that she made the choice.

WHEN TO HAVE RECONSTRUCTION

You can start talking about reconstruction with your doctor as soon as you're diagnosed with cancer. Your oncologist may recommend a plastic surgeon or you may select a plastic surgeon on your own. The ideal scenario, from your perspective, would be to have these two specialists working together to map out a mastectomy strategy that leaves your chest in the best possible condition for reconstruction. (However, keep in mind that this strategy may change once the mastectomy has begun, as your surgeon surveys the extent of the cancer.) Mastectomies are becoming less extensive and less complicated as time goes by.

Most mastectomy patients are eligible, medically speaking, for immediate reconstruction. The *best* candidate is one whose surgeon has every reason to believe the cancer will be completely eliminated by the mastectomy. (However, the need for further cancer therapy won't necessarily rule you out as a candidate.)

Women who have immediate reconstruction wake up with a breast mound already in place and never experience the shock of having no breast at all, nor do they go through as much of a grieving process. Studies at the National Cancer Institute found that these women were less anxious, less depressed, and less hostile. They were as happy with the results of their reconstruction as were the women who waited.

Still, there are legitimate reasons to wait. As mentioned earlier, getting a cancer diagnosis can be so devastating that some women do not want to think beyond their mastectomy. Some plastic surgeons feel they get a better cosmetic result if they wait, which may be particularly true if the breast is being rebuilt using flaps of skin, fat, and other tissue—a more complicated procedure. If prolonged radiation therapy is needed, doctors may prefer to postpone reconstruction for six months to a year, when the chest skin will be healthier. Finally, certain other health conditions may make you a less-than-ideal candidate for immediate reconstruction, such as obesity, high blood pressure, or smoking (especially after the age of sixty).

Regardless of when you decide to have reconstruction, knowing your options can help you go into mastectomy with a positive outlook for the future.

COSTS

The cost of breast reconstruction varies widely depending on the technique used. Expect to pay anywhere from $1,000 to $8,000 or more. Reconstruction using flaps—which are extensive, lengthy procedures—is the most expensive. Hospital fees and anesthesiology are extra. Most insurance companies will pay for breast reconstruction; however, have that confirmed in writing before your operation. Also check to see if your carrier has limits on what types of reconstruction it will cover.

THE PROCEDURES

Breast reconstruction usually involves more than one operation. The initial stage, in which the breast mound is created, usually takes place in a hospital under general anesthesia. One or two additional operations, such as surgery to replace a tissue expander with an implant (see below) or to reconstruct the nipple and areola, take place at a later date. These additional procedures can be done in the hospital, but may also be performed in your surgeon's in-office facility or other type of outpatient surgery center.

The length of the operation is dependent on the technique used. A flap procedure can take as long as eight hours. Nipple and areola reconstruction may take about an hour.

Depending on the type of procedure being performed, a local anesthesia plus sedation may be sufficient for breast reconstruction. General anesthesia is used if the procedure is extensive. Reconstruction using flaps is always done under general anesthesia.

Sixty-two percent of all breast reconstructions use a tissue expander to create additional skin, followed by insertion of a permanent implant. In another 17 percent of cases, enough healthy chest skin remains to allow creation of a breast mound using an implant, without stretching the tissue first with an expander. The final 21 percent represent a variety of reconstructive techniques, often using the body's own tissue (instead of an implant), commonly referred to as flap operations. The percentage of flap procedures is expected to grow as more and more plastic surgeons become familiar with the techniques.

Standard Reconstruction

Skin expansion is the most popular method for rebuilding a breast after a mastectomy. The plastic surgeon inserts a silicone-rubber balloon beneath your chest skin. The expander is attached to a tube that leads to a self-sealing valve buried in the skin, located near or in the armpit.

Over a period of several weeks, the physician injects saline solution through the valve to gradually fill the expander. This office procedure takes just minutes and is relatively painless, though you may feel some discomfort for a few hours afterward.

After the skin has stretched enough, the expander may be removed in a second operation and a permanent implant of the desired size inserted. The skin's natural elasticity causes it to contract sharply (from 30 to 50 percent) when the expander is removed; therefore, your doctor may overstretch the area or per-

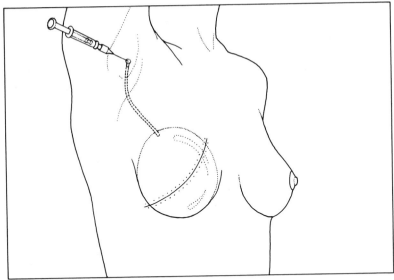

One of the most common uses for tissue expansion is to create new skin after mastectomy. Here a silicone balloon has been placed beneath the skin. The balloon is gradually filled with saltwater solution through a valve located just beneath the skin's surface. Alternatively, the salt water may be injected directly into the balloon.

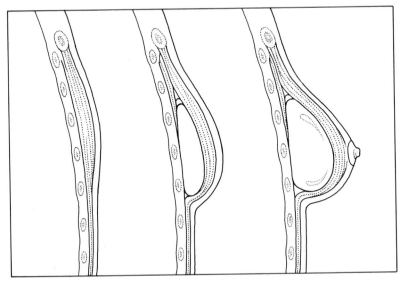

A cross-section of the breast shows the skin stretching as the balloon gradually expands. When the skin has expanded to the desired degree, the balloon is removed and an implant is inserted. Some types of expanders can be left in place as permanent implants. Reconstruction of the nipple (far right) occurs at a later stage in the process.

form a booster expansion when the final implant is inserted. A third procedure is required to rebuild the nipple and areola.

If the expander itself is to become the permanent implant, your surgeon will adjust the volume so that your breasts match as evenly as possible, remove the valve, and close the incision. Some surgeons are now using new directional expanders: Two separate balloons are inserted, with one pushing forward and one pushing down. Some believe the directional expanders create a more natural-looking breast and are especially good for patients who have little chest skin remaining after mastectomy.

Sometimes, if your cancer surgeon is able to leave an adequate supply of chest skin behind after mastectomy, your plastic surgeon may be able to skip the expansion process and immediately insert a permanent implant. The nipple and areola are then rebuilt in a second procedure.

Generally, implants used in reconstruction are larger than those used in breast augmentation, in order to compensate for the lack of supportive tissue. For reasons that are not yet understood, implants cause a higher percentage of capsular contracture (breasts that feel unnaturally firm) when they are used in reconstruction than when they are used for augmentation. (For more information on breast implants, see chapter 19.)

TISSUE EXPANSION

Tissue expansion "grows" skin that can be put to cosmetic and reconstructive use. Today it is used in plastic surgery procedures all over the body. Its most common use is for breast reconstruction. Skin expansion is also used in certain types of hair replacement and, by a few doctors, in certain facelifts and breast enlargements. Expansion can help repair injuries to the scalp, arms, and other areas of the body caused by tumors, radiation therapy, or accidents. Perhaps the most famous recent expansion patient was Jessica McClure, the child trapped in a well. Doctors used four expanders to stretch enough skin to close a two-and-one-half-inch gash in her forehead.

Tissue expansion is similar to the stretching of a woman's abdominal skin during pregnancy. A silicone-rubber balloon is inserted under the skin near the spot that needs repair and then gradually filled with a saltwater solution over a period of weeks or months. At first, the top layer of skin thickens and the underlying tissue thins. Fat and muscle also compress. Collagen, a connective tissue that gives structure to the skin, builds up, creating scar tissue that adds bulk to the area. Hair may become more sparse.

Once the skin has expanded to the desired degree and the expander is removed, these conditions naturally reverse themselves; however, some people will see small dents where the fat remains depressed. Hair follicles do not increase in number, but disperse themselves evenly over the skin surface. Muscles gradually regain their strength. Overall, slow expansion creates an increase in skin surface of up to 110 percent. The new skin is stretched over the defect and is then sutured into place.

Tissue expansion offers several advantages over skin grafts. First, expansion offers a near-perfect color and texture match. Second, because the skin remains connected to the donor area's blood and nerve supply, it retains all sensory capabilities and there is little risk that it will die. Because the skin is not moved from one site to another, there is less scarring.

Despite these advantages, skin expansion has significant drawbacks, chiefly the length of time it usually takes for skin to stretch sufficiently, which is anywhere from three to four months. At least two operations are needed: one to insert the expander and another to remove it. Also, expect repeated office visits for injections of saline to inflate the balloon. The worst part for most people is the temporary deformity created as the expander gradually puffs out like a balloon. While not much of a problem in breast reconstruction, it can be uncomfortable and embarrassing when the scalp, arm, or other areas of the body are involved.

Although your doctor can estimate how long expansion will take for you, it is impossible to specify the precise number of weeks required. Children and women tend to be more motivated and patient; men are far less so.

When only small amounts of extra skin are needed the tissue may be stretched quickly, in one session (intraoperative expansion). The surgeon inflates the expander until the skin is taut and white—about ten to fifteen minutes—and then deflates it. This may be repeated several times. Intraoperative expansion can create a 30 percent increase in skin surface.

Some plastic surgeons believe this rapid approach may prolong the effects of facelifts in patients over age sixty or in those who have sun-damaged skin. Once the facial skin is stretched using rapid expansion, these plastic surgeons say they can safely remove *more* of it (up to two inches instead of the standard one to one and a half inches) and the remaining skin drapes more easily. This keeps skin tauter longer, without creating unnatural tightness.

Skin expansion can be done on anyone, but works best on the very young and the very old—in other words, on those with very elastic or loose skin. Women have an advantage over men, whose skin is thicker and less supple. For the same reason, Caucasian skin tends to respond to tissue expansion better than Asian or black skin. Expansion doesn't work well on the back, torso, or other areas where skin is thick. If the affected area is severely damaged or scarred, skin expansion is probably not an option either.

Tissue expansion has a complication rate of about 1 percent. The greatest danger comes from exposure of the implant to bacteria or other contamination at the time of the operation.

Some patients also worry that the expander might explode, an extremely rare occurrence. However, an expander can occasionally pop through the skin if the tissue covering it is sparse and tight. As with all plastic surgery procedures, your best protection against complications is choosing a qualified, experienced plastic surgeon.

Flap Reconstruction

Flap procedures are far more complex operations, but many plastic surgeons think they give the most beautiful, natural-looking results. This technique rebuilds the breast with tissue taken from other parts of the body, such as the abdomen, buttocks, or back. Frequently, the donor tissue contains enough fat to provide filler for the new breast and an artificial implant is not necessary. (Although injections of liquefied fat are not safe, the fat in flaps of skin and muscle has a healthy blood supply and can therefore survive without causing problems.) However, flap procedures carry higher risks than simple implants; they leave more scars, and there's a risk of tissue loss in about 10 percent of the cases. If the transplanted tissue dies, it must be surgically replaced, subjecting patients to psychological loss all over again. (If you are not willing to stop smoking for at least two weeks before and after surgery, or you have high blood pressure or a disease like diabetes that affects blood flow to the chest, you cannot have a flap operation because of your body's inability to heal well.)

Flap surgery is performed using a pedicle flap (in which the donor tissue remains tethered to its original site, retaining its blood supply) or a free flap (in which skin, muscle, and arteries are completely detached and transplanted to the chest).

Pedicle Flap

A pedicle flap may be taken from the back or the abdomen. If from the back, a strip of skin and/or muscle is partially lifted, pushed underneath the skin of the armpit, and brought around to the chest. When this type of flap is used to rebuild the breast, however, an implant is usually needed as well.

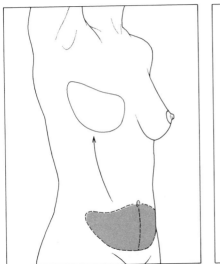 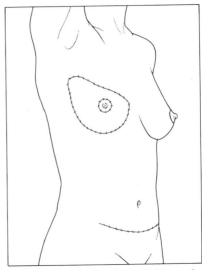

(LEFT) *In the pedicle-flap form of breast reconstruction, a piece of skin and fat is removed from an area such as the abdomen (shaded area). The flap is tunneled under the upper abdomen to the chest wall, creating a breast mound without an implant.*

(RIGHT) *The abdominal incision is closed and the flap is sutured into its new shape. The nipple and areola are reconstructed in a later procedure.*

The most innovative version of a pedicle flap is called the TRAM (transverse rectus abdominal muscle) flap, devised in the early 1980s and now performed by many skilled plastic surgeons around the United States. In this procedure, a large section of skin and muscle is partially separated from the lower or central abdomen, using half for filler and half to create the outside surface of the new breast. The flap remains attached to the abdomen, but it is artfully twisted and tunneled under the skin to the chest wall. Results from the TRAM flap are quite refined and predictable, and carry the added advantage of flattening a paunchy abdomen just as in a tummy tuck.

Some of the drawbacks of a TRAM flap include a large, low scar stretching from hip bone to hip bone; a hernia that may develop in the weakened abdominal wall; and loss of abdominal strength. You should also be aware that you are not a good candidate for a TRAM flap if you don't have excess skin in your abdomen, and that having one breast rebuilt with such a flap precludes the possibility of using the same technique for the other breast if needed.

Free Flap

This procedure must be performed by a plastic surgeon who is a microsurgeon as well, because the transplanted arteries and veins must be reconnected to their counterparts in the chest. A free flap often is taken from your abdomen; it may also come from your buttocks or thigh. Although the skin color and texture will be slightly different from the surrounding chest skin, the results are usually good. Compared to the pedicle TRAM flap, a free flap is less destructive to the muscle in the donor site and can provide a better blood supply to the reconstructed breast.

However, if the blood vessels are not reconnected properly, or if a problem develops later on, the entire flap may die and the breast will have to be rebuilt. That is why it is so important to choose a plastic surgeon who is skilled in microsurgery as well or who works in tandem with a microsurgeon.

Flaps are long, extensive operations with all the potential complications that any major surgery entails. However, the new breast may feel softer and more natural than a breast recon-structed with an implant. It may also have a more sculpted shape, since living tissue is flexible. Women who have had flap recon-structions are usually overjoyed with the result, even though they had to go through a lot to get it.

SURGERY ON THE NATURAL BREAST

Since most mastectomy patients are in their fifties or older, their breasts have begun to sag with age. A reconstructed breast is likely to be higher and firmer than the opposite, natural one (assuming only one breast was removed). Thus it's common for surgeons to enlarge, reduce, or lift the natural breast. This will be done in a later operation, after the reconstructed breast has had time to settle. It's important to be aware of this possibility from the beginning, since it may leave scars on the otherwise normal breast and may not be covered by insurance.

NIPPLE AND AREOLA RECONSTRUCTION

Nipple and areola reconstruction is an art that can dramatically improve the look of the new breast. It may take place six weeks to six months or more after the initial breast reconstruction depending on whether you've had any complications.

New nipples are made from tiny flaps of adjacent skin and fat. If you have a very large nipple on an opposite, natural breast, it may be possible to use a portion of it for the reconstruction. However, the donor nipple may be damaged in the process.

To create a new areola, the surgeon may use a skin graft from your inner thigh or remove a thin strip from the areola on your natural breast. If the latter option is chosen, the tissue to be transplanted can be removed at any time and preserved in a skin bank until you are ready for the final step of your breast reconstruction. This technique, called cryopreservation, saves tissue for two years or longer, as long as it is frozen within twelve to twenty-four hours after removal.

A new technique still under development involves a nipple implant, a silicone implant shaped exactly like a nipple and areola. It is believed that these implants soon will be available in various sizes, so that they will match the opposite nipple once inserted under the skin.

The biggest problem with nipple and areola reconstruction is creating a natural color. A skin graft turns white after a while. Some plastic surgeons tattoo the graft to match the other breast, but a totally natural-looking pigment has not yet been formulated. Other doctors forego nipple reconstruction altogether and simply tattoo the skin, but this can look a bit like a bull's-eye target.

If you have had a skin graft, it will be covered with a dressing and monitored for about seven days. If the graft dies, which occurs only rarely, it can be replaced. If no other surgery was performed at the same time, you should be able to go home the same day.

RECOVERY

Many variables affect recovery, including the extent of your surgery, your physical condition, and the impact of additional cancer treatments. Your plastic surgeon and cancer surgeon should review the recovery process with you thoroughly so you know what to expect.

You are sure to be tired and sore for several days or weeks after a reconstruction. Your incisions, covered with a dressing, require no special care. Stitches on your chest are removed after seven to ten days. Your only visible chest scar will be from the mastectomy, since the same incision is used for the reconstruction. However, if your breast was reconstructed with a flap, you will have a scar in the donor site as well.

The initial reconstruction operation takes the most out of you. It takes four to six weeks to recover from a combined mastectomy and reconstruction, or from a flap reconstruction alone. If implants are used without flaps, and if the reconstruction is done apart from the mastectomy, recovery may only take two to three weeks.

Don't plan on going to any parties for about a month after reconstruction. Follow your surgeon's advice about when to begin stretching exercises and when to resume sexual relations, sports, and other vigorous activities.

A second operation, to replace a tissue expander with a permanent implant or to reconstruct the nipple and areola, may only require recuperation of a week or less. Nipple reconstruction shouldn't slow you down for more than a few days, but if a skin graft was used the donor site will be tight and sore for about a week. Stitches are removed after a week or so.

It may take four to six weeks after a flap operation until you feel up to going back to work. You probably won't want to accept any party invitations either for at least two months. Your chest muscles will be quite sore and you may not have any sensation in your new breast. The area from which the flap was taken will also be sore; if the donor site was your abdomen, you may need to abstain from sexual relations for at least a month.

TROUBLESHOOTING: WHAT CAN GO WRONG

Potential complications following breast reconstruction are the same as with any major surgery. There may also be a difference in size between a reconstructed and natural breast. Postoperative bleeding sometimes occurs as well as infection, but that is rare. If an implant has been used, the scar tissue that forms around the device may squeeze tightly around it, causing a condition called capsular contracture that leaves the breast feeling unnaturally firm. (For more information on the treatment of this condition, see chapter 19.) If an infection develops around an implant, it will probably have to be removed while you undergo treatment with antibiotics. With flap procedures, there is roughly a 10 percent danger of tissue loss.

Women who postpone reconstruction may go through a period of emotional readjustment after receiving a new breast. Just as it took time to get used to loss of a breast following mastectomy, it will take some time before a woman begins to think of the reconstructed breast as her own. She may feel anxious during that period and may confuse her psychological distress with unhappiness about the operation. If this happens to you, be reassured that this period of confusion and anxiety is normal; it will pass within a few months as you get used to being a new size and shape.

SUCCESS

All breast reconstruction procedures offer permanent results. Though implants may change shape slightly over time, they won't lose their volume. (Contrary to common belief, leading cancer surgeons and plastic surgeons agree that mammography is usually not required for reconstructed breasts because so little of the natural breast tissue remains.) The advent of breast reconstruction has dramatically improved the quality of life for cancer patients. Today, virtually every woman who must lose her breast(s) to cancer can have it rebuilt.

23

Suction-Assisted Lipectomy (Liposuction)

THE GOOD NEWS IS THAT A LOW-FAT DIET AND REGULAR EXERCISE will keep you healthy, hearty, and fairly shapely. The bad news is that there are some localized fat deposits that no amount of aerobics or fasting can remove.

Fatty deposits are often the result of genetics and aging. As we grow older, body fat redistributes itself, muscle mass diminishes, and skin loses its elasticity. Unsightly accumulations of fat often collect in saddlebags, love handles, and double chins.

In the early 1980s, the French technique for suction-assisted lipectomy revolutionized the ability to recontour the body, proving to be safer and more effective than previous, cruder approaches. Also called liposuction, fat suction, or suction lipectomy, this procedure has been embraced by American plastic surgeons and their patients.

In less than a decade, suction lipectomy has become the most commonly performed cosmetic surgery procedure in America; certified plastic surgeons perform more than 100,000 procedures a year to remove unwanted fat from double chins, hips, thighs, abdomens, buttocks, and legs. About 10 percent of these operations are performed on men, usually under the chin or around the waist, and 12 percent are done on people over fifty.

Liposuction is becoming a common added feature in operations like facelifts, tummy tucks, and some breast reductions in men. It's rarer for suction lipectomy to be used on ankles or knees.

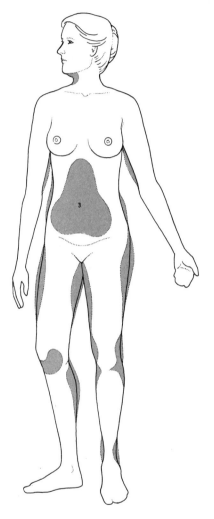

Liposuction can be used to remove fatty deposits from the chin, hips, thighs, stomach, ankles, and knees.

The results of liposuction are permanent—at least as long as a sensible diet and exercise program are followed. Some physicians believe that by the time we reach puberty the *number* of fat cells in the body is fixed, although they can and do *grow* larger if we overeat. However, there are studies that have contradicted this theory, suggesting that in some instances (such as when weight increases by 50 percent or more), the number of fat cells can increase later in life.

Fifty percent of our fat is tucked away deep within the body. The other half lies between muscle and skin. Suction lipectomy can remove up to 10 percent of this superficial fat. The basic procedure requires a small incision just big enough to allow entry of a hollow tube called a cannula. The cannula is attached to a machine that creates a high-powered vacuum. When the cannula is manipulated back and forth beneath the skin, fat is broken up and suctioned out.

The earliest liposuction procedures, performed in the 1970s, used very wide cannulas with low-intensity suction. Today's instruments come in a range of sizes and tend to be thinner. They are used in conjunction with a pump that's twice as powerful.

The total amount of fat that can be removed at one time is limited, so liposuction cannot be used as a substitute for weight control. It rarely produces a significant weight loss, nor is it used as a cure for obesity. Liposuction alone also will not improve the dimpled skin called cellulite. Cellulite forms when the skin thins and becomes less resilient with age. Since it can no longer hold down the small globules of fat that collect around the bands of connective tissue that run from the skin to the underlying muscles, the fat bulges out around these "anchoring points." It is thought that heredity, as well as the natural aging process, contribute to the development of this condition.

Many qualified plastic surgeons continue to think there is *no* satisfactory solution to cellulite. However, there are some who have developed techniques they think are promising. These techniques involve "disconnecting" the fibrous bands between skin and muscle, then injecting fat that has been removed from elsewhere in the body to smooth out the surface.

Most patients underestimate the trauma that fat suction can cause. It can produce severe complications when large areas of the body are suctioned at one time. Although serious problems occur in only about 1 percent of cases, illness and even death can result from excessive fluid loss, blood clots, or infection.

However, suction-assisted lipectomy is normally safe as long as patients are carefully selected, the operating facility is properly equipped, and the physician is adequately trained in both body contouring and general surgery (see chapter 2). Unfortunately, storefront liposuction centers abound, where the procedure may be performed by doctors inexperienced in managing complications. If you choose to have suction lipectomy done in an office or freestanding surgical facility, make certain that your doctor also has been given privileges to perform liposuction in an accredited hospital.

BEST CANDIDATES

The best candidates for suction lipectomy have pockets of fat concentrated in particular areas, as well as firm, elastic skin. More than any other factor, skin quality determines the success of the operation. Loose skin will not reshape to your body's new contours. The excess skin will then have to be cut away, sometimes leaving significant scars. Age is not a criterion so long as a person's skin is in good shape. Experienced plastic surgeons can evaluate skin elasticity by feeling, pinching, and looking at it.

Suction lipectomy is not advised for individuals with a history of significant health problems. For example, it is generally not an option if you have had recent surgery on the spot to be sculpted, if you have poor blood circulation in that area (such as phlebitis in your legs), or if you have heart or lung disease.

THE CONSULTATION

Your doctor will examine you to determine where your fat deposits lie. Most people fall into three main categories of body type: the tall, thin ectomorph; the more muscular mesomorph; and the endomorph whose fat is distributed throughout the body.

Most plastic surgeons don't recommend suction lipectomy for people who have excess fat all over the body and are considered obese. However, some leaders in this field believe that carefully controlled liposuction might be beneficial for obese people, with positive results encouraging them to begin a weight-loss program. This type of high-volume fat removal is done under strictly controlled conditions in a hospital; even so, it is risky and only a relatively small amount of fat is removed at any one time.

Your plastic surgeon should review the various body-contouring methods available. For some people, particularly those who have sagging skin, suction lipectomy alone is not the answer. For example, you may need an abdominoplasty, or tummy tuck, to remove excess skin as well as fat. Your surgeon should also explain the risks and limitations of suction lipectomy, so that your expectations do not exceed the possibilities.

COSTS

Surgical fees range from $500 to $5,000, depending on how much fat is suctioned and how many parts of your body are treated. Charges for the surgical facility and anesthesiologist, if needed, are extra.

Ask your surgeon beforehand if there is an additional charge for secondary touch-ups, if needed, or if they are included in the overall fee.

BEFORE SURGERY

If you smoke or take birth-control pills, hormone replacement therapy, or any other medication that affects blood coagulation, be certain to discuss this with your doctor. Smokers are encouraged to stop for one to two weeks before and after the operation.

If you opt to undergo body contouring below the neck, your body may be measured while you are in your bathing suit. This will allow your surgeon to determine where to place the incisions so the tiny half-inch scars will not show later.

For more extensive procedures, you will need to have blood drawn in advance of the operation. Generally, you will need a transfusion of one to two units of blood for every five pints of fat/fluid removed.

THE PROCEDURE

Depending on the extent of the procedure, liposuction is often performed in a surgeon's office, freestanding outpatient facility, or hospital. In most cases, no more than one and a half pints of fat and fluid are removed, and the procedure can be performed using local anesthesia and sedation. If your doctor plans to suction a large area or will be treating several sites, liposuction is usually done under general anesthesia. Suction lipectomy takes between one and two hours to perform, but varies with the amount of work being done.

The cannulas used on the face and neck are slender, whereas those used on the abdomen, hips, and thighs are much larger. Cannulas can range in size from one-eighth to three-eighths of an inch thick. Small, stablike incisions allow insertion of the cannula. The number of incisions used depends on how accessible the fat is, how much is being removed, and the size of the cannula.

The surgeon manipulates the cannula back and forth to free your skin from the underlying tissue and to loosen the fat cells, creating tunnels that radiate out like a spoke. Although the tissue contains nerves and blood vessels, the blunt-tipped cannula pushes them aside.

A vacuum pump attached to the cannula pulls out the fat through the tunnels. Suction lipectomy is considered a "blind" procedure because most of the work is performed out of direct sight. That's one important reason why liposuction should only be performed by an experienced surgeon. It is essential to stop suctioning when more blood than fat comes through the tube. A new, computerized device is now available to measure the quantities of fat and blood as they're removed, but most experienced plastic surgeons feel that such devices cannot replace their eyes, their instinct, and their experience.

When used on the lower body—the thighs, hips, and buttocks—suction lipectomy can be a very strenuous procedure. It requires force to push the cannula back and forth through fat and other tissues. (In men, the fat tends to be denser, and more than one procedure may be required to achieve the desired result.) The surgeon moves the cannula from site to site until the excess fat has been removed. In brief, some of the areas on which suction lipectomy is commonly used are described below.

Neck and Face

Excellent results can be achieved on the neck and under the chin; recovery time is fast, making this a common site for suction lipectomy. Incisions are made on either side of the jaw and sometimes under the chin. For chubby cheeks, incisions are made at the temples, below the earlobes, or just inside the nostrils. A very thin cannula is used for these facial procedures.

Suction lipectomy may be used alone on the chin or cheeks,

but more commonly it is performed in conjunction with a face-lift. Liposuction allows the surgeon to create a smoother, cleaner contour than he could by simply removing excess skin. It also may reduce the number of incisions needed and therefore the number of scars.

Abdomen

Fat suction is often done in conjunction with a tummy tuck (see chapter 25). However, in individuals with firm skin and excess fat below the navel, liposuction may be all that's needed. Incisions are made around the navel and/or just above the pubic triangle.

Suction lipectomy can also be used to reduce a "spare tire" or eliminate the "love handles" that many men develop above their hips. Small incisions are made just above the buttocks or on the sides.

Buttocks, Hips, and Thighs

These areas may be suctioned individually or in combination. "Saddlebags," as well as indentations just below the hips, are common reasons for performing suction lipectomy, especially

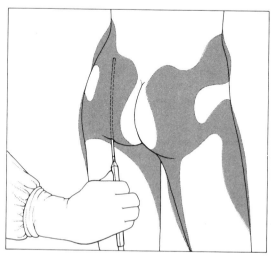

Short incisions are made in the skin through which the cannula is inserted to remove fat in the shaded areas. The cannula is a long hollow tube with an opening at one end that is tunneled through the fat to break it up. At the tube's opposite end, a vacuum pressure unit suctions off fat.

in women. The crease just under the buttocks is another area that people often wish to have suctioned.

Incisions may be made on the lower half or in the crease of the buttocks, on the hips, alongside the pubic area, or inside the thigh.

Knees, Calves, and Ankles

Fatty deposits around the knees can be readily suctioned, although the little scars will be visible. Suction lipectomy also can be helpful when reconstructing injured knees, since suctioning away extra fat allows a clearer field of vision and speeds healing. Incisions are made in the back of the knee, just above and below the center.

In the calves, the incision is also made behind the knee. Since the blood supply to the legs is poor, each calf may be done in two stages starting with the sides, leaving a center strip that is suctioned several months later.

Ankles are the most difficult site to suction since there's very little margin for error. Your surgeon will press on your ankles to see if fatty deposits are really the problem or if the fullness is caused by fluid buildup. If your skin springs back immediately after being pressed, there's fat below. If it remains indented, it's fluid. Incisions are made near the Achilles tendon.

Replacing Body Fluids

During suction lipectomy, it's crucial to replace lost body fluids. You will be given fluids intravenously, up to three times the amount lost through liposuction. This keeps the body from going into shock. You may also receive blood transfusions (usually using blood you donated yourself, in advance). Some surgeons administer intravenous alcohol as well, which they believe may help prevent clots of fat from forming.

Liposuction itself is not usually painful. However, if local anesthesia has been used, you will feel some vibration and friction during the procedure, and possibly a stinging sensation as the cannula moves closer to the muscle near the conclusion of the operation. Typically, the surgeon works on one side of the body at a time. Later in the operation, resuctioning may be done to create a more even match.

A single suture usually will close each incision. A drainage tube is sometimes inserted beneath your skin for twenty-four to seventy-two hours to prevent fluids from collecting. A snug elastic dressing is placed over the treated area to encourage the skin to shrink back against the underlying tissue, to prevent bleeding, and to control swelling. Many surgeons use an elastic girdle or long-legged body stocking when liposuction is done on the lower body. The garment or dressing chosen should provide uniform, steady compression. You should expect to wear this compression garment around the clock for several weeks, then during just the daytime hours for a few more weeks, depending on your surgeon's instructions. You usually will be given infection-fighting antibiotics for a short while following surgery.

RECOVERY

Don't expect instant gratification from suction lipectomy. Suction is trauma to the body tissues and you will look much worse before you start looking better. The suctioned areas will be swollen and heavily bruised. Contrary to what you might expect, you actually will weigh *more* right after surgery, thanks to the increased fluid pumped into your system.

When the anesthesia wears off, you may feel a burning sensation in the suctioned area. Your surgeon will prescribe narcotics for the first day and milder pain medication for subsequent days.

Any significant pain should ease after one or two days, but for three to four days after surgery the area will remain stiff and sore. If you had suction lipectomy on the thighs, buttocks, or hips, you may be uncomfortable for several days when sitting, standing, and lying down. If you were hospitalized for the procedure and have no complications, expect to be released within two to three days. The incisions themselves do not need any special care.

When suction is performed on the lower body, surgeons advocate a speedy return to normal activity and work. Begin walking as soon as possible. Sitting still with your feet hanging down allows fluid to collect, increasing the chances of clot formation.

You'll be most comfortable in loose clothing until the swelling subsides. Although walking and moving around is good for you, avoid strenuous activities for two to four weeks. Stitches will be removed after seven to ten days.

You may return to work after one or two weeks, depending on your strength and how the anesthesia affects you. You will tire quickly and your legs may swell if contouring was done on your lower body. After the second or third week, you can resume your social life, but avoid dancing.

Wait about two weeks before resuming low-intensity exercises like stretching. Swimming is excellent, but avoid aerobics, dancing, and other strenuous activities for about a month. Sex will probably be uncomfortable; wait two weeks or longer before resuming your usual sexual activity.

TROUBLESHOOTING: WHAT CAN GO WRONG

Complications fall into two categories: medical problems and variations from ideal results. True complications of a serious nature have occurred in a relatively small percentage of patients.

Medical Complications

Clots. The majority of serious complications involve clots (emboli) of blood or fat that block the flow of blood to the heart, brain, or lungs. Clots are more likely to develop following suction lipectomy on the lower body, particularly if you remain immobile for too long.

Clots cannot be absolutely prevented, but plastic surgeons take every known precaution to reduce the incidence. Your doctor will probably give you a compression garment to wear and suggest that you begin walking a day after the operation. Some surgeons also advocate intravenous alcohol.

Infection. Infection is rare if your surgeon is a highly skilled practitioner working in a sterile environment, but it rises dramatically if suction is poorly performed. Infections are treated with antibiotics, drainage, and the use of plenty of intravenous fluids to flush out your system.

Fluid Accumulation. Excess blood and fluid in the suctioned area can be drained with a needle in the doctor's office. The risk of excess fluid increases if you do not wear your compression bandage or if you do not get enough rest.

Skin Loss. The shedding of skin is uncommon, but it can occur if too much fat is suctioned off. Risk of skin loss increases if suction lipectomy is done in conjunction with surgery that creates and lifts a skin flap (such as abdominoplasty). Smokers also run a greater risk of skin loss because of their reduced blood circulation in the suctioned area.

Shock. Because fat has a plentiful blood supply, you can go into shock if too much fat is removed without a transfusion. This is a real risk when large areas are suctioned, but completely avoidable if your surgeon understands the techniques of fluid replacement.

Perforation. It's rare for a skilled surgeon to perforate one of your organs. Suction lipectomy can be a rough technique; the cannula must be pushed through the fat with force. If a surgeon doesn't have a good feel for the instrument and the technique, it's possible for him to push too hard and perforate an organ or the surface of the skin.

Minor Side Effects

Pain. Chronic pain is unusual, but as mentioned, you may experience a burning sensation in the skin around the suctioned area for up to a month after surgery.

Swelling. When fat is removed, the space left below your skin fills with fluid. The elastic dressing you are usually asked to wear helps to minimize this normal swelling. The swelling usually subsides after six to eight weeks, but it can last as long as three months in the torso and six months in the lower body.

Bleeding. The elastic bandage also helps lessen bleeding, although your incisions may seep slightly. If you develop little collections of blood under the skin, don't worry. These tiny hematomas are unavoidable and dissolve by themselves. However, if your incisions break open and a lot of bleeding occurs, call your surgeon immediately.

Numbness. You may temporarily lose all feeling in the suctioned area. Sensation will eventually come back.

Cosmetic Problems

Waviness. The skin over the suctioned sites may appear rippled like a washboard. Rippling may be caused by suctioning too close to the skin's surface, particularly in the lower legs where fat layers are thinner. Skin is less likely to ripple if the surgeon removes the fat from deeper layers, leaving a cushion just under the surface. The use of smaller cannulas is cutting down instances of wavy skin, but not eliminating them. Waviness may also appear as a delayed reaction as you grow older. This is a wild card that no doctor can reasonably predict.

Spotty Pigmentation. Suction lipectomy irritates the skin. It can cause brown discoloration, most often on the inner thighs and ankles. Sun exposure can "fix" pigmentation and it will be permanent. Avoid the sun until all discoloration fades.

Bagginess. The skin may appear baggy if the volume of fat removed exceeds the capacity of your skin to contract. No doctor removes *all* the fat from any area and most err on the side of caution, since once fat is removed, it's gone for good. Doctors can remedy bagginess by injecting fat from other parts of the body into the needy site. However, this is only a temporary solution. Most of the injected fat dies or is reabsorbed by the body and eventually the correction will have to be repeated. Cutting away baggy skin is an option, but this will leave scars.

Asymmetry. Suction lipectomy is imprecise and it is impossible to perfectly match both sides of the body. Since swelling sets in immediately, it may be impossible for your doctor to spot a problem during the operation. Months later, if a discrepancy becomes obvious, the area can be resuctioned, usually as an outpatient procedure using a local anesthetic. It is estimated that additional suctioning is necessary in 5 to 20 percent of cases. You may have to pay for this, but the cost is much less than the original suctioning.

SCARS

Scars are small—between one-fourth and one-half of an inch—and are strategically placed (in the navel, groin, or at the bottom of the buttocks). Usually pink or brown in color, scars vary from person to person. They fade, but never disappear. Most people can wear even a scanty bathing suit without their being visible.

SUCCESS

The results of fat suctioning are generally permanent. It is still possible to gain weight again in the suctioned areas, but these areas will remain proportionally smaller than they were previously. Remember, however, there's no accounting for the way your body will redistribute or eliminate other fatty deposits over time.

Liposuction is a powerful plastic surgery technique. It gives plastic surgeons the freedom to go beyond surface skin removal and recontour the body without leaving significant scars. In practiced hands, the results are excellent and patient satisfaction is high.

Body Lifts

LIFTS TRIM EXCESS FAT AND SKIN FROM THE ARMS, THIGHS, BUT-
tocks, and abdomen. They also leave long, visible scars. Since
suction lipectomy leaves barely perceptible scars, lifts are becoming less popular.

However, certain problems cannot be fixed without a lift. For
example, aging can cause skin to sag on the lower abdomen,
buttocks, upper arms, and inner thighs. Sometimes baggy skin
is left behind after large fat deposits are removed with liposuction or after a lot of weight is lost. The only way to correct this
problem is to trim off the excess skin.

ARM LIFT

An arm lift, or brachioplasty, tightens skin on the upper arms.
Women who have had a mastectomy are usually not good candidates for an arm lift, since their lymph glands may have been
injured and permanent, severe swelling could result.

In about half the cases, arm lifts are done on an outpatient
basis, under local anesthesia plus sedation. The procedure takes

about two hours; results are permanent. The surgical fee ranges from $1,000 to $6,500.

The Procedure

The surgeon may first suction fat from the area, then cut away excess skin. Some physicians prefer to remove fat and skin with the scalpel in one maneuver. Either way, the incision is made inside your arm, from armpit to inner elbow. It may be straight or slightly S-shaped.

Care is taken to avoid deeper layers of fat to protect nerves, veins, and other delicate structures. The goal is to improve contour without damage. The incisions are closed in three layers: a deep layer of stitches that eventually dissolves, a midlayer of strong sutures that actually close the incision, and a delicate superficial layer to create a thin scar. The stitches are covered by several layers of gauze and your arms are wrapped in elastic bandages.

Recovery

After the operation, your arms will be sore. You may get some relief if you can support your elbows, but for the most part you have to live with the ache. Your surgeon will prescribe strong pain medication for the first two days and nonaspirin pain reliever after that.

Swelling and bruising will be prominent for at least two weeks. After five days or so the bulky gauze dressing is replaced by a compression bandage, to be worn for another week. The stitches are removed in five days to two weeks.

You can probably return to work about a week after surgery unless you use your arms a lot on the job, in which case it's better to wait about ten days. Don't lift or carry anything until your incisions are fully healed.

Even if you feel up to going out socially, it's best to postpone engagements for about two weeks. Your arms may ache and swell by night's end. Sexual activity can loosen or snap stitches, so it is probably wise to wait two weeks before engaging in sex.

You can begin moderate lower-body exercises after a week, but avoid using your arms. Walking and pedaling on a stationary bicycle are good choices. If you swim, wait ten days, and then use a kickboard to support your arms until they are completely healed. Wait a month before doing any weight lifting, contact sports, or tennis.

Troubleshooting: What Can Go Wrong

Numbness caused by swelling is common. It usually subsides, but some patches of numbness can be permanent. Sometimes, indentations form in the skin where it was stitched, particularly if more skin was removed than necessary. These usually flatten out within a few months.

Rarely, some of the lymphatic vessels—which collect fluid from the tissues and return it to the blood—are inadvertently cut during an arm lift. This can result in permanent swelling in the arms. This condition, called lymphedema, is extremely rare, but may occur if too much deep fat is removed.

Scars

The most profound side effect of an arm lift is scarring. The location of the scar on the inner arm helps make it less obvious, but the scar may widen to a quarter inch or more. After a year or longer, it may blend with your skin or remain quite visible. Arm lifts are not routinely performed, but for someone troubled by unsightly skin folds, they may be the answer.

THIGH/BUTTOCK LIFT

Thigh and buttock lifts tighten droopy skin on the hips, thighs, and buttocks. They may become necessary if you lose a large amount of weight or if you previously had suction lipectomy and the skin did not contract.

If you have had phlebitis (a clot in a leg vein) in the past, your risk of developing it again after a thigh or buttock lift is greater than normal. Be sure to tell your surgeon about this aspect of your medical history. He may suggest wearing surgical support stockings and doing certain exercises before and after surgery to reduce this risk. If you currently have phlebitis, the lift should be postponed until the condition has cleared up.

The thigh lift, or a combination thigh and buttock lift, is done under general anesthesia in a hospital. You may have to stay several days. Surgery may take two to four hours and the surgeon's fee ranges from $1,000 to $5,000 depending on the extent of the operation. The buttock lift alone usually requires only local anesthesia plus sedation.

The Procedure

For a thigh lift, the surgeon makes two parallel, crescent-shaped incisions across the top of each thigh, running from the crease of the leg near the groin all the way around to the buttock. A thick layer of fat and excess skin is then removed and the remaining skin is stitched together as far up your leg as possible. If there has been much bleeding, a drainage tube may be inserted into the incision site. The incisions are covered with tape strips and an elastic bandage.

A lift can tighten skin on your inner, outer, or entire thigh. However, baggy skin around your knee will not be improved.

For a buttock lift, an incision is made above the crease to remove skin and fat. Eventually, the scar shifts downward. Drainage tubes may be placed in the incisions, and the wound is then taped and covered with a layer of gauze. You will be fitted with a surgical girdle or elastic bandage.

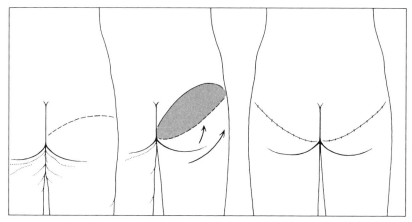

To improve sagging thighs, an incision is made along the upper dotted line. The skin is then separated from the underlying fat and muscle and pulled up. Excess skin (shaded area) is removed. Sutures close the incision, leaving a scar above the buttocks' crease.

Recovery

For several days the incision sites will ache and throb. Sitting will be uncomfortable and maybe impossible. You'll receive strong pain medication for several days at the hospital. After the first week, nonaspirin painkillers should be sufficient. Your legs will be swollen and you will need to wear knee-high support stockings for several weeks.

Surface stitches are removed after five to seven days; deeper sutures, which are taken out by pulling on the end that extends out of the skin, stay in two to three weeks.

A thigh lift is a major operation and requires a good deal of time to recover. You may be able to return to work after two weeks, but you will do better to allow more time. When you do go back to work, avoid draining activities such as parties and sports for at least a month.

Your doctor will ask you to wear support hose for about six weeks after surgery. You will also find you are more comfortable wearing skirts rather than slacks.

You can begin walking for exercise after two weeks. Swimming is also good during this period. Other exercise can be resumed after about three weeks, but avoid contact sports for at least a month. Sexual activity is likely to disturb the incisions for both thigh and buttock lifts. Avoid sex for at least three weeks, then resume with caution.

Lift results are permanent; however, if you gain weight later, the skin may stretch again and the scar may become wider.

Troubleshooting: What Can Go Wrong

Pain and hot, swollen skin in your lower leg suggests a blood clot. Call your doctor immediately.

Infection is uncommon, but if it occurs, it may be severe. Infection affects blood flow in the area and leaves scabs that further delay healing. The area can be drained and treated with antibiotics, but this treatment may worsen your scars. If you notice signs of infection—redness, pain, swelling around the incision—call your doctor at once; the faster it is treated, the less drastic the effect on scarring.

Scars

The scars from a thigh lift can be severe, although they are often confined to the inner surface. Clothing usually hides them, but the scars can widen or shift with time. Nerves may have been severed, leaving the skin numb for many months.

Abdominoplasty
(Tummy Tuck)

Don't be deceived by the merry nicknames "tummy tuck" and "mini-tummy tuck." These happy-go-lucky phrases minimize the extent of the surgery. Abdominoplasty cuts away excess skin and fat, tightens the abdominal wall, and repairs a hernia if one exists. This is a dramatic operation that requires a long convalescence and produces a long, permanent scar. Although liposuction may be done at the same time, abdominoplasty is a much more complicated procedure than fat suction alone.

Abdominoplasty came into its own in the 1960s and since the early 1980s liposuction has been used to further refine the procedure. Today, the procedure is often performed in men or women who are in relatively good shape, but are bothered by a *large* fat deposit on the abdomen that won't respond to diet or exercise, or by loose, sagging abdominal skin. The typical patient is a woman whose abdominal skin has been stretched by childbearing and who wants to look better in a bathing suit. (Young people rarely need abdominoplasty and men do not often request the procedure.)

No matter how much doctors stress the extensive, invasive nature of this operation, most patients are still shocked by the aftermath. Many women who have unobtrusive pelvic scars from gynecological surgery expect the same from a tummy tuck. However, the pubic area is slack and relaxed, without the tension characteristic of the abdomen. Scars that cross areas of tension tend to widen and take longer to heal than those in the pubic region.

As one abdominoplasty patient explained, "My doctor may have warned me—probably did warn me—but I just blocked it out. I was dead set on having it done and didn't listen." After her operation she was stunned by the soreness and amazed by the hip-to-hip scar. She spent four days in the hospital with uncomfortable drainage tubes in the wound and didn't begin to really feel good again for another two months. She still had no feeling in the area and numbness around her navel. Sometimes it takes six to nine months for feeling to return. Would she do it all over again? "Absolutely! I hated having a football for a stomach and now it's gone for good."

BEST CANDIDATES

The best candidate for abdominoplasty is a healthy individual whose weight is stable and, in the case of a woman, who no longer plans to become pregnant. The best candidate for a "mini-tuck" (partial abdominoplasty) is someone with loose skin and muscle only in the *lower* abdomen.

Abdominoplasty may remove stretch marks or previous scars from a hysterectomy, appendectomy, or cesarean section, but only if they're located in the skin being removed. The procedure will *not* slim your hips, thighs, or buttocks. Finally, your new abdomen will be flatter, but not completely taut.

If you plan to lose a lot of weight or to get pregnant, postpone the operation. (During abdominoplasty, the surgeon tightens the muscles that run up and down the abdomen; these can separate again during pregnancy.)

If you have abdominal scarring from previous surgery, every scar represents a reduction in blood supply, which means that circulation to the area may be diminished. This can cause your new incisions to heal poorly. Thus, your plastic surgeon may feel that abdominoplasty is not for you or may simply caution you that your new scars may be unusually prominent. In addition, if you have had phlebitis in the past, your risk of contracting it again as a result of abdominoplasty is higher.

THE CONSULTATION

As with every cosmetic procedure, your doctor should determine your goals and expectations at the time of the consultation, cautioning you about the trade-offs—in this case, a long recovery period and scarring. In preparation for surgery, the intended incision lines may be marked when you are wearing your bathing suit, so that they are as unobtrusively placed as possible.

COSTS

Surgical fees for abdominoplasty range from $2,500 to $8,500. A "mini-tuck" costs between $1,500 to $3,500. Additional charges include hospital and anesthesiology fees. Abdominoplasty is rarely covered by insurance.

BEFORE SURGERY

If you smoke, the risk of skin death is high, so plan to quit for at least one to two weeks before and after the operation. Do not get sunburned on your abdomen before a tummy tuck and do not go on a stringent diet—both inhibit your ability to heal.

THE PROCEDURE

A complete abdominoplasty is frequently performed in a hospital. You may remain in the hospital for several days. A mini-tuck is often done on an outpatient basis.

The operation takes two and a half to five hours depending on the extent of improvement needed and the amount of bleeding that occurs. A mini-tuck takes between one and two hours. Abdominoplasty is usually performed under general anesthesia; a mini-tuck may be done using general or local anesthesia (the latter with sedation added).

Just before the operation, you may have a catheter inserted to help keep your bladder empty during surgery. Every plastic surgeon has his own technique, but it's most common to make a long horizontal incision from hipbone to hipbone, just above

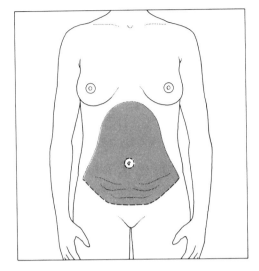

To tighten loose, wrinkled abdominal skin, an incision is made from hipbone to hipbone, across the pubic area. An additional incision is made around the navel. The shaded area of skin is separated from the abdominal wall and folded back so the surgeon has access to the underlying muscle.

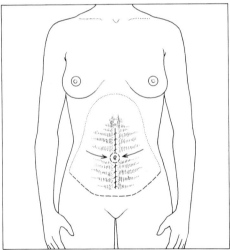

To tighten the abdominal wall, the surgeon pulls the underlying tissue and muscle together with sutures.

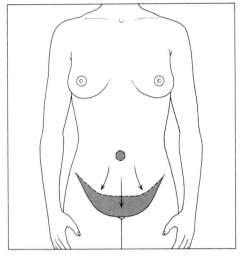

The skin is then drawn downward and the excess (shaded area) is removed. A small opening is made for the navel. Sutures close the incisions. The result is a flatter, trimmer abdomen.

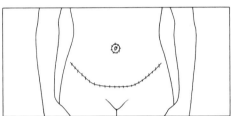

the pubic area. Though you may want your doctor to keep the incision short, a longer one actually gives a smoother result. If the incision line is too short, it may result in "dog ears"—little bulges of skin on the sides that can leave you with unsightly puckers.

The surgeon also cuts and releases the skin around the navel. The navel is anchored to a plantlike stalk of tissue and simply drops down inside the abdomen when it is freed. Retrieving and repositioning the navel later in the operation is one of the most delicate aspects of abdominoplasty and sometimes it is the most difficult. In a mini-tuck, the navel is not moved, but it may be pulled into an unnatural shape when the skin below it is tightened and stitched.

Abdominoplasties are often performed in conjunction with liposuction. A tube called a cannula is inserted through the navel incision; the surgeon then manipulates the cannula back and forth under the skin to remove excess fat before the operation proceeds.

Next, the surgeon frees the skin from underlying tissue all the way up to your ribs and lifts a large skin flap. Arteries are clamped to reduce bleeding, and the muscles running up and down your abdomen are completely exposed. These muscles are tightened by pulling them close together and stitching them into their new position. If you have a hernia, it also will be stitched closed.

The surgical table is built with hinges in the middle, so that both its head and its foot can be raised. When the surgeon "breaks" the table, your hips are elevated and tension on your abdomen is reduced. The skin flap is stretched down to the lower edge of the incision and clamped into place. (The old opening for the navel may now be in the excess skin below the incision line.) The extra skin is then removed.

A new hole is cut for the navel, which is stitched into place with fine sutures. A drainage tube may be inserted to collect excess fluids.

Finally, your horizontal incision is sewn shut. Your abdomen will probably be covered with a firm elastic dressing or support garment, although some doctors question the necessity for this.

Variations on Standard Abdominoplasty

A so-called mini-tuck removes only excess skin *below* the navel. The belly button remains in its original place. For a mini-tuck, a long, horizontal incision is made just above the pubic mound. Another small incision made near or in the belly button allows the surgeon to insert a cannula and suck out fat deposits. The skin is then separated only from the incision line up to the navel. This lower skin flap is then stretched down, the excess is cut away, and the flap is stitched back into place.

Another variation on the standard abdominoplasty is occasionally used if improvement is primarily needed in the center of your abdomen. A vertical incision is made from your ribs to the pubic area and the excess skin is removed. This is a much easier procedure from which to recover; however, although somewhat less pronounced, the long vertical scar that results from this incision can be difficult to hide.

A more extensive version of abdominoplasty may alleviate chronic back pain in those whose muscles are so weak that their spine is no longer properly supported. This may be particularly true in women who have given birth to several children. However, conservative treatments such as bracing should be tried first.

RECOVERY

The recovery process for full abdominoplasty and the modified version known as a mini-tuck are nearly identical, though recovery from the latter is usually faster. You may need to remain immobilized in the hospital for two or three days, with your hips bent to reduce tension on the abdomen. Your abdomen may be very swollen and you will probably feel pain. If hospitalized, you can have narcotic injections to control your pain for a day or more; then tablets may be prescribed for another two weeks. General anesthesia may induce nausea, and if you stay in the hospital, you will be fed intravenously for the first day or two. You will also be given medication to prevent vomiting, which could cause your stitches to pull loose.

Follow your doctor's instructions on how to sit up and do breathing exercises during the first forty-eight hours after surgery. The drain and catheter (if one was inserted) are removed after a day or two, and you usually can return home within one to five days.

At home, you will spend most of your time resting and sleeping. You will need someone to help you with everyday tasks such as bathing and dressing. Your doctor will give you instructions for showering and changing the bandages (no tub baths are allowed until all the stitches are out). It's important for you to start walking, even though you will be unable to straighten up for several weeks and may walk with a stoop. Carrying or lifting heavy things is limited for a month to six weeks. Avoid climbing stairs for at least a week. You will be surprised at how long it takes before your energy level returns to normal.

Surface stitches are removed after five to seven days; deeper sutures (in which both ends protrude through the skin) come out in two to three weeks. Your entire abdomen will be very bruised and swollen for several weeks. Avoid tight clothing; it may be months before your clothes fit properly. You may continue to feel pain for two weeks and it can take three weeks before you're able to straighten up fully.

All major surgery leaves you feeling exhausted. It may be months before you feel like your old self. If you start out in top physical condition with strong abdominal muscles, you will re-cover faster. Some people are able to return to work after two weeks, but many require three or four weeks of rest and recu-peration. Expect to be more tired than usual.

After about two weeks, you can walk for exercise, but you won't get far. Some people begin stretching and swimming ex-ercises. Even if you've never been active before, you should be-gin an exercise program, since it helps reduce swelling, lowers the chances of blood clots, and tones your muscles. If you were active before surgery, it will be one or two months before you're exercising with your usual intensity. Avoid contact sports for two months.

It's critical that your stitches be protected, so avoid sexual relations for at least three weeks after surgery. After a month, sex is possible, but it will probably hurt. Wait until you feel comfortable. Low-key, sit-down parties are fine after two weeks, but wait a couple of months before attempting a truly festive event that will require prolonged standing or dancing. If you are a smoker or if you have lung problems it may take you longer to recover and you may be more prone to postop diffi-culties.

TROUBLESHOOTING: WHAT CAN GO WRONG

Abdominoplasty is a major operation that carries a risk of seri-ous complications. About one in a hundred patients develops blood clots after surgery, which are dangerous because they can travel to the heart, lungs, or brain.

If detected, clots can be treated with medication. Symptoms can include chest pain and shortness of breath. Compression garments and motion minimize the potential for clot formation, but because abdominoplasty patients cannot move much after surgery, the risks multiply. Follow all of your doctor's instruc-tions about when and how to resume physical activity.

Other potential complications are internal bleeding, which may require further surgery, and infection. Infection not only prolongs your hospital stay but can damage the blood vessels feeding the abdominal skin, worsening the scar. Infection must be treated with drainage and antibiotics.

SCARS

Horizontal abdominal scars are almost always prominent because the skin in this area is moderately thick and it's virtually impossible to immobilize. However, long postoperative bed rest is out of the question, since mobility is essential to avoid clots and to speed recovery. As a result, the abdomen is under constant tension and the scar can pull and widen until it is a quarter inch or more thick. Abdominal scars may take two years or more to fade and flatten.

The scar will be red and lumpy for several weeks and your new navel may not match its predecessor. Most clothing, even a swimsuit, hides the abdominoplasty scar, but a very skimpy bikini probably will not cover all of it. Some doctors advocate injecting steroids into these scars to soften them, but this can also cause them to stretch. In addition, some people hesitate before getting even one steroid injection because of the thinning that can occur in adjacent skin.

SATISFACTION

Abdominoplasty produces excellent, permanent results on patients with weakened muscles, baggy skin, or hernias. However, some patients are unhappy with the results, especially if they had a relatively small problem from the start. If you have a *significant* paunchiness to your abdomen, and you're realistic about the consequences of the operation, abdominoplasty may be a good choice for you.

INDEX

Abdomen, liposuction of, 280
Abdominoplasty, 293–302
  before surgery, 295
  best candidates for, 294
  consultation, 295
  costs, 295
  liposuction, in conjunction with, 296
  potential problems, 301
  procedure, 295–99
  recovery, 299–300
  satisfaction, 302
  scars, 301
  variations, 298–99
Accreditation Association for Ambulatory Health Care (AAAHC), 62
Accreditation, of outpatient facility, 61–62
Acne scars, dermabrasion for, 156
Advertising, plastic surgery and, 32–33
Aging
  plastic surgery and, 142–44
  rhinoplasty and, 106
Allergies
  anesthesia and, 65
  collagen and, 169
  rhinoplasty and, 99
American Association for Accreditation of Ambulatory Plastic Surgery Facilities (AAAAPSF), 61–62
  phone number of, 62
American Board of Medical Specialties (ABMS), 28, 34–35
  phone number of, 36
American Board of Plastic Surgery (ABPS), 34–35
  physician requirements for membership in, 37
American Society of Aesthetic Plastic Surgery, 37
American Society for Plastic and

Reconstructive Surgeons (ASPRS), 13, 37
  advertising and, 32
  camouflage cosmetics brochure, 76
  financial plan, 69–70
  finding a surgeon and, 33
  phone number of, 36, 62
Anesthesia, 62–64
  for abdominoplasty, 295
  allergies and, 65
  for arm lift, 287
  for blepharoplasty, 177
  for breast enlargement, 240
  for breast reconstruction, 264
  for breast reduction for men, 259
  for browlift, 186
  for chemical peel, 149
  for chinbone surgery, 132
  for chin implant, 129
  choice of, 63–64
  for dermabrasion, 155
  for facelift, 194, 196
  general, 63
  for hair-replacement surgery, 210
  illness and, 65–66
  injectables and, 166
  for liposuction, 278
  local injection, 62
  local injection plus sedation, 62–63
  for lower-jaw implants, 124
  for otoplasty, 112
  postop planning and, 72
  for rhinoplasty, 99
  risk, 64
  smoking and, 67
  for thigh/buttock lift, 290–91
Anesthesiologist
  defined, 63
  payment to, 68
Anesthetics, administration of, 64–65
Ankles, liposuction of, 281
Areola reconstruction, 271–72
Arm lift, 287–89
  costs, 288

replacing body fluids and, 281–
  282
scars, 286
side effects and, 284–85
success, 286
Lip plumping, 171
Local injection anesthesia, 62
Local injection plus sedation
    anesthesia, 62–63
  administration of, 64–65
"Lop ear," 116
"Love handles," liposuction of, 280
Lymphedema, 289

Makeup. *See* Cosmetics, camouflage
Mammography, cancer detection
    after breast implants and, 245
Mastectomy, breast reconstruction
    and, 261–62
Mastopexy, 247–51
  best candidates for, 247–48
  breast-feeding and, 251
  consultation, 248
  costs, 248
  procedure, 248–50
  recovery, 250–51
  satisfaction, 251
  scars, 251
Medical history, 44
Medical societies, as credentials, 37
Medications, surgery and, 49, 66
Men
  breast reduction in, 259–60
  cosmetic surgery and, 26
  facelift and, 191, 199
Microplugs, 204
  finishing hairline with, 214
Microtia (missing ear), 117–18
Miniplugs, 204
  finishing hairline with, 214
Mini-tuck. *See* Abdominoplasty
Minoxidil, 220–21
Missing ear (microtia), 117–18
Models/actors, and rhinoplasty, 93
Myotonology, 192

Nasal congestion, following
    rhinoplasty, 102
Nasal packs, 100, 101
  removing, 102
Neck, liposuction of, 279–80
Nerve damage, from facelift, 199
Nipple implant, 271
Nipple placement

breast reduction and, 254, 255
  mastopexy and, 248
Nipple reconstruction, 271–72
Nonsteroidal antiinflammatory
    drugs (NSAID), 66
Nose(s)
  blowing after rhinoplasty, 102
  improvement possibilities of, 86
  protecting after rhinoplasty, 104
  shut, 86
  small, 89
  tip revision, 87–88
  See also Rhinoplasty
Numbness. *See recovery for individual
    surgeries*

Otolaryngology, specialists in, 35
Otoplasty, 109–16
  best candidates for, 110–11
  consultation, 111
  costs, 112
  exercise and, 114–15
  potential problems, 115
  procedure, 112–14
  recovery, 114–15
  satisfaction, 116
  scars, 115
  success, 115–16
Outpatient facility, choosing, 60–
    62

Pain. *See recovery for individual
    surgeries*
Paraffin, as injectable, 167
Patients, cosmetic surgery
  dissatisfied, 22–23
  satisfied, 21–22
Payment
  anesthesiologist and, 68
  ASPRS financial plan and, 69–70
  estimated fee and, 68
  for surgeon, 67–68
  training institutions and, 69
  See also Insurance
Pedicle flap, breast reconstruction
    and, 269
Perfectionists and cosmetic surgery,
    25
Perforation, from liposuction,
    284
Personal relationships and cosmetic
    surgery, 24–25
Phenol peel, 147, 150–51
Phlebitis